# THE 16PF® FIFTH EDITION ADMINISTRATOR'S MANUAL

Mary T. Russell and Darcie L. Karol

*Institute for Personality and Ability Testing, Inc.*
*Champaign, Illinois*

ISBN 0-918296-21-8

Institute for Personality and Ability Testing, Inc.
P.O. Box 1188, Champaign, Illinois 61824-1188

SECOND EDITION 1994. THIRD IMPRESSION 1999.

# TABLE OF CONTENTS

# FIGURES

## CHAPTER 6
## 16PF® BASIC INTERPRETIVE REPORT (BIR)

## APPENDIX A

## APPENDIX B

## APPENDIX C

# MANUAL AUTHORS' ACKNOWLEDGMENTS

*The authors would like to thank the many people who contributed vast amounts of time and effort to this manual. Most especially, we would like to recognize those who provided key input and reviews of manual drafts: A. Karen Cattell, Heather E. P. Cattell, Mark L. Rieke, Steven R. Conn, and James C. Slaughter, who also provided crucial input on the "look and feel" of the manual and its publication process. Editor Judy O'Donnell minimized differences in the authors' styles and made the text more accessible. Mary Ann Hussong and Mary Cattell were stalwarts when we could no longer see the forest, never mind the trees. Thanks to Dody Bullerman, who drafted and redrafted materials and figures, and to Brian Priest for his role in typesetting the manual and conceiving its cover and look. Special thanks to Richard Robinson for programming the Basic Interpretive Report (BIR) at all of its evolutionary stages, and for translating countless files and data.*

*The authors would also like to acknowledge the test authors, whose most recent revision of the 16PF has been eagerly awaited. Thank you, also, to those whose research contributions provide the back-bone for the reliability and validity chapters presented here, especially Mark L. Rieke, Ph.D., Steven R. Conn, Ph.D., and Stephen J. Guastello, Ph.D.*

*Finally, thanks to our friends for listening to our stories during this process, to Mary Cattell for her endless supply of brownies, and to Roget's Thesaurus.*

*Darcie Karol*
*Mary Russell*

# TEST AUTHORS' ACKNOWLEDGMENTS

*A project on the scale of this 16PF revision cannot occur without the help of many people outside of the test publisher's offices. It is a pleasure to express our appreciation to at least a few whose ideas have been invaluable:*

Randall Bergen, Ph.D.
Geneva College

Janet Bijou
Tucson, Arizona

Menucha Birenbaum, Ph.D.
Tel Aviv University

Heather Birkett Cattell, Ph.D.
Honolulu, Hawaii

Elden Chalmers, Ph.D.
Yountville, California

Herbert W. Eber, Ph.D.
Atlanta, Georgia

Barbara Ellis, Ph.D.
University of Texas, El Paso

Philip Farber, Ph.D.
Florida Institute of Technology

John Gillis, Ph.D.
St. Thomas University

Richard L. Gorsuch, Ph.D.
Fuller Theological Seminary

Stephen J. Guastello, Ph.D.
Marquette University

Zonya C. Johnson, Ph.D.
The Wright Institute

Charles Lardent, Ph.D.
Millbrook, Alabama

Barbara Tyler, Ph.D.
 and Ken Miller, Ph.D.
London, England

Norm Murphy, Ph.D.
San Luis Obispo, California

Janiece Pompa, Ph.D.
University of Utah

Marcel Ponton, Ph.D.
Pasadena, California

James Schuerger, Ph.D.
Cleveland State University

Ann Sweney, Ph.D.
 and Art Sweney, Ph.D.
Wichita State University

Maurice Tatsuoka, Ph.D.
Princeton, New Jersey

Fred Wallbrown, Ph.D.
Kent State University

David Watterson, Ph.D.
Cleveland, Ohio

*Raymond B. Cattell*
*A. Karen S. Cattell*
*Heather E. P. Cattell*

# C H A P T E R

# 1

INTRODUCTION

TO THE 16PF®

FIFTH EDITION

# 1

## INTRODUCTION

## TO THE 16PF®

## FIFTH EDITION

**T**he *Sixteen Personality Factor Questionnaire* (16PF) represents Dr. Raymond Cattell's endeavor to identify the primary components of personality by factor analyzing all English-language adjectives describing human behavior. The 16PF Fifth Edition, although updated and revised, continues to measure the same 16 primary personality factor scales identified by Cattell over 45 years ago. Factor scales remain denoted by letters as assigned by Cattell, such as "Factor A," but they also are designated by more descriptive labels, such as "Warmth." The broad personality domains under which primary factors cluster are now called "Global Factors" instead of "Second-Order Factors"; however, these domains still exhibit an underlying factor structure similar to that found previously, reaffirming Cattell's original findings.

The 16PF Fifth Edition contains 185 items that comprise the 16 primary personality factor scales as well as an Impression Management (IM) index, which assesses social desirability. Each scale contains 10 to 15 items. The test, which can be administered individually or in a group setting, takes 35 to 50 minutes to complete by hand or 25 to 35 minutes to complete by computer. Overall readability is at the fifth-grade level. Like its predecessors, the fifth edition can be easily handscored with a set of keys. The test also can be computer-scored by IPAT, the publisher, or at the site of administration using software available from IPAT. Computer-generated reports as well as numerous source books and articles are available to enrich the interpretation of test results.

While remaining true to the original objectives of the 16PF, the fifth edition includes these improvements:

1. Item content has been revised to reflect modern language usage and to remove ambiguity, and it also has been reviewed for gender, race, and cultural bias. The resultant test is more contemporary than previous editions.

2. Response choices are consistently organized for all personality items, with the middle response choice always being a question mark (?).

3. Normative data have been updated to reflect the 1990 U.S. Census, and, in accordance with federal civil rights legislation, combined-gender norms are available as a scoring option.

4. New administrative indices have been designed to assess response bias. An Impression Management (IM) index, which is comprised of items not found on the 16 primary personality factor scales, replaces the "Faking Good" and "Faking Bad" scales of the fourth edition. The fifth edition also contains indices of Acquiescence (ACQ) and Infrequency (INF). Personality scores are no longer adjusted on the basis of validity indices.

5. Psychometric properties have improved. Internal consistency reliabilities average .74, with a range from .64 to .85. Test-retest reliabilities average about .80 for a 2-week interval and .70 for a 2-month interval. Familiar criterion scores such as Adjustment and Creativity have been updated, and new ones such as Empathy and Self-Esteem have been added.

The 16PF Fifth Edition also offers a revised answer sheet that is compatible with both hand- and computer-scoring options. In addition to this manual, these are the testing materials used with each of the scoring options:

- For tests to be handscored: test booklet, answer sheet, four scoring keys and norm table, and Individual Record Form

- For tests to be computer-scored by IPAT: test booklet, answer sheet, and report certificates

- For tests to be computer-scored at the site of administration: test booklet, answer sheet, report certificates, and IPAT's OnSite System software

- For tests faxed to IPAT for scoring: test booklet, answer sheet, report certificates, and activated IPAT OnFax System (requires sign-up, password, and use of special cover sheet)

Two new computer-generated interpretive reports are available for the fifth edition: (1) the Basic Interpretive Report (BIR), which provides profiles, scores, and descriptive comments, and (2) the Basic Score Report (BSR), which presents scores only. IPAT's other popular reports are available from the fifth edition as well.

As a broad measure of personality, the 16PF is useful in a variety of settings to predict a wide range of life behaviors. Counselors and clinicians use results as an aid in clinical decision making. Vocational counselors find the links to occupational and other interests helpful in guiding clientele. Human resource personnel consider the test a useful component of selection batteries and essential for personal development planning.▾

# CHAPTER 2

# ADMINISTRATION AND SCORING

# 2

## ADMINISTRATION

## AND SCORING

**T**he 16PF Fifth Edition is designed to be administered to adults (aged 16 and older), individually or in a group setting. Available in both paper-and-pencil and computer-software versions, the test has an overall readability estimated at the fifth-grade level.

Normative data for the 16PF are based on an age range of 15 through 92 years. Whether the test is appropriate for an individual younger than 16 is a decision that should be based on professional consideration of the client's maturity level. Usually, the adolescent version of the 16PF—the High School Personality Questionnaire (HSPQ)—is most appropriate for ages 12 through 18.

## ADMINISTRATION

Although the 16PF Fifth Edition is virtually self-administrable, the test administrator is advised to take time to establish a comfortable rapport with examinees, since the creation of a favorable test-taking attitude is worth as much or possibly more in the production of accurate data as any number of response style indices. With this in mind, the administrator should give thoughtful attention to examinees' questions and should reinforce the test objectives by telling examinees that, in the long run, they will do the most good for themselves by being frank and honest in their self-descriptions.

### Response Format

Test questions have a three-choice response format. Except for the Factor B items, the middle response choice is always a question mark (*?*). The 15 Factor B items, which assess reasoning ability, are grouped together at the end of the test booklet following the personality items. This arrangement not only allows continuity in item content but also enables separate assessment of reasoning ability from that of personality in those instances when this may be desirable.

### Test-Completion Time

The test is untimed, but examinees should be encouraged to work at a steady pace. About 10 minutes into the testing session, the administrator may want to discourage examinees from agonizing over possible responses by reiterating this caution included in the test directions, "Remember, don't spend too much time thinking over any one question. Give the first, natural answer as it comes to you." Average test-completion time is 35 to 50 minutes by pencil and 25 to 35 minutes by computer.

### Computer Administration

The 16PF Fifth Edition can be administered via an IBM or IBM-compatible personal computer using IPAT OnSite System software. The program features on-line help and practice questions, item-by-item test administration, routines that allow examinees to change the previous answer, and a test interrupt and resume option. Research has demonstrated that 16PF scores obtained from computerized administration are equivalent to scores obtained via paper-and-pencil administration (Wade & Guastello, 1993).

The OnSite System also offers the capabilities of immediately scoring tests and processing reports. Additional information regarding OnSite can be obtained by calling IPAT at 800-225-4728.

### Paper-and-Pencil Administration

Testing materials include the fifth edition test booklet and the corresponding answer sheet, which may be hand- or computer-scored. Simple and clear instructions for examinees are printed in the test booklet. The administrator may either read aloud the instructions or request examinees to read the instructions silently, responding to their questions as necessary. Briefly, the instructions advise examinees not to make any marks in the test booklet, which is reusable. Examinees also are cautioned to avoid skipping any questions and to choose the first response that comes to mind rather than spending too much time on any single question.

Before starting the test, examinees are asked to complete the grids for name and gender on the left-hand side of the answer sheet (see Figure 1). If confidentiality is desired for tests to be computer-scored, the grid for I.D. number should be completed in lieu of the name grid.

During testing, the administrator should check that examinees are marking responses appropriately. Response circles must be darkened completely with a No. 2 or softer lead pencil, particularly if the test is to be computer-scored.

At the conclusion of testing, the administrator should review each answer sheet to ensure that the name (or I.D. number) and gender grids have been completed and that all responses are scorable. Examinees should be asked to erase any extraneous marks, to fix incomplete erasures, to complete missing answers, and to correct multiple answers to a single item.

### SCORING

Before being handscored or computer-scored, each answer sheet should be verified for completeness:

1. That the identification grid information has been provided: name (or I.D. number) and gender.

2. That all 185 items have been answered. Although completion of all items is desirable, an answer sheet having 12 or fewer incomplete items is still scorable by hand or by computer. An answer sheet having 13 or more incomplete items must be completed before it can be hand- or computer-scored.

FIGURE 1

SCORING KEY AND ANSWER SHEET

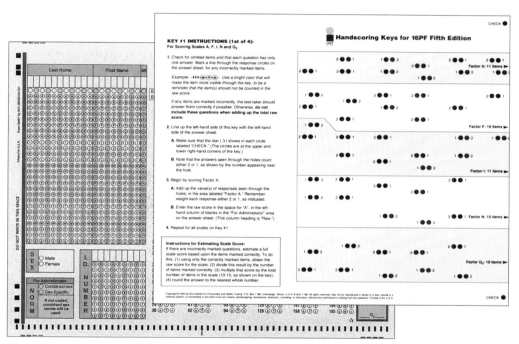

**3.** That the norm grid has been completed. This grid includes two choices, combined-sex norms and sex-specific norms. (Refer to Table 39 in Appendix B.) When combined-sex norms are chosen, the examinee's scores for all 16 personality factors are compared to the normative group containing both men and women. When sex-specific norms are selected, the examinee's scores for 13 of the personality factors are compared to the combined-sex normative group, and his or her scores on the 3 personality factors of A (Warmth), E (Dominance), and I (Sensitivity) are compared only to the normative group compatible with his or her gender. Sex-specific norms are available for the latter 3 factors because their score distributions are different for men and women. In relation to these 3 factors, selection of sex-specific versus combined-sex norms depends on professional judgment and the testing application (e.g., combined-sex norms for all 16 factors may be preferable in job selection applications).

### Handscoring

These materials are needed for handscoring the 16PF: set of four scoring keys, norm table, and an Individual Record Form.

As mentioned previously, an answer sheet having 13 or more unanswered items must be completed before it can be handscored. Although completion of all items is desirable, an answer sheet is still scorable if 12 or fewer items remain unanswered. In this situation, the full scale score can be estimated for any affected scale by averaging item scores on the scale. The procedures are as follows:

1. Using the appropriate scoring key, obtain the total raw score of the items in the scale that have been completed. (Directions for using the scoring keys are given in the section that follows, "Step 1: Score the Test.")

2. Divide the total raw score by the number of items completed.

3. Multiply the quotient obtained in procedure 2 by the total number of items in the scale.

4. Round the product obtained in procedure 3 to the nearest whole number, which becomes the *estimated* full scale score.

The sections that follow describe the steps involved in handscoring the 16PF Fifth Edition: (1) obtain raw scores for the 16 personality factors and the Impression Management (IM) index, (2) convert personality factor raw scores into sten scores and convert the IM raw score into a percentile, (3) calculate the 5 global factor sten scores, and (4) profile sten scores for the global factors and primary personality factors.

### Step 1: Score the Test

A sample scoring key is also shown in Figure 1. Each of the first three scoring keys in the set of four is used to score five of the primary personality factors; the fourth key is used to score Reasoning (Factor B) and the Impression Management (IM) index, which is a response style scale that reflects social desirability.

Detailed instructions for obtaining raw scores for the 16PF are provided on the scoring keys. This is a summary of the handscoring procedures, using the first scoring key as an example:

1. Align the left edge of the first scoring key over the answer sheet, making sure that the stars on the right side of the answer sheet appear through the corresponding holes on the right side of the key.

2. Count the marks visible through the holes in the area labeled "Factor A," allowing 1 or 2 points as indicated by the number adjacent to each hole. Total the points, and enter the total in the space for the Factor A raw score (as indicated by an arrow on the scoring key).

3. Continue scoring the remaining four factors that correspond with the first key, following procedures 1 and 2.

Raw scores for the other personality factors are determined in the preceding manner, using the next two keys in sequence. The IM and Factor B raw scores are obtained by using the fourth answer key; Factor B responses are scored as 0 (incorrect) or 1 (correct).

There is no key for scoring the response style indices of Infrequency (INF) and Acquiescence (ACQ), for which the scoring routine is somewhat laborious. Appendix C provides instructions for handscoring these indices when they are needed.

### Step 2: Convert Raw Scores to Sten Scores

Raw scores are converted into standardized (sten) scores by using the norm table included with the set of handscoring keys. Stens are based on a 10-point scale with a mean of 5.5 and a standard deviation of 2, and are described in the next chapter. The raw scores are printed in the body of the table, and their corresponding sten scores are located at the top of each column. This table is reproduced as Table 39 in Appendix B of this manual.

These are the procedures followed in converting raw scores into stens, using Factor A as an example:

1. Determine whether combined-sex or sex-specific norms for Factor A are more appropriate for the testing application. (Recall that both types of norms are available for Factor A [Warmth], Factor E [Dominance], and Factor I [Sensitivity] since gender differences exist on these scales.)

2. Locate the examinee's raw score for Factor A in the row that corresponds to the norms selected: the *A* row (combined-sex norms), *Male* row, or *Female* row.

3. Draw your finger up the column in which the raw score appears. The score at the top of the column is the sten for Factor A. For example, if a male examinee received a raw score of 19 on Factor A, his sten score would be 8 using male sex-specific norms, and his sten score would be 7 using combined-sex norms. Sten scores for the remaining factors are determined in the preceding manner.

The norm table also is used in converting the raw score for the Impression Management (IM) index; however, the IM score is converted into a percentile rather than a sten.

### Step 3: Calculate Global Factor Sten Scores

This step involves calculating sten scores for the five global factors of personality: Extraversion, Anxiety, Tough-Mindedness, Independence, and Self-Control. Since these global factors are comprised of combinations of related primary factors, they describe personality in broader, more general terms than do the primary factors.

Global factor sten scores can be calculated by following the instructions at the top of side 1 of the Individual Record Form

(Figure 2), or by using the equations listed in Table 13 in Chapter 5. The instructions that follow correspond to those printed on the Individual Record Form:

1. Transfer the examinee's primary factor sten scores from the answer sheet to the left-hand column labeled "Sten" on the Individual Record Form.

2. Begin by scoring Factor A, which is the first row. Follow the dashed line to the right, and each time you reach a decimal in a black box, multiply the examinee's Factor A sten score by that decimal. Enter the resultant product in the empty box adjacent to the black box.

3. Repeat procedure 2 for each factor. Note that you calculate and record only one product in some factor rows and two in others, and that some boxes are clear whereas others are shaded.

4. After you have calculated and recorded the products for all 16 factors, add the numbers in each pair of vertical columns (clear and shaded) separately. When you total the decimals, be sure to include *any given constant* appearing in the first empty box at the base of the column pair. Enter the sum of the decimals from the shaded column in the shaded box at the base of the column pair.

5. After you have totaled all the columns, subtract each sum in a shaded box from the sum in a clear box. Enter the remainder (a decimal) in the empty box that follows. This decimal represents the sten score to the nearest tenth of a sten for the global factor indicated.

### Step 4: Profile Sten Scores

Sten scores for the 5 global factors and the 16 primary factors can be graphed to achieve a pictorial representation, or profile, of the examinee's overall personality pattern. Such a profile is quite helpful in interpretation.

FIGURE 2

INDIVIDUAL RECORD FORM

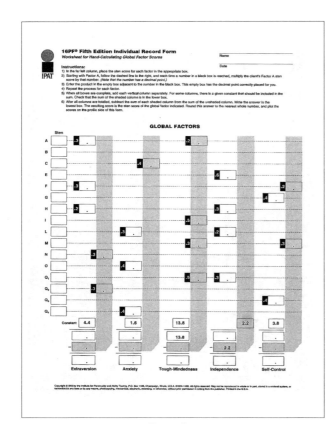

SIDE 1                    SIDE 2

The grid for developing the profile is on side 2 of the Individual Record Form (Figure 2). These are the procedures to be followed:

1. Write the examinee's primary and global factor sten scores in the Sten column at the left of the profile sheet. You will need to round the examinee's decimal sten score for each global factor to the nearest whole number. (Decimal sten scores are determined by completing the global factor scoring worksheet on side 1 of the Individual Record Form.)

2. In the appropriate spaces on the grid, mark a dot that corresponds to each rounded global factor sten score and to each personality factor sten score.

3. Connect the dots using a series of short straight lines.

**Computer-Scoring**

As an alternative to handscoring, the 16PF answer sheet can be scored and interpreted via computer using IPAT's mail-in scoring service or IPAT's OnSite System software.

12

Computer-scoring and interpretation of the 16PF has several important advantages over handscoring, such as (1) quick turnaround of results, (2) less possibility for error, and (3) the ability to report additional administrative indices and other composite scores that enrich test results.

To be computer-scored, an answer sheet must be marked with a No. 2 or softer lead pencil; responses marked with ballpoint or felt-tip pens cannot be scanned accurately. As mentioned previously, an answer sheet having 13 or more unanswered items must be completed before it can be computer-scored. Although completion of all items is desirable, an answer sheet is still computer-scorable if 12 or fewer items remain unanswered.

Prior to being submitted for computer-scoring, the answer sheet's demographic grids must be completed: name (or I.D. number) of examinee, sex of examinee, and norm choice. The sex of the examinee should be indicated so that appropriate pronouns will appear in the interpretive report. If combined-sex norms are selected, the test will be processed using combined-sex norms for all 16 personality factors. If sex-specific norms are selected, the test will be processed using sex-specific norms for Factors A, E, and I and combined-sex norms for the remaining factors. If neither norm choice is selected, the test will be processed using combined-sex norms.

Answer sheets mailed to IPAT for scoring should be accompanied by a red-and-white processing request form. The information necessary to complete this form includes the professional's name and address, the type of interpretive report desired, and method of return shipment desired.

16PF Fifth Edition answer sheets can also be faxed to IPAT; reports are returned within minutes. Users must sign up for the system,

and an OnFax cover sheet must accompany faxed answer sheets. Full instructions are provided at the time of signing up.

The 16PF also can be processed on IBM or IBM-compatible personal computers using IPAT OnSite System software or on Macintosh computers via TeleTest, a telephone-modem connection.

Additional information regarding these scoring options can be obtained by calling IPAT at 800-225-4728.

## COMMONLY ASKED QUESTIONS ABOUT 16PF TESTING

*When should a client be retested?*

Personality traits should be relatively stable over time. However, the possibility of fluctuations in scores always exists, whether due to maturational effects, learning, or psychological state (Cattell, Eber, & Tatsuoka, 1970). Under normal circumstances, the recommendation is that a client be retested after a six-month time period. If the client has experienced a major life event that could be expected to influence his or her psychological state, retesting after a shorter time interval is strongly advised.

*How long does IPAT keep customer test data?*

Since enormous amounts of data are processed daily at IPAT, storage space for processed answer sheets is limited. The present policy is to store answer sheets for a maximum of four months. ▼

CHAPTER

3

PROFILE

INTERPRETATION

# PROFILE

# INTERPRETATION

**I**ntended as a user-friendly guide for interpreting 16PF Fifth Edition results, this chapter provides general interpretive information, a profile interpretation strategy, and specific scale descriptions. The content synthesizes findings from a number of different studies included in *The 16PF Fifth Edition Technical Manual* (Conn & Rieke, 1994f).

## GENERAL INTERPRETIVE INFORMATION

The interpretive information that follows is based on the preliminary body of evidence available for the fifth edition. As users begin to develop a database on this edition, scale definitions will be refined to reflect the incoming data.

### Factor Analysis

The evolution of the 16PF has reflected Cattell's use of the factor-analytic approach in identifying the basic structure of human personality. Understanding this method of test development as the theoretical base of the 16PF aids in using the test. Chapter 4 of this manual helps to build a foundation for this understanding as do other resource books on the history and applications of the 16PF. Professionals may want to consult the latter for information regarding development of the factors, relevant research, and interpretive findings.

### Primary Factor Scales

Historically, the basic scales of the 16PF have been labeled with letters (e.g., Factor A, Factor B, etc., through Factor Q4). The fifth edition continues the tradition of using factor letters and also provides "common-language" names for each scale (see Figure 3).

### Bipolar Scales

As shown in Figure 3, the 16PF scales are bipolar in nature; that is, both high and low

## FIGURE 3

### PRIMARY FACTOR SCALE DESCRIPTORS

| Factor | | Left Meaning | Right Meaning |
|---|---|---|---|
| A | Warmth | Reserved, Impersonal, Distant | Warm, Outgoing, Attentive to Others |
| B | Reasoning | Concrete | Abstract |
| C | Emotional Stability | Reactive, Emotionally Changeable | Emotionally Stable, Adaptive, Mature |
| E | Dominance | Deferential, Cooperative, Avoids Conflict | Dominant, Forceful, Assertive |
| F | Liveliness | Serious, Restrained, Careful | Lively, Animated, Spontaneous |
| G | Rule-Consciousness | Expedient, Nonconforming | Rule-Conscious, Dutiful |
| H | Social Boldness | Shy, Threat-Sensitive, Timid | Socially Bold, Venturesome, Thick-Skinned |
| I | Sensitivity | Utilitarian, Objective, Unsentimental | Sensitive, Aesthetic, Sentimental |
| L | Vigilance | Trusting, Unsuspecting, Accepting | Vigilant, Suspicious, Skeptical, Wary |
| M | Abstractedness | Grounded, Practical, Solution-Oriented | Abstracted, Imaginative, Idea-Oriented |
| N | Privateness | Forthright, Genuine, Artless | Private, Discreet, Non-Disclosing |
| O | Apprehension | Self-Assured, Unworried, Complacent | Apprehensive, Self-Doubting, Worried |
| Q1 | Openness to Change | Traditional, Attached to Familiar | Open to Change, Experimenting |
| Q2 | Self-Reliance | Group-Oriented, Affiliative | Self-Reliant, Solitary, Individualistic |
| Q3 | Perfectionism | Tolerates Disorder, Unexacting, Flexible | Perfectionistic, Organized, Self-Disciplined |
| Q4 | Tension | Relaxed, Placid, Patient | Tense, High Energy, Impatient, Driven |

scores have meaning. Generally, professionals should not assume that high scores are "good" and that low scores are "bad." For example, high scorers on Factor A tend to be warm interpersonally, whereas low scorers tend to be more reserved interpersonally. In some situations, being reserved might be quite fitting or useful. In other situations, being warm might be more suitable.

Throughout this chapter, the right-side pole, or high-score range, of a factor is described as the plus (+) pole. The left-side pole, or low-score range, is the minus (–) pole. For example, high scorers on Factor A are described as Warm (A+); low-scorers are described as Reserved (A–).

Usually, the correlation of one 16PF scale with another is framed in terms of the

FIGURE 4

GLOBAL FACTOR SCALE DESCRIPTORS

| Factor | Left Meaning | Right Meaning |
| --- | --- | --- |
| EX Extraversion | Introverted, Socially Inhibited | Extraverted, Socially Participating |
| AX Anxiety | Low Anxiety, Unperturbed | High Anxiety, Perturbable |
| TM Tough-Mindedness | Receptive, Open-Minded, Intuitive | Tough-Minded, Resolute, Unempathic |
| IN Independence | Accommodating, Agreeable, Selfless | Independent, Persuasive, Willful |
| SC Self-Control | Unrestrained, Follows Urges | Self-Controlled, Inhibits Urges |

positive correlation. For example, Warmth (A+) is positively correlated with the Extraversion global factor. That is, being high on Warmth (A+) contributes to being high on Extraversion. On the other hand, Sensitivity (I+) is negatively correlated with the Tough-Mindedness global factor; that is, being high on Sensitivity (I+) contributes to being low on Tough-Mindedness. Thus, Sensitivity (I+) could be said to be negatively correlated with Tough-Mindedness or positively correlated with Receptivity, the minus pole of Tough-Mindedness. In most cases involving such an option, the correlation is described in the positive manner (e.g., being Sensitive (I+) contributes to Receptivity).

## Global Factors

In addition to the primary scales, the 16PF contains a set of five scales that combine related primary scales into global factors of personality. (The global factors historically have been called "second-order factors" in 16PF literature and result from a factor analysis of the test's primary scales.) Figure 4 lists the global factors and gives brief descriptors of each factor pole.

## Sten Scales

The 16PF uses "standardized ten" (sten) score scales. Sten scores range from 1-10, with a mean of 5.5 and a standard deviation of 2. Scores that fall farther from the mean (either in the high or the low direction) are considered more extreme. The more extreme a score is toward a given factor pole, the more likely that the descriptors for the scale's pole will apply for that score and that the trait will be apparent in the examinee's behavior.

Historically, 16PF stens of 4-7 have been considered to be within the average range; stens of 1-3, in the low range; and stens of 8-10, in the high range. (See Figure 5.) These same ranges continue to be used for the fifth edition, with a sten score of 4 being described as "low-average" and a sten score of 7, as "high-average." (Similar categorizations are used in the profile sheet and interpretive reports for the fifth edition.) In a sten distribution, most people are expected to score in the middle (theoretically, about 68% obtain a score within plus-or-minus one standard deviation from the mean). About 16% score at the low end, and another 16% score at the high end. The

FIGURE 5

STEN DISTRIBUTION

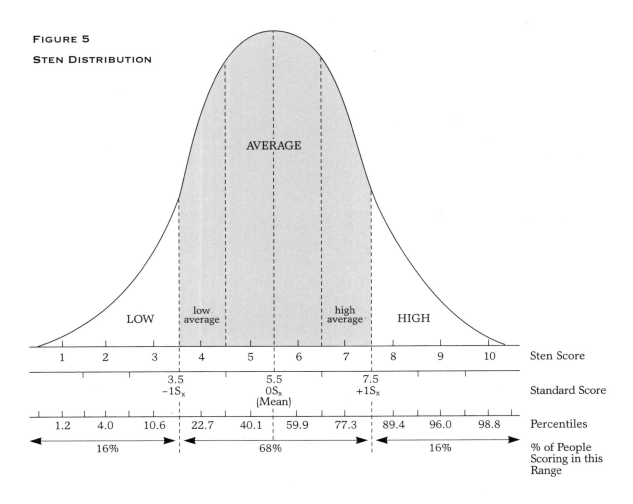

| | | | | | | | | | | |
|---|---|---|---|---|---|---|---|---|---|---|
| 1 | 2 | 3 | 4 | 5 | 6 | 7 | 8 | 9 | 10 | Sten Score |

AVERAGE

LOW    low average    high average    HIGH

| | | |
|---|---|---|
| 3.5 −1S$_x$ | 5.5 0S$_x$ (Mean) | 7.5 +1S$_x$ |

Standard Score

| 1.2 | 4.0 | 10.6 | 22.7 | 40.1 | 59.9 | 77.3 | 89.4 | 96.0 | 98.8 |
|---|---|---|---|---|---|---|---|---|---|

Percentiles

◄——— 16% ———► ◄——— 68% ———► ◄——— 16% ———►   % of People Scoring in this Range

actual percentages may vary somewhat, depending on the shape of the distribution for any given factor scale.

## Measurement Limits

Professionals need to integrate an understanding of measurement limits when interpreting 16PF Fifth Edition profiles. Because the scales are short (between 10 and 15 items each), they necessarily are an estimate of a person's true score on any given personality factor. Theoretically, a person's true score falls, 68% of the time, in a band of plus-or-minus one standard error unit. Most 16PF scales have a standard error of measurement ($SE_M$) that is close to 1 sten score point. (See Tables 37 and 38 in Appendix A for standard errors of measurement for the scales.) Thus, 68% of the time, the true score for a person falls within the score range of plus-or-minus 1 sten score point around his or her obtained score. That is, the true score for a sten score of 8 on a factor would be expected to fall, 68% of the time, within a sten score range of 7-9. For a 95% confidence interval, the score band expands to plus-or-minus two standard error units; that is, for a sten of 8, the true score falls, 95% of the time, within a sten range of 6-10.

Professionals should be careful not to over-interpret sten-score differences. This caution especially applies to interpreting scores at the extremes of the distribution where, in a few cases, a mere 2-point raw score difference (the answer to one item) can account for a 2-point sten score difference. See Table 39 in Appendix B for data concerning score distributions.

As mentioned previously, scores of 4 and 7 are termed "low-average" and "high-average," respectively. Professionals should realize that an examinee's true score might fall outside the average range because it is on the line between "average" and "distinctive" scores and because the scales are not perfect measures of traits. For example, an examinee's sten of 4 might shift down a sten-score point, thus falling outside the average range, if he or she were to be retested. Similarly, scores of 3 and 8, which fall outside the average line but along the line between average or extreme, should not be overinterpreted as extreme because the true scores might actually fall in the average range.

## INTERPRETIVE STRATEGY: APPROACH TO A 16PF PROFILE

### Recommended Strategy

The recommended strategy for 16PF profile interpretation involves evaluating the following in the sequence indicated:

1. Response style indices
2. Global factor scales
3. Primary factor scales

Each of the interpretive steps is described in the sections that follow. In general, response style indices are evaluated first as a check for atypical test-response styles. The global factors are examined next because they provide a broad picture of the person. Finally, the primary factor scales are evaluated to obtain details of the personality

picture. Scoring both the global dimensions and the primary scales is recommended for handscore users. Interpretive report programs score both sets of scales automatically. Chapter 2 of this manual describes how to administer and score the 16PF Fifth Edition.

### Step 1: Evaluate Response Style Indices

The fifth edition has three response style indices: Impression Management (IM), Infrequency (INF), and Acquiescence (ACQ). For full details on the development and use of these scales, professionals can consult *The 16PF Fifth Edition Technical Manual* (see Conn & Rieke, 1994e). The report findings are summarized here.

According to the authors of the scales, reviewing all three scales provides data about test-taking response styles. If an examinee's score on any of the indices is extreme, the professional should generate hypotheses about the examinee's test-taking attitude and, if possible, review information concerning the examinee (e.g., background data, other test results, notes from previous interactions and discussions after the testing). In some cases, retesting may be necessary.

Instructions on handscoring the response style scales are included in Appendix C. Fifth edition computer-based interpretive reports automatically score all three scales.

Interpretive information for each of the response style indices is given in the sections that follow. This information is based on the preliminary body of evidence available for the fifth edition. As users begin to develop a database on this edition, scale definitions will be refined to reflect the incoming data.

### Impression Management (IM) Scale

This bipolar scale consists of 12 items. The items are scored only on the IM scale and do not contribute to any of the primary personality scales.

## General Scale Meaning

IM is essentially a social-desirability scale, with high scores reflecting socially desirable responses and low scores reflecting willingness to admit undesirable attributes or behaviors. The item content reflects both socially desirable and undesirable behaviors or qualities.

Social-desirability response sets include elements of self-deception as well as elements of other-deception (Conn & Rieke, 1994e). Thus high scores can reflect impression management (presenting oneself to others as tending to behave in desirable ways), or they can reflect an examinee's self-image as a person who behaves in desirable ways. In both cases, the possibility exists that the socially desirable responses might be more positive than the examinee's actual behavior (i.e., a form of response distortion that may be conscious or unconscious) or that the examinee really might behave in socially desirable ways (i.e., the response choices accurately reflect the person's behavior).

## Item Content/Typical Self-Report

The IM scale includes items such as "Sometimes I would like to get even rather than forgive and forget;" and "I have said things that hurt others' feelings." Answering "false" to such items contributes to a higher score on IM, indicating a socially desirable response set, whereas answering "true" indicates a willingness to admit to less socially desirable behaviors. On the other hand, responding "true" to an item such as "I am always willing to help people" contributes to a higher score on IM. Items scored on the IM scale are listed in Table 42, Appendix C.

## Correlations with Other Measures

Table 1 presents correlations of the fifth edition's IM scale with the response style scales of other measures and those of the 16PF Form A and Form C. IM correlates significantly with other social desirability

TABLE 1

IM CORRELATIONS WITH OTHER DESIRABILITY SCALES (N=156 UNIVERSITY STUDENTS)

| Desirability Scale | Correlation with Impression Management |
|---|---|
| Self-Deception Enhancement | 0.54* |
| Other-Deception | 0.49* |
| Marlowe-Crowne | 0.54* |
| Faking Good (16PF, Form A) | 0.45* |
| Faking Bad (16PF, Form A) | −0.55* |
| Faking Good (16PF, Form C) | 0.48* |

Note. Self-Deception Enhancement and Other-Deception from Paulhus' Balanced Inventory of Desirable Responding (BIDR; Paulhus, 1990); Marlowe-Crowne scale (Crowne & Marlowe, 1964); Faking Good and Bad from the 16PF Fourth Edition, Forms A & C. Table from "Response Style Indices" by S. R. Conn and M. L. Rieke, 1994e. In S. R. Conn & M. L. Rieke (Eds.), *The 16PF Fifth Edition Technical Manual.* Champaign, IL: IPAT.

*$p < .01$.

measures (Conn & Rieke, 1994e), including
Marlowe-Crowne's social desirability scale
(.54) and Paulhus's Balanced Inventory of
Desirable Responding (BIDR). BIDR is a
measure of social desirability that contains
two subscales: Self-Deception Enhancement
(SDE), with which IM correlates (.54), and
the Other-Deception scale, with which IM
correlates (.49).

The fifth edition's IM scale correlates with
16PF Form A's Faking Good Scale (.45) and
with Faking Bad (–.55), and with Form C's
Faking Good Scale (.48).

*Correlations with Other 16PF Factors*
The IM scale correlates with several fifth
edition primary personality scales (Conn &
Rieke, 1994e). Its main relationships are to
primary scales that contribute to the Anxiety
and Extraversion global factors. (See Table
2.) IM correlates most highly with Emotional
Stability (C+) and Relaxedness (Q4–). In
fact, high IM scorers may tend to score in
the nonanxious direction on all scales related
to the Anxiety global factor, including Trust
(L–) and Self-Assurance (O–). Moreover,
high IM scorers also may tend
to score in the Extraverted direction on
scales related to this global factor. The
highest correlations are with Warmth (A+),
Social Boldness (H+), and Group-
Orientation (Q2–), and the correlation
with Forthrightness (N–) is also significant.
Finally, high IM scorers may tend to score in
the controlled direction on Seriousness (F–),
Rule-Consciousness (G+), Groundedness
(M–) and Perfectionism (Q3+), the primary
scales related to the Self-Control global
factor. Conversely, low scores on IM tend to
correlate with the same primaries, but in the
direction of admitting Anxiety, Introversion,
and less Self-Control.

*Use of the IM Scale*
Full elaboration of the use of the IM scale is
given by its authors in *The 16PF Fifth Edition
Technical Manual* (see Conn & Rieke, 1994e).

**TABLE 2**

**IM CORRELATIONS WITH 16PF PRIMARY
FACTOR SCALES
(N=4569, 2205 MALES, 2364 FEMALES)**

| Factor Scale | | Correlation with Impression Management |
|---|---|---|
| A | Warmth | .16* |
| B | Reasoning | –.01 |
| C | Emotional Stability | .50* |
| E | Dominance | –.02 |
| F | Liveliness | –.09* |
| G | Rule-Consciousness | .34* |
| H | Social Boldness | .20* |
| I | Sensitivity | –.03 |
| L | Vigilance | –.39* |
| M | Abstractedness | –.36* |
| N | Privateness | –.12* |
| O | Apprehension | –.39* |
| Q1 | Openness to Change | .06* |
| Q2 | Self-Reliance | –.21* |
| Q3 | Perfectionism | .17* |
| Q4 | Tension | –.53* |

Note. From "Response Style Indices" by S. R. Conn and M. L. Rieke, 1994e. In S. R. Conn & M. L. Rieke (Eds.), *The 16PF Fifth Edition Technical Manual*. Champaign, IL: IPAT.

*$p < .01$

In brief, if an examinee's score exceeds a certain level (usually the 95th percentile for the high end of the IM scale and the 5th percentile for the low end), the professional should consider possible explanations for the extreme response set. For the fifth edition, raw scores of 20 or higher fall at or above the 95th percentile compared to the norm sample. (See Appendix C, Table 41 for the set of possible raw scores and their corresponding percentile values.) Depending on the reasons for testing and the criticality of accurate test data, the professional might consider retesting, especially if deliberate distortion is suspected.

**Infrequency (INF) Scale**

The INF scale consists of 32 items taken from the full set of personality items in the fifth edition. Item selection was based on analyses of statistical frequencies of item response choices within a large sample ($\underline{N} = 4,346$), with the criterion being that a given response choice for an item should be selected infrequently, falling at or below a 6.5% endorsement rate. Even though the 16PF has a three-choice response format (*a*, *b*, or *c*), all infrequently chosen response choices were *b* responses (a question mark [?], representing the "uncertain or cannot decide" option). Therefore, when an *a* or *c* response is chosen for an INF scale item, that response does not contribute to the INF scale. (Finally, scale score percentile ranks were devised for the norm sample.)

*General Scale Meaning*

High scores on the INF scale indicate that an examinee answered a relatively large number of items in a way different from most people. Possible explanations for high INF scale scores include random responding, inability to decide, reactions to specific item content, reading or comprehension difficulties, or trying to avoid making the "wrong impression."

*Item Content/Typical Responses*

High INF scorers choose the middle response (?) to the following kinds of items, most of which are true or false and offer distinct choices: "I have said things that hurt others' feelings;" "In a situation where I'm in charge, I feel comfortable giving people directions;" "I don't usually mind if my room is messy;" "When I do something, I usually take time to think of everything I'll need for the job first." Items scored on the INF scale are listed in Table 44 in Appendix C.

*Use of the INF Scale*

The total raw score on the INF scale is converted to a percentile that compares the examinee to the normative sample for the fifth edition. Raw scores of 8 or greater fall at or above the 95th percentile relative to the norm sample, and are considered to be high. (Possible raw scores and their corresponding percentile values are presented in Table 43 in Appendix C.)

The importance of correctly identifying invalid protocols varies in different situations. Professionals may choose to set their own cutoffs for classifying protocols as invalid in accordance with the information presented here and relative to individual client cases. Base rate and hit rate considerations are included in the technical report on the development of the INF scale (Conn & Rieke, 1994e). In general, considering a protocol to be invalid if the raw score is 6 or greater would result in 90.4% of valid protocols being classified as valid and 9.6% being classified as random. To avoid misclassifying a protocol as valid when it is truly random, the cutoff should be more conservative. Comparable hit rates are presented for all raw score values in Table 45, Appendix C.

If an examinee's INF score is above the 95th percentile or above another designated cutoff, the professional should try to determine why the uncertain response choice (?)

was selected so frequently. Possible explanations for high INF scale scores are listed in the preceding "General Scale Meaning" section.

## Acquiescence (ACQ) Scale

The Acquiescence (ACQ) scale measures the tendency to answer "true" to an item, no matter what its content. This scale, which consists of 103 true-or-false items, is unique to the 16PF Fifth Edition. Its utility will be determined by test users in applications of the fifth edition.

### General Scale Meaning

An acquiescent response set reflects an examinee's tendency to answer "true" to incongruous items such as these: "I tend to like to be in charge" and "I tend to be more comfortable taking orders than being in charge." This response set may denote a misunderstanding of item content, random responding, difficulty in attending to self-evaluative questions, or inability to choose a self-descriptive response. An acquiescent response set also might indicate an unclear self-image or a high need for the testing professional's approval (or approval by people in general).

### Item Content/Typical Responses

All items on the ACQ scale are true-false items. Thus, a high score indicates an overall pattern of tending to respond "true" to items rather than choosing answers based on the item content. Items scored on the ACQ scale are listed in Table 47 in Appendix C.

### Use of the ACQ Scale

As with the other response style scales, scores above the 95th percentile on the ACQ scale signify the possibility of an acquiescent response set. Raw scores of 71 or higher exceed the 95th percentile and are considered high. (See Table 46 in Appendix C for the set of raw scores and their corresponding percentile values.) The testing professional

should try to determine whether the high score reflects random, inconsistent or indecisive responding, or a high need for approval.

### Step 2: Evaluate Global Factor Scales

Table 13 in Chapter 5 presents the factor pattern for the five global factors along which the primary scales cluster: Extraversion, Anxiety, Tough-Mindedness, Independence, and Self-Control. Descriptions of both poles of each global factor are listed in Figure 4. Readers may recognize links between the 16PF global factors and the "big five" model of personality that is discussed in personality literature. For more technical details about the global factors, see *The 16PF Fifth Edition Technical Manual* (Conn & Rieke, 1994f).

For each global factor, a set of primary scales "load on" the global construct; that is, the scale set contributes to, or makes up, the global construct. For example, Warmth (A+), Liveliness (F+), Social Boldness (H+), Forthrightness (N−), and Group-Orientation (Q2−) compose the scale set that contributes to the Extraversion global factor.

An understanding of the primary factor scales is critical to understanding the global factor scales. Therefore, 16PF users should become familiar with such test characteristics as scale reliabilities, score distributions and standard errors of measurement ($SE_M$), and correlations with other measures. Evidence for these characteristics is summarized in this manual's text and tables and examined fully in *The 16PF Fifth Edition Technical Manual* (Conn & Rieke, 1994f).

The sections that follow discuss how to evaluate broad trends evident at the global factor level in a 16PF profile. Each global factor is described in terms of the primary scales that contribute to it and its meaning. The pole of the bipolar primary scale that contributes to the global factor will be identified by a plus (+) or minus (−) following the factor name. For example, scoring high (+) on Warmth (Factor A), Liveliness (Factor F), and Social Boldness (Factor H) contributes to being Extraverted on the global factor. Scoring low (−) on Privateness (Factor N) and Self-Reliance (Factor Q2) also contributes to the Extraversion global factor score. Equations for calculating global factor scores are presented in Table 13 in Chapter 5.

Many, but not all, significant other-measure correlations that support the global factor constructs are described in the text that follows. Each of these correlations is significant at least at the $p < .01$ level. Table 3 selects the highest correlations with other

measures but does not include all correlations significant at $p < .01$. Tabular information concerning all global factor correlations with other measures is presented in Chapter 5.

**Broad Trends**

Before examining the specific global scale scores in a 16PF profile, testing professionals are encouraged to look at broad trends within the profile.

*Evaluate Number of Extreme Scores*

As noted in prior explanations of the sten distribution, the extreme scores in a profile usually indicate an examinee's most distinctive traits. Thus, the greater the numbers of extreme scores, the more distinctive the personality expression is likely to be.

TABLE 3

HIGHEST CORRELATIONS BETWEEN GLOBAL FACTORS AND OTHER PERSONALITY MEASURES

| 16PF Global Factor | PRF Content Scale ($\underline{N} = 225$) | CPI Folk Scale ($\underline{N} = 212$) | NEO Facet ($\underline{N} = 257$) | MBTI Type ($\underline{N} = 119$) |
|---|---|---|---|---|
| Extraversion | Affiliation (56) | Sociability (59) | Gregariousness, E2 (70) | Extraversion (68) |
| | Exhibition (54) | Social Presence (54) | Warmth, E1 (61) | Introversion (−61) |
| | Nurturance (40) | Self-acceptance (49) | Positive Emotions, E6 (47) | Judging (−26) |
| | Succorance (39) | Empathy (48) | Assertiveness, E3 (45) | Feeling (19) |
| | Play (38) | Capacity for Status (40) | Excitement-Seeking, E5 (39) | Thinking (−18) |
| | Autonomy (−25) | Dominance (31) | Trust, A1 (38) | |
| | Impulsivity (23) | Independence (25) | Altruism, A3 (32) | |
| | Dominance (20) | Flexibility (21) | Self-Consciousness, N4 (−31) | |
| | Cognitive Structure (−20) | Well-being (19) | Depression, N3 (−28) | |
| | Change (18) | Tolerance (18) | Fantasy, O1 (26) | |
| | | | Aesthetics, O2 (24) | |
| | | | Feelings, O3 (24) | |
| | | | Tender-Mindedness, A6 (24) | |
| | | | Vulnerability, N6 (−22) | |
| | | | Deliberation, C6 (−22) | |
| | | | Anxiety, N1 (−21) | |
| | | | Activity, E4 (21) | |

<u>Note.</u> Decimals omitted. Other measures include Personality Research Form (PRF) content scales, California Psychological Inventory (CPI) folk scales, NEO Personality Inventory, Revised (NEO PI-R) facets, and Myers-Briggs Type Indicator (MBTI) types. Data summarized from "Construct Validation of the 16PF Fifth Edition" by S. R. Conn & M. L. Rieke, 1994b. In S. R. Conn & M. L. Rieke (Eds)., *The 16PF Fifth Edition Technical Manual*. Champaign, IL: Institute for Personality and Ability Testing, Inc. Correlations are presented in parentheses following a scale name.

All correlations are significant at the $p < .01$ level.

TABLE 3, CONTINUED

HIGHEST CORRELATIONS BETWEEN GLOBAL FACTORS AND OTHER PERSONALITY MEASURES

| 16PF Global Factor | PRF Content Scale | CPI Folk Scale | NEO Facet | MBTI Type |
|---|---|---|---|---|
| Anxiety | Defendence (42) | Independence (−54) | Depression, N3 (66) | Extraversion (−38) |
| | Aggression (36) | Capacity for | Anxiety, N1 (63) | Introversion (23) |
| | Exhibition (−22) | Status (−50) | Angry Hostility, N2 (59) | |
| | Cognitive | Psychological- | Self-Consciousness, N4 (55) | |
| | Structure (21) | mindedness (−50) | Vulnerability, N6 (51) | |
| | Social | Well-being (−49) | Trust, A1 (−47) | |
| | Recognition (20) | Empathy (−48) | Impulsiveness, N5 (30) | |
| | Affiliation (−18) | Good Impression (−47) | Positive Emotions, E6 (−29) | |
| | | Social Presence (−46) | Assertiveness, E3 (−26) | |
| | | Achievement via | Warmth, E1 (−24) | |
| | | Independence (−45) | Gregariousness, E2 (−23) | |
| | | Intellectual | Compliance, A4 (−23) | |
| | | Efficiency (−45) | Actions, O4 (−21) | |
| | | Sociability (−41) | Straightforwardness, A2 (−19) | |
| | | Tolerance (−38) | Self−Discipline, C5 (−19) | |
| | | Achievement via | | |
| | | Conformance (−37) | | |
| | | Dominance (−34) | | |
| | | Self-acceptance (−33) | | |
| | | Femininity/Masculinity (30) | | |
| | | Self-control (−28) | | |
| | | Responsibility (−24) | | |
| | | Socialization (−22) | | |
| | | Flexibility (−22) | | |
| Tough-Mindedness | Change (−34) | Flexibility (−32) | Aesthetics, O2 (−53) | Sensing (56) |
| | Understanding (−32) | Capacity for Status (−27) | Fantasy, O1 (−41) | Intuitive (−56) |
| | Cognitive | Self-acceptance (−26) | Feelings, O3 (−37) | Feeling (−26) |
| | Structure (27) | Empathy (−26) | Values, O6 (−33) | Thinking (24) |
| | Order (26) | Independence (−21) | Actions, O4 (−31) | |
| | Sentience (−26) | Achievement via | Order, C2 (28) | |
| | Nurturance (−23) | Independence (−21) | Tender-Mindedness, A6 (−26) | |
| | Impulsivity (−19) | Social Presence (−19) | Achievement Striving, C4 (23) | |
| | | Sociability (−18) | Deliberation, C6 (23) | |
| | | Self-control (18) | Altruism, A3 (−22) | |
| | | | Self-Discipline, C5 (21) | |

HIGHEST CORRELATIONS BETWEEN GLOBAL FACTORS AND OTHER PERSONALITY MEASURES

| 16PF Global Factor | PRF Content Scale | CPI Folk Scale | NEO Facet | MBTI Type |
|---|---|---|---|---|
| Independence | Dominance (54) | Dominance (53) | Assertiveness, E3 (60) | Extraversion (39) |
| | Exhibition (47) | Self-acceptance (53) | Self-Consciousness, N4 (-44) | Sensing (-36) |
| | Aggression (29) | Independence (51) | Compliance, A4 (-44) | Introversion (-35) |
| | Change (29) | Sociability (45) | Activity, A4 (40) | Intuitive (32) |
| | Abasement (-28) | Social Presence (40) | Modesty, A5 (-34) | Thinking (22) |
| | Harm Avoidance (-23) | Capacity for Status (33) | Gregariousness, E2 (32) | Feeling (-19) |
| | Play (22) | Psychological-mindedness (29) | Straightforwardness, A2 (-31) | |
| | Defendence (21) | Femininity/Masculinity (-27) | Vulnerability, N6 (-28) | |
| | Impulsivity (19) | Self-control (-22) | Excitement-Seeking, E5 (25) | |
| | | Intellectual Efficiency (22) | Actions, O4 (24) | |
| | | Empathy (19) | Anxiety, N1 (-23) | |
| | | | Depression, N3 (-22) | |
| | | | Positive Emotions, E6 (22) | |
| | | | Competence, C1 (22) | |
| | | | Warmth, E1 (20) | |
| | | | Ideas, O5 (20) | |
| Self-Control | Impulsivity (-60) | Self-control (54) | Order, C2 (57) | Perceptive (-57) |
| | Cognitive Structure (54) | Flexibility (-54) | Deliberation, C6 (57) | Judging (54) |
| | Order (54) | Good Impression (46) | Achievement Striving, C4 (44) | Sensing (38) |
| | Play (-39) | Achievement via Conformance (44) | Self-Discipline, C5 (44) | Intuitive (-35) |
| | Autonomy (-34) | Socialization (40) | Dutifulness, C3 (42) | |
| | Change (-34) | Responsibility (32) | Competence, C1 (39) | |
| | Endurance (33) | Social Presence (-25) | Fantasy, O1 (-35) | |
| | Harm Avoidance (32) | Well-being (20) | Impulsiveness, N5 (-32) | |
| | Achievement (31) | | Actions, O4 (-32) | |
| | Exhibition (-25) | | Excitement-Seeking, E5 (-25) | |
| | | | Values, O6 (-24) | |
| | | | Gregariousness, E2 (-23) | |
| | | | Positive Emotions, E6 (-22) | |
| | | | Straightforwardness, A2 (20) | |

Table 4 presents the numbers of extreme global factor sten scores (scores that fall outside the average range of 4-7). The majority of examinees (78.6%) obtain all average scores at the global factor level or are extreme on only one or two global factors. This outcome is compatible with sten distributions, in which, theoretically, 68% of people tend to score in the average range. That an examinee would have extreme scores on four or all five global factors is rare. Only about 6% of the fifth edition norm sample had global factors scores that were so distinctive.

*Remember the Primary Factor Scale Relationships*

When interpreting a global factor score, the testing professional should identify (1) contributing primary scale scores that are in the expected direction for the global factor, and (2) primary scale scores that are in the opposite direction. With a knowledge that certain scales are expected to contribute to a given global factor, the professional can begin to identify unusual factor combinations and can form hypotheses about possible ways that conflicting scores might be expressed in an examinee's life.

For example, if an examinee is extraverted and all the related primary scale scores are in the extraverted direction, he or she probably moves toward other people in a consistent manner. On the other hand, if an examinee is extraverted on some relevant primary scales and introverted on others, he or she may experience conflict. That is, the examinee may be extraverted in some situations or ways but not in others, or may be ambivalent about how to or whether to move toward others.

Another example involves an overall global Extraversion score that is low-average. Such a score can reflect various combinations of the primary scales since several primary scales contribute to the global factor score.

TABLE 4

NUMBER OF EXTREME GLOBAL FACTOR SCORES ON 16PF PROFILES (BASED UPON NORM SAMPLE, $\underline{N}$=2500)

| Number of Extreme Scores | Percent of Sample | Cumulative Percent |
|---|---|---|
| 0 | 26.4 | 26.4 |
| 1 | 29.5 | 55.9 |
| 2 | 22.7 | 78.6 |
| 3 | 15.1 | 93.8 |
| 4 | 5.0 | 98.7 |
| 5 | 1.3 | 100.0 |

For instance, one person with this score might be Reserved (A–), average on Liveliness (Factor F) and Social Boldness (Factor H), and high on Self-Reliance (Q2+). This person could be expected to be reserved, serious, and self-sufficient, but not timid. If there is no sign of anxiousness or lack of self-confidence, the person may be comfortable with his or her introversion. Another person with a low-average Extraversion score might be average on Warmth (Factor A) and Liveliness (Factor F), but also Shy (H–) and Group-Oriented (Q2–). This introvert shows more timidity and dependency on other people and less orientation away from people than the introvert in the previous example. A fair hypothesis would be that the second introvert might enjoy being around people but that his or her reticence and shyness intrude. Another possibility is that this person would like to be group-oriented so that he or she can get lost in a crowd (Q2–) as a way to deal with the evident timidity.

The global factor interpretive information that follows is based on the preliminary body of evidence available for the 16PF Fifth Edition. As test users begin to develop a database, scale definitions will be refined to reflect the incoming data.

## Extraversion (Extraverted Versus Introverted)

| Introversion | Weight in Scoring Equation | Extraversion |
|---|---|---|
| Reserved (A–) | .3 | Warm (A+) |
| Serious (F–) | .3 | Lively (F+) |
| Shy (H–) | .2 | Socially Bold (H+) |
| Private (N+) | .3 | Forthright (N–) |
| Self-Reliant (Q2+) | .3 | Group-Oriented (Q2–) |

*General Factor Meaning*

Extraversion has been included in even the earliest descriptions of personality. The construct is largely attributed to Jung (1971), but has been found and described in many subsequent studies such as those by Eysenck (1960) and Cattell (1957, April). Extraversion continues to be measured in the "big five" model of personality so popular in current personality literature (Goldberg, 1992). In the original 16PF Handbook, Extraversion was said to orient around a general social participation (Cattell et al., 1970, p. 117). Extraverts tend to be people-oriented and to seek out relationships with others. Introverts tend to be less outgoing and sociable; they tend to spend more time in their own company than in that of others. Extraversion has several contributing aspects, as reflected in the primary factor scales that play a role in the overall global factor. Extraversion includes interpersonal Warmth (A+), a stimulation-seeking type of sociability called Liveliness (F+), Social Boldness (H+), Forthrightness (N–), and the need to affiliate with other people, especially in groups, called Group-Orientation (Q2–).

A strong relationship exists between social desirability and the Extraversion global factor; several of the extraversion-related primary factors are correlated with the fifth edition Impression Management (IM) scale. (See individual primary scale descriptions for further evidence.) Even though introversion is seen as less desirable than extraversion, it may be associated with independence of thought and a tendency to think and deliberate, as demonstrated by correlations.

*Correlations with Other Measures*

Extraversion correlates highly with numerous other measures of social participation and extraversion: PRF's Affiliation, Exhibition, Nurturance, and Succorance; all of NEO's Extraversion facets; CPI's Sociability, Social Presence, and Capacity for Status; and MBTI's Extraversion. Extraversion can have a flavor of being oriented to feelings and to being empathic, as suggested by correlations with CPI's Empathy and with NEO's Feelings (O3) and Tender-Mindedness (O6). Extraversion also can have a more dominant flavor with a commanding social presence, as evidenced by links between PRF's Dominance and CPI's Dominance and Capacity for Status. A flavor of playfulness, flexibility, and tolerance may be evident in Extraversion, perhaps supported by positive correlations with CPI's Tolerance and Flexibility scales, PRF's Play, and the two NEO Openness facets of Fantasy (O1) and Aesthetics (O2). Extraversion is related to measures of well-being, as evidenced by a positive correlation with CPI's Well-being and negative correlations with four of the five NEO Neuroticism facets—Anxiety (N1), Depression (N3), Self-Consciousness (N4), and Vulnerability (N6). Introversion, on the other hand, can have the opposite qualities: nonsociability and lower flexibility. Sometimes, Introversion may be associated with independence of thought and a tendency to think and deliberate, as evidenced by negative correlations with PRF's Autonomy and Cognitive Structure scales, MBTI's Thinking and Judging scales, and NEO's Deliberation (C6).

## Anxiety (Anxious Versus Unperturbed)

| Low Anxiety | Weight in Scoring Equation | High Anxiety |
|---|---|---|
| Emotionally Stable (C+) | .4 | Reactive (C–) |
| Trusting (L–) | .3 | Vigilant (L+) |
| Self-Assured (O–) | .4 | Apprehensive (O+) |
| Relaxed (Q4–) | .4 | Tense (Q4+) |

*General Factor Meaning*

Like Extraversion, Anxiety has been described since early studies of personality, and continues to be described in studies of the "big-five" dimensions of personality (Goldberg, 1992). Anxiety has several contributing aspects, as reflected in its related primary factor scales. Anxiety includes a tendency to be Reactive (C–) rather than adaptive, distrustful and Vigilant (L+), worrying and Apprehensive (O+), and Tense (Q4+).

Anxiety can be aroused in response to external events, or it can be internally generated. Anxiousness may be an activation of the "fight-or-flight" state associated with perceived or actual threat, as suggested by the correlations. Low-anxious people tend to be unperturbed; however, they may minimize negative affect or be unmotivated to change because they are comfortable. Since anxious people often experience more negative affect, they may have difficulty controlling their emotions or reactions and may act in counterproductive ways, as suggested by the correlations.

A strong relationship exists between social desirability and Anxiety; several of the anxiety-related primary factors are correlated with the fifth edition Impression Management (IM) scale as well as with CPI's Good Impression scale. (See individual primary scales for further evidence.)

## Correlations with Other Measures

This global factor is linked to several other measures of anxiety, including all NEO Neuroticism facets. Anxious people may tend to make a poor social impression and may appear to lack confidence or assertive ambition, as supported by positive correlations with NEO's Self-Consciousness scale and by negative correlations with CPI's Dominance, Social Presence, Capacity for Status, Achievement via Conformance or via Independence, and Good Impression scales. Links between anxiousness and subjective discomfort are supported by correlations with CPI's Well-being and Self-acceptance scales and with NEO's Vulnerability scale. Feeling anxious may preclude seeing oneself and other people clearly, as suggested by negative correlations with CPI's Empathy and Psychological-mindedness scales. Fight-or-flight impulses may be supported by correlations with PRF's Aggression and Defendence scales. In fact, the PRF's Defendence scale description is "Ready to defend self against real or imagined harm..." (Jackson, 1989, p. 6). A tendency to be unable to prevent pent-up tensions from spilling out is suggested in links with NEO's Impulsiveness (N5) and PRF's Aggression scale and in negative correlations with CPI's control measures of Socialization, Responsibility, and Self-control.

As mentioned previously, the Anxiety global factor is linked with social desirability, as measured by CPI's Good Impression scale and the fifth edition Impression Management (IM) scale. In fact, several of the anxiety-related primary factors are correlated with the IM scale. (See individual primary scales for further evidence.)

## Tough-Mindedness (Tough-Minded Versus Receptive)

| Receptive | Weight in Scoring Equation | Tough-Minded |
|---|---|---|
| Warm (A +) | .2 | Reserved (A–) |
| Sensitive (I +) | .5 | Utilitarian (I–) |
| Abstracted (M +) | .3 | Grounded (M–) |
| Open to Change (Q1 +) | .5 | Traditional (Q1–) |

### General Factor Meaning

Cattell originally called this global factor "Cortertia," an abbreviation for "Cortical alertness" (Cattell et al., 1970, p. 119). High scorers on Cortertia were described as alert and tending to deal with problems at a dry, cognitive level. The factor later assumed the more popularized term "Tough Poise."

In the fifth edition, this global factor is called Tough-Mindedness, and it has several contributing aspects, as reflected in its related primary factor scales. Tough-Minded people tend to be Reserved (A–), Utilitarian (I–), Grounded (M–), and Traditional (Q1–). In addition to operating at a dry, cognitive level, extremely Tough-Minded people may portray a sense of being "established," possibly to the degree of being set or fixed. That is, they may not be open to other points of view, to unusual people, or to new experiences. Receptive people, on the other hand, are Warm (A +), Sensitive (I +), Abstracted (M +) and Open to Change (Q1 +). While they may be more open than their Tough-Minded counterparts, Receptive people may overlook the practical or objective aspects of a situation.

Users of previous 16PF editions may recall that the Tough-Minded label had been given to Factor I, one of the main primaries that contributed to this global factor. For the fifth edition, Tough-Mindedness has become the name of the high pole of the global factor because it appropriately represents the overriding thread that runs through all the contributing primary scales. Factor I continues to contribute to Tough-Mindedness; however, its contribution is more specific to sensitivity and aesthetic values on the high end and to utilitarian values and objectivity on the low end. Hence, the primary scale Factor I has been renamed "Sensitivity" for the fifth edition. The low pole of the Tough-Mindedness global factor is named Receptive in the fifth edition. Receptive people tend to deal with problems in a cultured, refined, or sensitive way. They also tend to be open to interpersonal involvement (Warmth, A+), to sensitive perceptions (Sensitivity, I+), to ideas and fantasy (Abstractedness, M+), and to change (Openness to Change, Q1+). Correlations provide supporting evidence, including strong correlations with NEO's Openness to Experience dimension and all but one of its facets and with MBTI's Intuition and Feeling scales.

A certain inflexibility and lack of openness may be apparent in Tough-Mindedness. In fact, toughness and resoluteness can border on inflexibility and entrenchment, as suggested by the correlations. Tough-Minded people may have difficulty in accepting new viewpoints, including those that involve emotions. In contrast, Receptive people can be more open to experiencing feelings, possibly even negative affective states. As a result, Receptive people may experience difficulty in setting aside their feeling reactions to attain objectivity, and consequently, may overlook the practical aspects of situations. Gender stereotypes are associated with Tough-Mindedness and Receptivity, the former being more "masculine" and the latter being more "feminine."

*Correlations with Other Measures*

The link between Tough-Mindedness and the tendency to deal with life at a dry, cognitive level is supported in positive correlations with MBTI's Sensing and Thinking scales and with PRF's Cognitive Structure scale. Several NEO Conscientiousness facets are positively correlated with Tough-Mindedness, including Order (C2), Achievement Striving (C4), Self-Discipline (C5), and Deliberation (C6), as is CPI's Self-control scale; PRF's Impulsivity scale is negatively correlated with Tough-Mindedness. Tough-Mindedness may come at the cost of understanding, self-acceptance, or pleasure, as evidenced by negative correlations with PRF's Understanding and Sentience scales and with CPI's Flexibility and Self-acceptance scales. The inflexibility of Tough-Mindedness is suggested by negative correlations with CPI's Flexibility scale and with PRF's Change and Understanding scales. The link between Receptivity and being open to experience is suggested by correlations with all but one of NEO's Openness facets, including Fantasy (O1), Aesthetics (O2), Feelings (O3), Actions (O4), and Values (O5). That Receptive people tend toward emotionality and empathy is supported by the correlations with MBTI's Intuitive and Feeling scales and with CPI's Empathy scale. Receptive people also may tend to be warm and caring, as suggested by correlations with PRF's Nurturance scale, CPI's Empathy and Sociability scales, and NEO'S Altruism (A3) facet.

## Independence (Independent Versus Accommodating)

| Accommodating | Weight in Scoring Equation | Independent |
|---|---|---|
| Deferential (E–) | .6 | Dominant (E+) |
| Timid (H–) | .3 | Bold (H+) |
| Trusting (L–) | .2 | Vigilant (L+) |
| Traditional (Q1–) | .3 | Open to Change (Q1+) |

*General Factor Meaning*

Independence revolves around the tendency to be actively and forcefully self-determined in one's thinking and actions. Independence has several contributing aspects, as reflected in its primary factor scales. This global factor includes tendencies to be Dominant (E+), Socially Bold (H+), Vigilant (L+), and Open to Change (Q1+). Independent people tend to enjoy trying new things and exhibit an intellectual curiosity, as shown in correlations with other measures. A strong element of social forcefulness is evident in Independence. Independent people tend to form and to express their own opinions. They often are persuasive and forceful, willing to challenge the status quo, and suspicious of interference from others. Extreme Independence—especially when not tempered with Self-Control or the sociability of Extraversion or the sensitivity of Receptivity—can assume a certain amount of disagreeableness. In the fifth edition, Independence may have flavors of inflexibility and domination, as supported by correlations with other measures. Independent people may be uncomfortable or ineffective in situations that involve accommodating other people.

In contrast to Independent people, Accommodating people tend to be Deferential (E–), Shy (H–), Trusting (L–), and Traditional (Q1–). They tend not to question; instead, they value agreeableness and accommodation more than self-determination or getting their way. External situations and other people tend to influence them, both in terms of forming opinions and shaping behavior. They may be very uncomfortable or ineffective in situations that call for self-expression, assertiveness, or persuasion. Accommodation may be linked with the wish to avoid harm or with anxiousness, as suggested by the correlations.

*Correlations with Other Measures*

Independent people can have a strong social presence, as indicated by positive correlations with CPI's Capacity for Status, Sociability, and Social Presence scales; with PRF's Exhibition scale; and with all of NEO's Extraversion facets. A possibly aggressive or domineering component also may be suggested by positive correlations with PRF's Aggression, Dominance, and Defence scales and CPI's Dominance scale, and by negative correlations with three of NEO's Agreeableness facets—Straightforwardness (A2), Compliance (A4), and Modesty (A5). Independent people's intellectual curiosity and desire to try new things are supported in positive correlations with PRF's Change and Play scales, CPI's Intellectual Efficiency and Psychological-mindedness scales, and NEO's Actions (O4) and Ideas (O5) scales. An element of noncompliance in Independence can be supported by negative correlations with NEO's Compliance (A4) and by positive correlations with CPI's Independence scale. An element of unrestrictedness and lack of self-control may be suggested by negative correlations with CPI's Self-control scale and PRF's Impulsivity scale. On the other hand, a link between Accommodation and Anxiety is shown by negative correlations with four of the five NEO Neuroticism facets, including Anxiety (N1), Depression (N3), Self-Consciousness (N4), and Vulnerability (N6). Additionally, Accommodation is related to PRF's Harm-Avoidance and Abasement scales.

## Self-Control (Self-Controlled Versus Unrestrained)

| Unrestrained | Weight in Scoring Equation | Self-Controlled |
|---|---|---|
| Lively (F+) | .2 | Serious (F-) |
| Expedient (G-) | .4 | Rule-Conscious (G+) |
| Abstracted (M+) | .3 | Grounded (M-) |
| Tolerates Disorder (Q3-) | .4 | Perfectionistic (Q3+) |

*General Factor Meaning*

Self-Control concerns curbing one's urges. High scorers tend to be able to inhibit their impulses and may do so in several ways, depending on the pattern of scores on the related primary factor scales. For example, Self-Controlled people can be Serious (F-), Rule-Conscious (G+), practical and Grounded (M-), and/or Perfectionistic (Q3+) as a means to Self-Control. Either Self-Controlled people simply do not value flexibility or spontaneity, or they may have acquired self-control at the expense of these qualities. The link between Self-Control and being rigid in certain ways is supported by correlations with other measures. A link also exists between Self-Control and social desirability, with higher control being more socially desirable.

In contrast to Self-Controlled people, Unrestrained people tend to follow their urges more. This Unrestrainedness can be reflected in several ways: in spontaneity and Liveliness (F+), in Expedience (G-), in Abstractedness (M+), and/or in a Tolerance of Disorder (Q3-). Unrestrained people may be flexible in their responses; however, in situations that call for self-control, they may find it difficult to restrain themselves. They may be perceived as self-indulgent, disorganized, irrepressible, or irresponsible, depending on whether they can muster

resources for self-control when doing so is important.

*Correlations with Other Measures*

The Self-Control global factor is related to several other measures of self-control, being positively correlated with all of NEO's Conscientiousness facets—Competence (C1), Order (C2), Dutifulness (C3), Achievement Striving (C4), Self-Discipline (C5), and Deliberation (C6). Self-Control also is positively correlated with CPI's Responsibility, Socialization, Self-control, and Achievement via Conformity scales. In relation to PRF's scales, Self-Control correlates positively with Achievement, Harm Avoidance, and Endurance and negatively with Impulsivity. Self-Control also correlates with CPI's Social Presence and Good Impression scales, confirming the link between social desirability and Self-Control. Some scale correlations may suggest that elements of sociable self-expression and of openness to experience might be restricted when Self-Control is high. For example, Self-Control shows negative correlations with CPI's Flexibility scale, with PRF's Play, Autonomy, and Change scales, and with MBTI's Intuition and Perception scales. Self-Control also correlates negatively with NEO's Extraversion facets of Gregariousness (E2), Excitement-Seeking (E5), and Positive Emotions (E6) and negatively with NEO's Openness to Experience facets of Fantasy (O2), Actions (O4), and Values (O6).

### Step 3: Evaluate Primary Factor Scales

To fully understand the 16PF Fifth Edition primary scales, testing professionals not only should study this chapter but also scale information presented elsewhere in this manual. For example, professionals should understand scale reliabilities, score distributions and standard errors of measurement ($SE_M$), intercorrelations among the scales, correlations with other measures, and so forth. These data, which are presented in tables throughout this manual and in the appendixes, are synthesized in the sections that follow. For each primary scale, the general scale meaning is defined, items contributing to the scale are discussed, and supporting correlations are presented. (Note: A correlation must be significant at the $p < .01$ level. Many, but not all, of the significant correlations are discussed here.

Table 5 selects the highest correlations with other measures; tables showing all correlations with other measures are in Chapter 5.) The interpretive information that follows is based on the preliminary body of evidence available for the fifth edition. As users begin to develop a database on this edition, scale definitions will be refined to reflect the incoming data.

TABLE 5

HIGHEST CORRELATIONS BETWEEN PRIMARY FACTORS AND OTHER PERSONALITY MEASURES

| 16PF Primary Factor | PRF Content Scale ($\underline{N}$ = 225) | CPI Folk Scale ($\underline{N}$ = 212) | NEO PI-R Facet ($\underline{N}$ = 257) | MBTI Type ($\underline{N}$ = 119) |
|---|---|---|---|---|
| Warmth (A) | Nurturance (39) Affiliation (35) Exhibition (30) Succorance (27) Autonomy (–26) | Empathy (42) Sociability (37) Social Presence (32) Self-acceptance (32) | Gregariousness, E2 (46) Warmth, E1 (44) Altruism, A3 (33) Positive Emotions, E6 (31) Feelings, O3 (29) Tender-Mindedness, A6 (27) | Extraversion (41) Introversion (–36) Thinking (–32) |
| Reasoning (B) | Order (–26) | Intellectual Efficiency (22) | Intuitive (27) | |
| Emotional Stability (C) | Affiliation (27) Defendence (–27) Dominance (26) Exhibition (26) | Well-being (52) Independence (51) Social Presence (47) Psychological-mindedness (47) Capacity for Status (42) Achievement via Conformance (42) Intellectual Efficiency (42) Achievement via Independence (40) Empathy (40) | Depression, N3 (–69) Vulnerability, N6 (–59) Anxiety, N1 (–57) Self-Consciousness, N4 (–53) Angry Hostility, N2 (–49) Trust, A1 (40) | Extraversion (36) |
| Dominance (E) | Dominance (48) Aggression (34) Abasement (–33) Exhibition (31) | Dominance (50) Self-acceptance (45) Independence (45) Sociability (35) Social Presence (33) | Assertiveness, E3 (55) Compliance, A4 (–48) Modesty, A5 (–40) Self-Consciousness, N4 (–39) Activity, E4 (38) Straightforwardness, A2 (–31) Competence, C1 (31) | Extraversion (31) |

Note. Decimals omitted. Other measures include Personality Research Form (PRF) content scales, California Psychological Inventory (CPI) folk scales, NEO Personality Inventory, Revised (NEO PI-R) facets, and Myers-Briggs Type Indicator (MBTI) types. Correlations are presented in parentheses following a scale name. From "Construct Validation of the 16PF Fifth Edition" by S. R. Conn and M. L. Rieke, 1994b. In S. R. Conn & M. L. Rieke (Eds.), *The 16PF Fifth Edition Technical Manual.* Champaign, IL: Institute for Personality and Ability Testing, Inc.

All correlations are significant at the $p < .01$ level.

HIGHEST CORRELATIONS BETWEEN PRIMARY FACTORS AND OTHER PERSONALITY MEASURES

| 16PF Primary Factor | PRF Content Scale | CPI Folk Scale | NEO Facet | MBTI Type |
|---|---|---|---|---|
| Liveliness (F) | Play (52) Affiliation (50) Exhibition (49) Impulsivity (37) | Social Presence (51) Sociability (50) Self-acceptance (43) Self-control (−38) Empathy (36) | Excitement-Seeking, E5 (57) Gregariousness, E2 (55) Warmth, E1 (45) Positive Emotions, E6 (41) Assertiveness, E3 (35) Activity, E4 (30) | Introversion (−51) Extraversion (48) |
| Rule-Consciousness (G) | Impulsivity (−47) Autonomy (−37) Cognitive Structure (37) Order (33) Achievement (30) Endurance (30) Play (−30) | Self-control (39) Good Impression (37) Responsibility (36) Achievement via Conformance (34) Flexibility (−32) Socialization (31) | Deliberation, C6 (39) Dutifulness, C3 (36) Achievement Striving, C4 (32) | Perceptive (−37) Judging (25) |
| Social Boldness (H) | Exhibition (71) Dominance (46) Affiliation (39) Play (36) | Sociability (63) Self-acceptance (60) Social Presence (54) Independence (51) Capacity for Status (50) Dominance (48) Empathy (43) | Assertiveness, E3 (62) Gregariousness, E2 (51) Self-Consciousness, N4 (−49) Warmth, E1 (43) Excitement-Seeking, E5 (34) Anxiety, N1 (−33) Depression, N3 (−33) Positive Emotions, E6 (33) Vulnerability, N6 (−32) Activity, E4 (31) | Extraversion (65) Introversion (−52) |
| Sensitivity (I) | Understanding (25) | | Aesthetics, O2 (43) Fantasy, O1 (27) Feelings, O3 (26) | Intuitive (28) Feeling (28) |
| Vigilance (L) | Aggression (31) Defendence (30) | Tolerance (−47) Well-being (−42) Good Impression (−41) Achievement via Independence (−41) Empathy (−40) | Trust, A1 (−62) Depression, N3 (39) Angry Hostility, N2 (35) Straightforwardness, A2 (−33) Anxiety, N1 (31) | |
| Abstractedness (M) | Impulsivity (37) Cognitive Structure (−28) Change (26) Harm Avoidance (−26) Order (−26) Autonomy (25) | Self-control (−46) Socialization (−44) Achievement via Conformance (−41) Well-being (−39) Good Impression (−38) | Fantasy, O1 (44) Self-Discipline, C5 (−35) Order, C2 (−33) Deliberation, C6 (−33) Competence, C1 (−32) Aesthetics, O2 (26) Feelings, O3 (26) Actions, O4 (26) | Sensing (−41) Intuitive (41) Perceptive (31) Judging (−25) |

HIGHEST CORRELATIONS BETWEEN PRIMARY FACTORS AND OTHER PERSONALITY MEASURES

| 16PF Primary Factor | PRF Content Scale | CPI Folk Scale | NEO Facet | MBTI Type |
|---|---|---|---|---|
| Privateness (N) | Succorance (–41) Affiliation (–34) Exhibition (–32) | Sociability (–30) Social Presence (–30) Capacity for Capacity for Status (–28) Self-acceptance (–27) | Trust, A1 (–41) Warmth, E1 (–37) Gregariousness, E2 (–36) Assertiveness, E3 (–29) Positive Emotions, E6 (–29) | Extraversion (–40 Introversion (37) |
| Apprehension (O) | Dominance (–28) Exhibition (–26) Social Recognition (26) | Independence (–50) Femininity/ Masculinity (45) Social Presence (–33) Dominance (–32) Psychological-mindedness (–31) Capacity for Status (–27) Intellectual Efficiency (–27) Self-acceptance (–25) Well-being (–25) | Anxiety, N1 (61) Self-Consciousness, N4 (56) Depression, N3 (54) Vulnerability, N6 (41) Angry Hostility, N2 (33) Assertiveness, E3 (–28) | Thinking (–33) Extraversion (–32 Feeling (27) |
| Openness to Change (Q1) | Change (42) Sentience (30) Understanding (30) Cognitive Structure (–25) | Psychological-mindedness (35) Achievement via Independence (32) Capacity for Status (28) Intellectual Efficiency (27) Flexibility (26) Independence (25) Empathy (25) | Actions, O4 (43) Aesthetics, O2 (40) Ideas, O5 (30) Values, O6 (28) Fantasy, O1 (27) | Sensing (–59) Intuitive (54) Judging (–29) |
| Self-Reliance (Q2) | Affiliation (–45) Nurturance (–38) Autonomy (33) Succorance (–33) Play (–29) Exhibition (–26) | Sociability (–45) Social Presence (–39) Empathy (–34) Capacity for Status (–27) Self-acceptance (–26) Well-being (–25) | Gregariousness, E2 (–62) Warmth, E1 (–48) Positive Emotions, E6 (–36) Trust, A1 (–36) Altruism, A3 (–30) Excitement-Seeking, E5 (–28) Assertiveness, E3 (–26) Tender-Mindedness, A6 (–26) | Extraversion (–49 Introversion (42) |

TABLE 5, CONTINUED

HIGHEST CORRELATIONS BETWEEN PRIMARY FACTORS AND OTHER PERSONALITY MEASURES

| 16PF Primary Factor | PRF Content Scale | CPI Folk Scale | NEO Facet | MBTI Type |
|---|---|---|---|---|
| Perfectionism (Q3) | Order (66) Cognitive Structure (56) Impulsivity (−45) Achievement (35) Endurance (34) Play (−29) | Flexibility (−57) Self-control (29) Good Impression (27) Achievement via Conformance (26) | Order, C2 (68) Deliberation, C6 (49) Achievement Striving, C4 (44) Self-Discipline, C5 (40) Competence, C1 (38) Dutifulness, C3 (35) Impulsiveness, N5 (−27) | Judging (57) Perceptive (−53) |
| Tension (Q4) | Aggression (46) Defendence (46) Abasement (−31) | Good Impression (−41) Empathy (−35) Capacity for Status (−33) Psychological-mindedness (−27) Tolerance (−26) Achievement via Independence (−26) Self-control (−25) | Angry Hostility, N2 (54) Compliance, A4 (−41) Anxiety, N1 (28) Trust, A1 (−28) Actions, O4 (−27) Impulsiveness, N5 (26) Depression, N3 (25) Aesthetics, O2 (−25) | |

## Broad Trends

Before examining the specific primary scale scores in a 16PF profile, testing professionals are encouraged to look at broad trends within the profile.

*Evaluate Number of Extreme Scores*

As noted previously, extreme scores in a profile usually indicate an examinee's most distinctive traits. Therefore, greater numbers of extreme scores are likely to indicate a more distinctive personality expression.

Table 6 presents the number of extreme sten scores (those outside the 4-7 average range) obtained by the norm sample for the fifth edition. An examinee not having at least one extreme score is a rare occurrence. Most profiles show extreme scores on three to seven primary scales. If the number of extremes is nine or more, the examinee is among only about 5% of people whose profiles are this distinctive. If the number of extremes is below two, the examinee is among only about 5% of people whose profiles are this flat.

If the profile shows few extreme scores, the examinee possibly chose a large number of undecided (?) responses, indicating uncertainty about which response choice better described him or her. If the number of (?) responses is not elevated, the examinee may have answered a given scale's questions inconsistently. In either case, the reasons for the "flat" profile can be pursued by the testing professional.

*Evaluate Slope*

Evaluating the slope of a profile involves obtaining a rather impressionistic overview of the 16PF profile. The method for evaluating slope is meant to be used as a rule of thumb only. With this caveat, imagine a 16PF profile sheet on which a horizontal line is drawn between Factors H and I, dividing the profile sheet more or less in half. In general, a profile tends to suggest a more

TABLE 6

NUMBER OF EXTREME PRIMARY FACTOR SCORES ON 16PF PROFILES (BASED ON NORM SAMPLE, N=2500)

| Number of Extremes | Percent of Sample | Cumulative Percent |
|---|---|---|
| 0 | 1.0 | 1.0 |
| 1 | 4.5 | 5.5 |
| 2 | 8.6 | 14.1 |
| 3 | 13.4 | 27.5 |
| 4 | 15.4 | 42.9 |
| 5 | 15.1 | 58.0 |
| 6 | 14.4 | 72.4 |
| 7 | 10.5 | 82.9 |
| 8 | 7.7 | 90.6 |
| 9 | 5.0 | 95.6 |
| 10 | 2.5 | 98.1 |
| 11 | 1.0 | 99.1 |
| 12 | 0.5 | 99.6 |
| 13-15 | 0.4 | 100.0 |

"positive" or socially desirable picture of an examinee if it contains more high scores in the top half than in the bottom half. This sort of profile slopes from higher at the top right to lower at the bottom left, a slope-left profile. A slope-right profile (more low scores in the top half and more high scores in the bottom half) hints at the possibility of a less socially desirable picture of an examinee.

The rule-of-thumb slope evaluation rests on the general tendency for social desirability (as measured by the Impression Management [IM] index) to be associated with lower Anxiety and higher Extraversion. Specifically, the bottom half of the profile contains more scales on which low scores correlate with social desirability, whereas the reverse is true for the top half of the profile. In the top half, the most involved scales are Warmth (A+), Emotional Stability (C+), Rule-Consciousness (G+), and Social Boldness (H+). In the lower half of the profile, the most involved scales are Vigilance (L+), Abstractedness (M+), Privateness (N+), Apprehension (O+), Self-Reliance (Q2+), and Tension (Q4+). Admittedly, some factors do not follow the rule of thumb since they have little or no social desirability component.

Used within its limits, slope evaluation can provide an overall sense of a profile; however, it should be regarded only as a general impression, not as a substitute for a thorough examination of a person's scores on the individual primary scales.

*Remember the Primary Factor Scale Relationships*

Because the 16PF uses oblique factors (i.e., Cattell assumed that the primaries would be related), the structure of the 16PF shows that the scales are indeed intercorrelated. These intercorrelations are predictable: the primary scales cluster along the five global factors of Extraversion, Anxiety, Tough-Mindedness, Independence, and Self-Control.

With a knowledge of how certain scales are expected to intercorrelate, the testing professional can identify unexpected factor combinations, thus adding a richness beyond an evaluation that involves only a single factor at a time. In general, primary factor scale scores that cluster on a given global factor tend to be consistent; that is, a person who scores in the introverted direction on the global factor often tends to score in the introverted direction on the primary factor scales that make up Introversion (Reserve [A–], Seriousness [F–], Shyness [H–], Privateness [N+], and Self-Reliance [Q2+]). However, it is not uncommon that one of the primary scale scores will be in the extraverted direction, even when the person's score on the global factor falls in the introverted direction. For example, a generally introverted person might be Reserved (A–), Shy (H–) and Private (N+), but Group-Oriented (Q2–). (The latter is a score in the extraverted direction.) This person might be reserved and timid but wishing for more group contact, or the person might rely on group interactions to get "lost in the crowd" because of his or her reserve and timidity. Given the likelihood that this person experiences a conflict between the urge to be in groups and the tendency to be timid, the testing professional can generate a number of hypotheses about the person's orientation to people.

In evaluating a profile, then, how conflicting tendencies are played out should be considered and hypotheses should be generated. Comparing the findings with other data about the examinee also can be helpful. Finally, in cases where findings are shared with the examinee, a discussion of conflicting patterns could be valuable.

## Factor A (Warmth): Warm Versus Reserved

*General Factor Meaning*

Factor A addresses the tendency to be warmly involved with people versus the tendency to be more reserved socially and interpersonally; both poles are normal. Reserved (A–) people tend to be more cautious in involvement and attachments. They tend to like working alone, often on mechanical, intellectual, or artistic pursuits. Warm (A+) people tend to have more interest in people and to prefer occupations dealing with people (as seen in the item content). They tend to be comfortable in situations that call for closeness with other people.

Warm (A+) behavior tends to be more socially desirable, and, in fact, Factor A correlates positively with the Impression Management (IM) scale. However, extremely high scores can indicate that the desirable aspect of warmth represents an extreme need for people and for close relating. Extremely Warm (A+) people may be uncomfortable in situations where the close relationships they seek are inaccessible. Low scorers, on the other hand, can be quite uncomfortable in situations that call for extensive interaction or for emotional closeness. In previous editions of the 16PF, Karson and O'Dell (1976, p. 36) point out that Reserved (A–) people can be quite effective (e.g., famous researchers are often reserved). Karson and O'Dell also state that, in some cases, an extremely low Warmth score may indicate a history of unsatisfactory or disappointing interpersonal relationships.

Warmth (A+) is one of three primary factors on which score distributions are significantly different for men and women. (The other two primaries exhibiting similar distributions are Dominance [E+] and Sensitivity [I+].) On A+, women's raw scores tend to be slightly higher than men's; that is, women are more Warm. Thus, both combined-sex and separate-sex norms are available on this factor.

*Item Content/Typical Responses*

High scorers might say that they enjoy people who show their emotions openly, that they prefer working in a busy office rather than in a quiet room, and that their friends describe them as warm and comforting. Low scorers might say that they would rather work on an invention in a laboratory than show people how to use it, that they would rather be an architect than a counselor, and that they're uncomfortable talking about or showing feelings of affection or caring.

*Correlations with Other 16PF Factors*

Warmth (A+) contributes to the Extraversion global factor, along with Liveliness (F+), Social Boldness (H+), Forthrightness (N–), and Group-Orientation (Q2–). It is related to seeking closeness to people, clearly a component of the general orientation to people that typifies Extraversion. Reserve (A–) also contributes to the Tough-Mindedness global factor, along with being Utilitarian (I–), Grounded (M–), and Traditional (Q1–). This combination of factors suggests a tough, unemotional pattern with which the lower warmth of A– is consistent.

*Correlations with Other Measures*

The correlations show a link between Warmth (A+) and other measures of Extraversion: positive correlations with NEO's Warmth (E1), Gregariousness (E2), and Altruism (A3) scales; with PRF's Affiliation, Nurturance, and Succorance scales; with CPI's Sociability, Social Presence, and Empathy scales; and with MBTI's Extraversion scale. (There is a corresponding negative correlation with MBTI's Introversion scale.) Correlations with NEO's Feelings (O3), Positive Emotions (E6), and

Tender-Mindedness (A6) facets support the feeling aspect of Factor A and its link with the Tough-Mindedness global factor. In this relationship, Warmth (A+) contributes to the Receptive pole of the Tough-Mindedness global factor.

## Factor B (Reasoning): Abstract Versus Concrete

### About the Scale

The Factor B scale is composed of 15 items concerning the ability to solve problems using reasoning. In the 16PF literature, Factor B is described as a brief measure of reasoning or intelligence, although it is not intended as a replacement for more reliable, full-length measures of mental ability. Therefore, cautious interpretations are in order (see "Score Meaning"). Even though Reasoning is not a personality trait, it is included in the 16PF because cognitive style moderates the expression of many personality traits.

### Item Content/Typical Responses

The scale equally represents three different types of items: verbal reasoning, numerical reasoning, and logical reasoning (Rieke & Conn, 1994). An example Factor B item is "Adult is to child as cat is to: (a) kitten, (b) dog, (c) baby." Nine of the 15 fifth edition Factor B items are new, and the remaining items are from previous forms of the 16PF.

### Score Meaning

High scorers tend to solve more of the reasoning problems correctly; low scorers tend to choose a higher number of incorrect answers. In previous editions of the 16PF, H. B. Cattell (1989, pp. 31-32) suggests that high scores frequently reflect higher reasoning ability because people are unlikely to obtain high scores by chance. At times, however, average or low scores may not accurately reflect people's reasoning ability. "These instances are apt to occur in exami-

nees who are educationally disadvantaged or who are depressed, anxious, or preoccupied with their troubles. They also occur when examinees are distracted by environmental stimuli, are wrong in their interpretations of the instructions, or are, for various reasons, not motivated to spend the time figuring out the correct answers" (Cattell, H. B., 1989, p. 32).

Because of the verbal nature of the items, a lower-than-expected score can result when an examinee has reading difficulties or speaks English as a second language. A low score also may indicate that an examinee did not pay full attention to the test, and review of the Infrequency (INF) scale score may support this possibility.

### Correlations with Other 16PF Factors

Even though reasoning is seen as a separate domain from personality, Factor B does show some small correlations with Emotional Stability (C+), Trust (L-), and Openness to Change (Q1+). This subtle pattern may be an artifact of the qualities of the people in the sample, or it may reflect a theoretic link between these qualities and higher reasoning scores.

### Correlations with Other Measures

Correlations of Factor B with other ability measures include a .61 with the Information Inventory and a .51 with the Culture Fair Intelligence Test (Rieke & Conn, 1994). Factor B is correlated with other personality measures' scales: CPI's Intellectual Efficiency, PRF's Need for Order, and MBTI's Intuition.

### Additional Considerations

In general, items do not show bias for gender or race, but level of education does seem to affect scale scores (Rieke & Conn, 1994). See Chapter 5 of this manual for relevant data, as well as *The 16PF Fifth Edition Technical Manual* (Conn & Rieke, 1994f).

## Factor C (Emotional Stability): Emotionally Stable Versus Reactive

*General Factor Meaning*

This factor largely concerns feelings about coping with day-to-day life and its challenges. High scorers tend to take life in stride and to manage events and emotions in a balanced, adaptive way. Low scorers feel a certain lack of control over life. Low scorers tend to react to life, whereas high scorers make adaptive or proactive choices in managing their lives. This factor has an element of emotional well-being that is supported by correlations with other measures. However, an extremely high score on this scale can indicate that an examinee may be strongly disinclined to report, or even to experience, so-called "negative" feelings.

Factor C shows a very strong correlation with the Impression Management (IM) scale. Presenting oneself as able to cope with life is socially desirable; admitting that one feels unable to manage feelings or adapt to life is socially undesirable. Whenever an examinee obtains an extremely low score, he or she is admitting undesirable feelings. In previous editions of the 16PF, Karson and O'Dell (1976, p. 43) suggest that an examinee always should be questioned about reported experiences of distress and reactivity. They also advise that interpretation of a high Emotional Stability (C+) score, especially when it is accompanied by a high score on the IM scale, should address whether the examinee denied any problems in order to present himself or herself favorably.

*Item Content/Typical Responses*

High scorers tend to say that they rarely meet problems with which they can't cope, that they usually go to bed at night feeling satisfied with their day, and that they recover from upsets quickly. Low scorers say that they have more ups and downs in mood than most people, that their emotional needs are not too satisfied, and that they feel as though they can't cope when small things keep going wrong.

*Correlations with Other 16PF Factors*

Reactivity (C–) is a strong contributor to the Anxiety global factor, along with Vigilance (L+), Apprehension (O+), and Tension (Q4+). Self-perceptions of feeling unable to adapt to life and its demands contribute to general anxiousness. Emotional Stability (C+) does not load significantly on the Self-Control global factor, but it does show some modest correlations with two primary scales related to Self-Control: Rule-Consciousness (G+) and Groundedness (M–).

*Correlations with Other Measures*

The relationship of Reactivity (C–) to Anxiety is supported by its correlations with other measures of anxiety and well-being: NEO Neuroticism facets of Anxiety (N1), Angry Hostility (N2), Depression (N3), Self-Consciousness (N4), and Vulnerability (N6). Of all the 16PF primary scales, Emotional Stability (C+) shows the highest correlation with Self-Esteem, as measured by the Coopersmith Self-Esteem Inventory (Conn & Rieke, 1994d). Other aspects of C+ behavior may be hypothesized when additional correlations are examined. For example, success and social presence are suggested by positive correlations with several CPI scales, including Achievement via Conformance, Achievement via Independence, Capacity for Status, and Social Presence. Emotional Stability also correlates positively with CPI's Psychological-mindedness and Intellectual Efficiency scales, possibly indicating that Emotionally Stable people tend to see more options. Resourcefulness also may be suggested by the positive correlation with CPI's Independence scale. Finally, a link between Emotional Stability and low vulnerability to stress may be suggested by the negative correlation with NEO's Vulnerability (N6). On the Reactive (C–)

side, the correlation with PRF's Defendence may suggest a readiness to defend against real or perceived threat.

## Factor E (Dominance): Dominant Versus Deferential

### General Factor Meaning

This factor involves the tendency to exert one's will over others (Dominance) versus accommodating others' wishes (Deference). Factor E is more about dominance than about simple assertiveness. Whereas assertiveness serves to protect one's rights, wishes, and personal boundaries, dominance serves to subjugate others' wishes to one's own (Cattell, H. B., 1989, pp. 68-69). A high score does not eliminate the possibility that an examinee can be assertive rather than aggressive. However, most high scorers tend to be forceful, vocal in expressing their wishes and opinions even when not invited to do so, and pushy about obtaining what they want. They feel free to criticize others and to try to control others' behavior. While dominance can lend a certain amount of commanding social presence, extreme dominance can alienate people who do not wish to be subjugated.

Low scorers tend to avoid conflict by acquiescing to the wishes of others. They are self-effacing and willing to set aside their wishes and feelings. Extreme deference can be alienating to those who wish for a more forceful or participating response.

Dominance (E+) is one of three primary factors on which score distributions are significantly different for men and women. (The other two primaries exhibiting similar distributions are Warmth [A+] and Sensitivity [I+].) On Dominance, women's raw scores tend to be slightly lower than men's; that is, women are more deferential. Thus, separate-sex norms as well as combined-sex norms are available on this factor.

### Item Content/Typical Responses

High scorers say that they feel comfortable giving people directions, that they can be tough and sharp if being polite and pleasant doesn't work, and that they point it out if they regard another person's reasoning as wrong. Low scorers say that they tend to be more cooperative than assertive; that if they were lost in a city and didn't agree with friends about which way to go, they'd make no fuss and follow their friends; and that when people do something that bothers them, they usually let it go.

### Correlations with Other 16PF Factors

Dominance (E+) is the strongest contributor to the Independence global factor, along with Social Boldness (H+), Vigilance (L+), and Openness to Change (Q1+). In being Independent, one is forcefully self-determined and attempts to influence others. The dominance element and the willingness to assert oneself contribute to this Independent stance.

### Correlations with Other Measures

Factor E as a measure of Dominance is supported by its positive correlations with PRF's Dominance and Aggression scales, CPI's Dominance scale, and NEO's Assertiveness (E3) scale. Factor E's elements of Independence are supported by its positive correlations with CPI's Independence and Self-acceptance scales and by its negative correlation with PRF's Abasement scale. If not perceived as too pugnacious, dominant people can assert a strong social presence, as suggested by positive correlations with CPI's Sociability and Social Presence scales, PRF's Exhibition scale, and NEO's Competence (C1) scale. However, dominant people's willingness to manipulate others in order to control them is suggested by the negative correlation with NEO's Straightforwardness (A2) scale.

## Factor F (Liveliness): Lively Versus Serious

### General Factor Meaning

In *The 16PF: Personality in Depth*, Factor F's exuberance is compared to the natural self-expression and spontaneity exhibited by children before they learn self-control (Cattell, H. B., 1989, pp. 90-91). High scorers are enthusiastic, spontaneous, and attention-seeking; they are lively and drawn to stimulating social situations. Extreme scores may reflect a flighty quality that is seen as unreliable or immature. The attention-seeking and liveliness of F+ people can assume proportions inappropriate for certain situations, especially those that call for restraint or decorum. In contrast, low scorers on Factor F tend to take life more seriously. They are quieter, more cautious, and less playful. They tend to inhibit their spontaneity, sometimes to the point of appearing constricted or saturnine. While they may be regarded as mature, they may not be perceived as fun or entertaining.

### Item Content/Typical Responses

High scorers say that they like being in the middle of excitement and activity; that they'd rather dress in an eye-catching, stylish way than neatly and quietly; and that they enjoy spending time talking with friends about social events. Low scorers tend to say that they prefer working on a quiet hobby rather than attending a lively party, that they don't enjoy racy or slapstick humor on television, and that they believe more in being properly serious than in living the saying "Laugh and be merry."

### Correlations with Other 16PF Factors

Factor F contributes positively to the Extraversion global factor, along with Warmth (A+), Social Boldness (H+), Forthrightness (N−), and Group Orientation (Q2−). Factor F's social exuberance has a more lively, impulsive, high-spirited flavor than other Extraversion-related primary scales. This may explain the contribution of Liveliness (F+) to the Unrestrained pole of the Self-Control global factor in the fifth edition.

### Correlations with Other Measures

The interpersonal aspects that support Factor F's link with Extraversion are seen in its positive correlations with all of NEO's Extraversion facets, especially Excitement-Seeking (E5) and Gregariousness (E2); with MBTI's Extraversion scale; with CPI's Sociability and Social Presence scales; and with PRF's Affiliation and Exhibition scales. In addition, positive correlations with PRF's Exhibition and Play scales support the childlike, self-expressive spontaneity of Liveliness (F+). The uncontrolled aspect of Liveliness (F+) is seen in its negative correlation with CPI's Self-control and in its positive correlation with PRF's Impulsivity.

## Factor G (Rule-Consciousness): Rule-Conscious Versus Expedient

### General Factor Meaning

This factor addresses the extent to which cultural standards of right and wrong are internalized and used to govern behavior (Cattell et al., 1970, p. 89). It has been associated with the psychoanalytic concept of superego, in which moral ideals from the culture and environment are internalized and used to control the id impulses of self-gratification. High scorers tend to perceive themselves as strict followers of rules, principles, and manners. In previous 16PF editions, high scorers are described as those who endorse conventional cultural values in their responses to Factor G items (Cattell, H. B., 1989, p. 110). These values are defined as those being endorsed by the majority of North Americans and northern Europeans and as having remnants of the Protestant Puritan ethic. Rule-Conscious people emphasize the importance of conformance to regulations, depicting themselves as rule-bound, conscientious, and persevering.

In reality, they can be perceived as staid, inflexible, or self-righteous because of their dogmatism. Low scorers tend to eschew rules and regulations, doing so either because they have a poorly developed sense of right and wrong (e.g., lack internalized moral values) or because they ascribe to values that are not solely based on conventional mores in deciding which rules and principles should govern their actions. Expedient (G–) behaviors seem to have elements of need for autonomy, need for play, and need for flexibility, as suggested by correlations with other measures. Low scorers might have difficulty in conforming to strict rules and regulations. It is important to evaluate whether low scorers have failed to develop moral standards or whether they simply follow unconventional standards. In either case, their behaviors may be perceived as unpredictable unless their guiding principles and motivations are known. Other primary factor scales can indicate resources that might influence the Expedient (G–) person's self-control, especially those scales with which this factor correlates.

A link exists between the cultural values endorsed by Rule-Conscious (G+) people and social desirability. Factor G shows a significant positive correlation with social desirability as measured by the Impression Management (IM) scale. That is, saying that one follows the rules is more socially desirable than admitting that one does not conform.

*Item Content/Typical Responses*

High scorers say that they always think carefully about what's right and proper in making a decision, they believe people should insist on strict adherence to moral standards, and they respect rules and good manners more than being free to do what they want. Low scorers say that they believe most rules can be broken when good reasons for doing so exist, that they become annoyed when told to follow minor safety rules, and that being free to do what they want is more important than good manners and respect for rules.

*Correlations with Other 16PF Factors*

Factor G contributes positively to the Self-Control global factor and correlates with the other contributing factors: Seriousness (F–), Groundedness (M–), and Perfectionism (Q3+). It also shows modest correlations with Emotional Stability (C+) and Relaxedness (Q4–), possibly suggesting that following convention tends to arouse less anxiety than challenging convention. A modest correlation exists with being Traditional (Q1–), indicating a relationship between the Rule-Conscious (G+) tendency to follow rules and the Traditional (Q1–) tendency to prefer the status quo.

*Correlations with Other Measures*

Rule-Consciousness (G+) shows strong correlations with measures of socialization, conformance, and conscientiousness. In relation to the PRF scales, Rule Consciousness (G+) correlates positively with Endurance, Order, and Achievement needs and negatively with Play, Impulsivity, and Autonomy needs. Rule-Consciousness also correlates positively with NEO's Conscientiousness facets of Dutifulness (C3), Achievement Striving (C4), and Deliberation (C6) and with CPI's Responsibility, Socialization, Self-control, Good Impression, Achievement via Conformance; G+ correlates negatively with CPI's Flexibility. These correlates indicate that Rule-Consciousness (G+) contains elements of perseverance, impulse control, need for order, and desire to impress others as responsible. They also suggest evidence of the inflexibility that can result from rigid rule-conformity.

Expedient (G–) correlations exist with PRF's Autonomy, Play, and Flexibility. Predictably, G– has negative associations with the controlled direction of other measures' conformance and conscientiousness scales (e.g., NEO's Dutifulness [C3]; CPI's Self-control, Responsibility, and Socialization; and PRF's Order, Cognitive Structure, and Endurance).

## Factor H (Social Boldness): Socially Bold Versus Shy

### General Factor Meaning

High scorers consider themselves to be bold and adventurous in social groups, and show little fear of social situations. They tend to initiate social contacts and aren't shy in the face of new social settings. A large element of need for self-exhibition is evident at the high pole, with a flavor of dominance more prevalent than in other extraversion-related factors. Low scorers tend to be socially timid, cautious, and shy; they find speaking in front of a group to be a difficult experience. The possibility of subjective experience of discomfort may relate to shyness (H–) as well as to some lack of self-esteem and discomfort in new settings, particularly interpersonal settings. In fact, Social Boldness (H+) is among the factors that show the strongest relationship with fifth edition predictions of Self-Esteem as measured by the Coopersmith Self-Esteem Inventory (Conn & Rieke, 1994d).

### Item Content/Typical Responses

High scorers tend to say that starting conversations with strangers is easy for them, they usually seem to immediately fit into a new group, and they typically aren't bothered by speaking in front of a large group. Low scorers tend to say that starting conversations with strangers is hard for them, they are shy and cautious when meeting people, and they tend to get embarrassed if they suddenly become the center of attention in a social group.

### Correlations with Other 16PF Factors

Social Boldness (H+) contributes positively to the Extraversion global factor, as do Warmth (A+), Liveliness (F+), Forthrightness (N–), and Group-Orientation (Q2–). Factor H's contribution to Extraversion seems to relate more to boldness, status, and self-exhibition in comparison to the contributions of the other four primary scales. Social Boldness (H+) also contributes positively to the Independence global factor, along with Dominance (E+), Vigilance (L+), and Openness to Change (Q1+). The ability to interact boldly with others plays a part in Independence, which involves elements of persuasion and self-expression.

### Correlations with Other Measures

Interpersonal aspects that link Social Boldness (H+) with Extraversion are evident in positive correlations with other Extraversion measures: PRF's Affiliation scale, CPI's Sociability and Social Presence scales, and all of NEO's Extraversion facets, especially Assertiveness (E3) and Gregariousness (E2). The single largest positive correlation is with PRF's Exhibition scale. H+ correlations with NEO's Aggressiveness, PRF's Dominance scale, and CPI's Dominance, Social Presence, and Capacity for Status scales suggest the flavor of dominance and the power aspects of Socially Bold (H+) self-expression. Factor H's presence on the fifth edition Independence global factor is supported by its correlation with CPI's Independence scale. The possible presence of subjective experience of discomfort at the Shy (H–) pole is suggested by correlations with four of NEO's Neuroticism facets (Anxiety [N1], Depression [N3], Self-Consciousness [N4], and Vulnerability [N6]) and by a negative correlation with CPI's Self-acceptance scale. Factor H is a main contributor to the fifth edition equation predicting Self-Esteem, as measured by Coopersmith's Self-Esteem Inventory.

## Factor I (Sensitivity): Sensitive Versus Utilitarian

### General Factor Meaning

The content of the fifth edition Factor I scale focuses on people's sensitivities and sensibilities; that is, high scorers tend to base judgments on personal tastes and aesthetic values, whereas low scorers tend to have a more utilitarian focus. Sensitive (I+) people rely on empathy and sensitivity in their considerations; Utilitarian (I–) people evince less sentimentality, attending more to how things operate or work. Sensitive (I+) people tend to be more refined in their interests and tastes and more sentimental than their Utilitarian (I–) counterparts. At the extreme, I+ people may be so focused on the subjective aspects of situations that they overlook more functional aspects. Low scorers, on the other hand, tend to be concerned with utility and objectivity, and may exclude people's feelings from consideration. Because they don't tend to indulge vulnerability, people with extreme I– scores may have trouble dealing with situations that demand sensitivity. In previous editions of the 16PF, the Sensitivity factor is linked to the Jungian concept of judging functions: Thinking versus Feeling (Cattell, H. B., 1989, pp. 153-154). This interconnection is supported by correlations with other measures.

The sensitivity of Factor I is related to gender stereotypes. Emotional sensitivity and refinement are perceived as qualities of the "feminine" stereotype; objectivity and toughness are seen as qualities of the "masculine" stereotype. Factor I is one of three primaries that exhibit significant gender differences in the distributions, and therefore, separate-gender norms as well as combined-gender norms are available for this factor. (The other two primaries exhibiting significant gender differences in the distributions are Warmth [A+] and Dominance [E+]).

### Item Content/Typical Responses

High scorers tend to say that they appreciate the beauty of a poem more than an expert football strategy, they find watching an artist at work more interesting than watching a building being constructed, and they become excited about good plays or novels. Low scorers say that they prefer reading action stories to sensitive, imaginative novels; they are interested in mechanical things and good at fixing them; and as children, they spent more time making things than reading.

### Correlations with Other 16PF Factors

Sensitivity (I+) is the strongest contributor to the Receptive aspect of the Tough-Mindedness global factor, but it shows only moderate correlations with other 16PF factor scales. Its highest correlations are with Openness to Change (Q1+), Abstractedness (M+), and Warmth (A+), which all load on the Tough-Mindedness global factor. Sensitivity (I+) also shows weak correlations with Reactivity (C–), Deference (E–), and Expedience (G–). Utilitarian (I–) people, then, might have some tendency to be emotionally mature, dominant, and norm-conforming. This pattern fits with the notion of unemotional objectivity that does not indulge vulnerability, which is inherent in the low pole of Factor I.

### Correlations with Other Measures

Sensitivity (I+) is most highly correlated with NEO's Openness facet of Aesthetics (O2), and it also correlates with the Fantasy (O1) and Feelings (O3) facets. A link between Sensitivity (I+) and feeling is shown by the positive correlation with MBTI's Feeling scale; Sensitivity (I+) also correlates positively with MBTI's Intuitive scale. Finally, Sensitivity (I+) correlates with PRF's Understanding scale, a measure of intellectual exploration, with CPI's Femininity/Masculinity scale, and with PRF's Harm Avoidance scale.

### Factor L (Vigilance): Vigilant Versus Trusting

*General Factor Meaning*

This factor relates to the tendency to trust versus being vigilant about others' motives and intentions. High scorers expect to be misunderstood or taken advantage of, and they experience themselves as separate from other people. High scorers may be unable to relax their Vigilance (L+) when it might be advantageous to do so. At the extreme, high scorers' mistrust may have an aspect of animosity, as suggested in correlations with other measures. Sometimes a Vigilant stance is in response to life circumstances (e.g., members of oppressed minority groups tend to score higher on Vigilance [L+]).

Low scorers tend to expect fair treatment, loyalty, and good intentions from others. Trust (L–) tends to be related to a sense of well-being and satisfactory relationships, as supported in correlations with other measures. However, extremely low scorers may be taken advantage of because they do not give enough thought to others' motivations.

Factor L is correlated with the Impression Management (IM) scale; Trust is the socially desirable pole for Factor L.

*Item Content/Typical Responses*

High scorers say that a difference usually exists between what people say they'll do and what they actually do, that being frank and open leads others to get the better of them, that more than half the people they meet can't be trusted, and that paying attention to others' motives is important. Low scorers tend to respond "false" to the preceding descriptions.

*Correlations with Other 16PF Factors*

Vigilance (L+) contributes to the Anxiety global factor along with the primaries of Reactivity (C–), Apprehension (O+), and Tension (Q4+). Vigilance (L+) also contributes to the Independence global factor, as do Dominance (E+), Social Boldness (H+), and Openness to Change (Q1+).

*Correlations with Other Measures*

The single largest correlation of Trust (L–) is with NEO's Trust (A1). Elements of interpersonal goodwill in Trust (L–) are reflected by correlations with CPI's Empathy and Tolerance scales. The element of good impression in Trust (L–) is reflected by the relationship with CPI's Good Impression scale. Vigilance (L+) correlates with three NEO Neuroticism facets that are measures of anxiousness: Anxiety (N1), Angry Hostility (N2), and Depression (N3). In addition, Vigilance (L+) negatively correlates with CPI's Well-being scale. Elements of aggression or animosity in Vigilance (L+) are reflected in positive correlations with NEO's Angry Hostility (N2) and with PRF's Aggression and Defendence scales.

### Factor M (Abstractedness): Abstracted Versus Grounded

*General Factor Meaning*

Factor M addresses the type of things to which people give thought and attention. Abstracted people (M+) are more oriented to internal mental processes and ideas rather than to practicalities. Grounded (M–) people focus on their senses, observable data, and the outer realities of their environment in forming their perceptions. In previous editions, this factor is linked to the Jungian perceiving functions, Sensation versus Intuition (Cattell, H. B., 1989, pp. 191-192).

In previous editions, high scores, reflecting an intense inner life rather than a focus on outer environment, are associated with the absent-minded professor image (Krug, 1981, p. 8). High scorers are Abstracted (M+); that is, they are occupied with thinking, imagination, and fantasy, and they often get lost in thought. In contrast, low scorers are Grounded (M−); that is, they focus more on the environment and its demands. Although low scorers may think in a practical and down-to-earth manner, they may not be able to generate possible solutions to problems. In fact, extremely Grounded (M−) people may be so overly concrete or literal that they "miss the forest for the trees." Abstracted (M+) thinking, on the other hand, often leads to plentiful idea generation and is related to creativity (Rieke, Guastello, & Conn, 1994b). However, high scorers may generate ideas without considering the practical realities of people, processes, and situations. Extremely Abstracted (M+) people sometimes seem less in control of their attention or of situations, and sometimes report that they have mishaps or accidents because they are preoccupied. In fact, Factor M loads negatively on the Self-Control global factor, with Abstracted (M+) people being less self-controlled.

### Item Content/Typical Responses

High scorers tend to say that they pay more attention to thoughts and imagination than to practical matters, they become so lost in thought that they misplace things or lose track of time, and they overlook practical details because they are so interested in thinking about ideas. Low scorers tend to say that their thoughts usually concern sensible, down-to-earth matters; they think about doing what needs to be done rather than daydreaming; and their ideas are realistic and practical.

### Correlations with Other 16PF Factors

Factor M's highest correlation is with Factor G; it correlates negatively, therefore suggesting a link between Abstractedness (M+) and Expedience (G−). Factor M also correlates with Openness to Change (Q1+), indicating that Abstracted (M+) people's thinking is related to new approaches or unconventional solutions. The remaining correlations suggest a link between

Abstractedness (M+) and lowered Self-Control: it correlates with Reactivity (C−) and Tolerance of Disorder (Q3−), and loads negatively on the Self-Control global factor in the fifth edition. Factor M also is an important contributor to the Tough-Mindedness global factor, along with Warmth (A+), Sensitivity (I+), and Openness to Change (Q1+). Groundedness (M−) contributes to a Tough-Minded stance; Abstractedness (M+) contributes to a Receptive stance. Finally, Factor M is negatively correlated with social desirability as measured by the Impression Management (IM) scale; that is, to say one is Grounded (M−) is more socially desirable than to say one is Abstracted (M+).

### Correlations with Other Measures

Correlations with the MBTI show a strong link between Abstractedness (M+) and Intuition and between Groundedness (M−) and Sensation. Additionally, Factor M is correlated positively with MBTI's Perceptive and Intuitive scales and negatively with MBTI's Judging and Sensing scales, thus supporting the Grounded (M−) person's tendency to focus on observable, objective processing as opposed to thinking, intuitive processing. While being Grounded (M−) is associated with social desirability, high scores on Factor M tend to be correlated with creativity and openness to ideas: Factor M correlates positively with PRF's Change scale and several of NEO's Openness facets, including Fantasy (O1), Aesthetics (O2), Feelings (O3), and Actions (O4). The unconventionality of Abstractedness (M+) is suggested by its positive correlation with PRF's Autonomy scale and its negative correlation with CPI's Socialization and Achievement via Conformance scales. Abstractedness (M+) also correlates negatively with CPI's Self-control and Socialization scales and with CPI's v.2, a broad measure of Conventionality; with PRF's Order scale; with several NEO Conscientiousness facets, including

Competence (C1), Order (C2), Self-Discipline (C5), and Deliberation (C6); and positively with PRF's Impulsivity scales. Finally, Factor M is negatively correlated with CPI's Well-being scale.

## Factor N (Privateness): Private Versus Forthright

### General Factor Meaning

This factor addresses the tendency to be Forthright (N−) and personally open versus being Private (N+) and nondisclosing. Related to the Extraversion global factor in the fifth edition, Factor N content addresses whether self-disclosure is part of one's orientation to people. High scorers say they "play their hand close to their chest," whereas low scorers "put all their cards on the table." Low scorers tend to talk about themselves readily; they are genuine, self-revealing, and forthright. At the extreme, low scorers may be Forthright (N−) in situations where doing so may not be to their advantage. High scorers, on the other hand, tend to be personally guarded. At the extreme, high scorers may maintain their privacy at the expense of developing close relationships with others. This may reflect disinterest in or fear of closeness, as suggested by correlations. Factor N shows a modest correlation with the Impression Management (IM) scale, with Forthrightness (N−) being the socially desirable pole.

### Item Content/Typical Responses

High scorers say that they tend to keep problems to themselves rather than discussing them with friends, that they have difficulty talking about personal matters, and that people find them hard to get close to. Low scorers say that they tend to talk about their feelings readily and that they give more than minimal responses to personal questions.

### Correlations with Other 16PF Factors

Correlations with Reserve (A−), Shyness (H−), and Self-Reliance (Q2+) and the negative loading of Factor N on the Extraversion global factor support the link between Privateness (N+) and Introversion, especially with Introversion's components of timidity, reserve, and self-reliance.

### Correlations with Other Measures

The link between Extraversion and Forthrightness (N−) is supported in correlations with other measures: with all of NEO's Extraversion facets and with CPI's overall Sociability scale (v.1) as well as with its Sociability, Social Presence, and Capacity for Status scales. Negative correlations with PRF's Nurturance and Succorance scales and with MBTI's Feeling scale suggest that Private (N+) people do not tend to be emotionally close. Private people may mistrust others, as reflected in the negative correlation with NEO's Trust (A1) facet. Private (N+) people may feel dissatisfied with themselves, as suggested by negative correlations with CPI's broad Self-realization index (v.3) and Self-acceptance scale in particular.

## Factor O (Apprehension): Apprehensive Versus Self-Assured

### General Factor Meaning

High scorers tend to worry about things and to feel apprehensive and insecure. Sometimes, these feelings are in response to a particular life situation. In other cases, these feelings are part of a characteristic response pattern, appearing across situations in a person's life. Worrying can have positive results, in that a person can anticipate dangers in a situation and can see how actions might have consequences, including interpersonal effects. However, Apprehensive (O+) people can make a poor social presence, as supported in correlations with other measures.

In contrast to high scorers, low scorers tend to be more self-assured, neither prone to apprehensiveness nor troubled about their sense of adequacy. Low scorers present themselves as confident and self-satisfied. If a person's score is extremely low, his or her confidence may be unshaken, even in situations that provide opportunities for self-evaluation and self-improvement. In such instances, the person's self-assurance may result from blocking out awareness of negative elements of self.

There also is an element of social desirability in Factor O, with Self-Assured (O–) response choices being the socially desirable pole.

*Item Content/Typical Responses*

High scorers tend to say that they're sensitive and worry too much about things they've done, that they're hurt if people dislike them, and that they tend to be too self-critical. Low scorers say they worry less than most people, they usually aren't upset if people dislike them, and they don't spend time thinking about what they should have said but didn't.

*Correlations with Other 16PF Factors*

Apprehension (O+) contributes to the Anxiety global factor, along with Reactivity (C–), Vigilance (L+), and Tension (Q4+). Thus, Apprehension (O+) seems to contribute to a general anxiousness.

*Correlations with Other Measures*

The presence of Apprehension (O+) on the Anxiety global factor is supported by positive correlations with four of six NEO Neuroticism facets, especially Anxiety (N1), Self-Consciousness (N4), and Depression (N3). The notion that O+ people may be uncertain of themselves in social situations or relative to others is supported by negative correlations with CPI's Self-acceptance, Independence, Capacity for Status, Social Presence, and Dominance scales; with PRF's Dominance and Exhibition scales; and with NEO's Assertiveness (E3) facet. Self-Assurance (O–) is correlated with CPI's Self-acceptance and Well-being scales.

## Factor Q1 (Openness to Change): Open to Change Versus Traditional

*General Factor Meaning*

High scorers tend to think of ways to improve things and to enjoy experimenting. If they perceive the status quo as unsatisfactory or dull, they are inclined to change it. Low scorers tend to prefer traditional ways of looking at things. They don't question the way things are done. They prefer life to be predictable and familiar, even if life is not ideal.

*Item Content/Typical Responses*

High scorers tend to say that they like thinking of new and better ways of doing things in contrast to following well-tried ways, they find people interesting if they express different viewpoints, and they are bored by work that is familiar and routine. Low scorers say that they feel secure and confident when they do work that is familiar and routine, they don't really like people who are "different" or unusual, and think more trouble arises from questioning and changing satisfactory methods than from rejecting promising new approaches.

*Correlations with Other 16PF Factors*

Openness to Change (Q1+) contributes to the Independence global factor, as do Dominance (E+), Social Boldness (H+), and Vigilance (L+). Q1+ also contributes to the Receptive pole of the Tough-Mindedness global factor, along with Warmth (A+), Sensitivity (I+), and Abstractedness (M+). Factor Q1's elements of nonconformity and openness to new ideas are reflected in its correlations with Expedience (G–) and Abstractedness (M+).

*Correlations with Other Measures*

The link between openness to new ideas and perception by way of insight is shown in Factor Q1's correlations with MBTI's Intuitive scale, PRF's Understanding scale, and CPI's Psychological-mindedness and

Intellectual Efficiency scales. This openness also is reflected in positive correlations with PRF's Change and Sentience scales, CPI's Flexibility scale, and nearly all of NEO's Openness facets, including Fantasy (O1), Aesthetics (O2), Actions (O4), Ideas (O5), and Values (O6). The element of independent-mindedness in Openness to Change (Q1+) is shown in the correlations with CPI's Independence, Achievement via Independence, and Capacity for Status scales and in the modest correlation with PRF's Autonomy scale.

## Factor Q2 (Self-Reliance): Self-Reliant Versus Group-Oriented

### General Factor Meaning

This factor tends to be about maintaining contact with or proximity to others. High scorers are Self-Reliant (Q2+); they enjoy time alone and prefer to make decisions for themselves. Low scorers are Group-Oriented (Q2-); they prefer to be around people and like to do things with others. It appears to be more socially favorable to present oneself as scoring in the Extraverted, Group-Oriented (Q2-) direction rather than in the Self-Reliant (Q2+) direction, as possibly reflected by the moderate but significant negative correlation of Self-Reliance with the Impression Management (IM) scale. Self-Reliant (Q2+) people may have difficulty in working alongside others, and they also may find it hard to ask for help when necessary. While Self-Reliant people can act autonomously when the need arises, those having extremely high scores may neglect interpersonal aspects and consequences of their actions. On the other hand, being extremely Group-Oriented (Q2-) may not be optimally effective in situations where help is unavailable or where others are providing poor direction or advice.

### Item Content/Typical Responses

High scorers say that they like to do their planning alone, without interruptions or suggestions from others; they easily can go a whole morning without wanting to speak to anyone; and they would rather work alone than with a committee. Low scorers say that they like to participate with people in doing something, they like it best when they're around other people, and they prefer playing games in which they're on a team or have a partner.

### Correlations with Other 16PF Factors

The Group-Orientation shown by low scorers is part of Extraversion, a general orientation toward other people. In the 16PF Fifth Edition, Group Orientation (Q2-) contributes to the Extraversion global factor, along with Warmth (A+), Liveliness (F+), Social Boldness (H+), and Forthrightness (N-).

### Correlations with Other Measures

Group-Orientation (Q2-) correlates with many other scales of sociability: CPI's v.1, a broad measure of sociability; CPI's Capacity for Status, Sociability, and Social Presence; PRF's Affiliation; MBTI's Extraversion; and nearly all of NEO's Extraversion facets, including Warmth (E1), Gregariousness (E2), Assertiveness (E3), Excitement-Seeking (E5), and Positive Emotions (E6). These correlations support Factor Q2's place on the 16PF Extraversion global factor.

Self-Reliance (Q2+) is positively correlated with PRF's Autonomy scale, supporting the individualistic element of self-reliance. It is negatively correlated with PRF's Nurturance and Succorance scales, CPI's Empathy scale, and NEO's Altruism facet. This pattern suggests the notion that Self-Reliant (Q2+) people may deemphasize caring connections with others. Finally, Self-Reliance (Q2+) is negatively correlated with CPI's Well-being and Self-acceptance scales, and shows modest but significant correlations with three of NEO's Neuroticism facets, including Angry Hostility (N2), Depression (N3), and Self-Consciousness (N4). By way of hypothesis, these qualities might be consequences of extreme Self-Reliance or contributing causes of it.

**Factor Q3 (Perfectionism): Perfectionistic Versus Tolerates Disorder**

*General Factor Meaning*
High scorers want to do things right. They tend to be organized, to keep things in their proper places, and to plan ahead. Perfectionistic (Q3+) people are likely to be most comfortable in highly organized and predictable situations and may find it hard to deal with unpredictability. At the extreme, they may be seen as inflexible.

In contrast to high scorers, low scorers leave more things to chance and tend to be more comfortable in a disorganized setting. However, low scorers may be perceived as lackadaisical, unorganized, or unprepared. They may not be able to muster a clear motivation for behaving in planful or organized ways, especially if these behaviors are unimportant to them.

*Item Content/Typical Responses*
High scorers say that they keep their belongings in tip-top shape, they like to have things done just right, they plan ahead, and they believe that any job should be done thoroughly if it's to be done at all. Low scorers say that they don't mind if their room is messy, they don't always take time to think ahead of everything needed for a job, and they think that some jobs don't have to be done as carefully as others.

*Correlations with Other 16PF Factors*
Perfectionism (Q3+) contributes to the Self-Control global factor, along with Seriousness (F-), Rule-Consciousness (G+), and Groundedness (M-). While Perfectionism (Q3+) correlates with the social desirability aspect of the Impression Management (IM) scale, it is not among the strongest of the correlations. Perhaps this reflects the fact

that Perfectionism, while it can have positive results, is not always desirable.

*Correlations with Other Measures*
Like Rule-Consciousness (G+), with which it is highly correlated, Perfectionism (Q3+) tends to correlate with other measures' control-related scales, including all NEO Conscientiousness facets. These correlations support Factor Q3's position on the Self-Control global factor. Some correlations are more unique to Perfectionism (Factor Q3) than to Rule-Consciousness (Factor G). For example, the two highest correlations for Factor Q3 relate to the need for order: PRF's Order scale and NEO's Order (C2). Nearly as high is the following cluster: positive correlations with PRF's Cognitive Structure and MBTI's Judging and negative correlations with CPI's Flexibility and MBTI's Perceptive. This cluster may suggest the need for predictability and the inflexibility of judgment that can accompany a strong need for order and dislike for ambiguity. Factor Q3's element of striving for achievement and perfection is suggested in correlations with PRF's Achievement scale and CPI's Achievement via Conformance. An element of social desirability also is suggested by the positive correlation with CPI's Good Impression scale.

**Factor Q4 (Tension): Tense Versus Relaxed**

*General Factor Meaning*
This scale is associated with nervous tension. High scorers tend to have a restless energy and to be fidgety when made to wait. While a certain amount of tension can be focused effectively and can motivate action, extremely high tension can lead to impatience and irritability, as seen in the item content. Correlations with other measures suggest the possibility that high tension may sometimes get in the way of self-control or may impede effective action. Professionals may want to address the source of tension

whenever high scores occur in a profile since such scores may reflect either tension that is characteristic of a person or tension that is specific to a person's present life situation.

Low scorers tend to feel relaxed and tranquil. They are patient and slow to become frustrated. At the extreme, their low level of arousal can make them unmotivated. That is, because they are comfortable, they may be disinclined to change or push themselves.

Social desirability can affect Factor Q4 results. Since the items are fairly transparent, they can be influenced by response sets to present oneself favorably (Q4–) as well as unfavorably (Q4+). In fact, the correlation between Factor Q4 and the Impression Management (IM) scale is the highest in the 16PF Fifth Edition.

*Item Content/Typical Responses*
High scorers tend to become frustrated too quickly with people, to get annoyed by changes in plans, and to become restless and fidgety when waiting for something. Low scorers aren't bothered by people interrupting them, find it easy to be patient, and don't tend to get as restless and fidgety as most people when waiting.

*Correlations with Other 16PF Factors*
Factor Q4 is the largest contributor to the Anxiety global factor, along with Reactivity (C–), Vigilance (L+), and Apprehension (O+).

*Correlations with Other Measures*
Factor Q4 correlates with several NEO Neuroticism facets, including Anxiety (N1), Angry Hostility (N2), Depression (N3), and Impulsiveness (N5). These correlations support the place of Factor Q4 on the Anxiety global factor. The notion that extreme tension may get in the way of self-control is suggested by a negative correlation with CPI's Self-control and a positive correlation with NEO's Impulsiveness (N5).

That Tension (Q4+) may impede effective action is suggested by negative correlations with NEO's Actions (O4) facet and CPI's Psychological-mindedness, Empathy, Tolerance, and Achievement via Independence scales. Based on Factor Q4's correlations with PRF's Aggression and Defendence scales and NEO's Angry Hostility (N2), a hypothesis might be that the tension involved in Q4 is akin to the arousal of the "fight or flight" impulse. Factor Q4 also negatively correlates with CPI's Good Impression scale, supporting the link with social desirability mentioned previously.▾

# CHAPTER

# 4

OVERVIEW OF

THE 16PF® FIFTH

EDITION REVISION

# 4

## CONCEPTUAL FOUNDATION OF THE 16PF®

**W**hen Dr. Raymond Cattell and his colleagues set out to measure the broad range of normal personality over 45 years ago, they reasoned that adjectives relating to personality had to correspond to English-language adjectives commonly used to describe people. Therefore, they began research on the basis of the Allport and Odbert (1936) trait lexicon, a set of some 18,000 adjectives that describe people. Their developmental work and findings are summarized broadly in the text that follows.

Initially, Cattell and his colleagues asked observers to rate subjects well known to them on the basis of a subset of adjectives reduced to eliminate similar terms in the Allport and Odbert set. The researchers then subjected the observers' ratings to factor analysis—a statistical technique used to discover, in a large set of variables, a smaller subset that explains the whole domain. Cattell performed this factor analysis with the intent of identifying the "primary" personality traits, or those that could explain the entire personality domain.

Factor analyses of the observers' ratings data, termed "Life-data" or "L-data," identified 12 traits that could account for the range of descriptors in the trait lexicon. These traits, called "factors," were named using letters of the alphabet, such as Factors A, B, C. (Within the alphabetical listing of factor names, some letters are skipped over. Factors corresponding to these skipped letters were found in parallel studies of child and adolescent personality, but were not found in descriptions of adults.) The adjectives rated for the factors were translated into multiple-choice questionnaire items and were termed "Questionnaire-data" or "Q-data." In a series of studies, responses to the questionnaire items were factor analyzed, and the resultant data were used in constructing the 16 primary scales of the 16PF. Twelve of the scales measure the factors labeled alphabetically and originally identified through analyses of the L-data. The remaining four scales measure factors labeled Q1, Q2, Q3, and Q4 because they originated from analyses of the Q-data.

Just as the chemical elements are considered the primary building blocks of all matter, Cattell conceptualized the 16 factor-analytically discovered personality factors to be the basic elements of personality. To describe qualities relevant to scores on the 16 factor scales, Cattell created distinctive names. For example, he denoted as "Sizothymia" the reserved quality reflected by low scores on Factor A, and he chose "Affectothymia" to capture the warm quality reflected by high scores on Factor A. In subsequent editions of the 16PF, vernacular names (e.g., Warmth for Factor A) also are used to describe the qualities corresponding to the factor scale scores.

For the first edition of the 16PF, as well as for subsequent ones, Cattell factor analyzed the 16 primary scales to derive global factors on which related primary scales cluster together. (The global factors were called "second-order factors" in previous 16PF literature.) The most-replicated 16PF global factors are Extraversion, Anxiety, Tough-Mindedness, Independence, and Self-Control. These global factors show how the 16 factor scales are interrelated, and also allow personality to be viewed at a simpler, broader level than do the individual factor scales.

In summary, the 16PF represents Cattell's intention to identify the primary traits of personality through factor analyzing the entire domain of personality descriptors. This use of factor analysis is distinct from other methods of constructing personality measures. For example, some inventories are composed of items that reflect constructs posited by a particular theory of personality (e.g., questionnaires that assess Murray's Needs). In other inventories, the content is designed to distinguish one group from another (e.g., tests that differentiate clinical groups from so-called "normals").

Because the 16PF is a broad measure of normal adult personality, it has been used in a variety of settings (clinical/counseling, industrial/organizational, research, and schools) to measure a wide range of life behaviors. Such measurements include predicting performance criteria and behavioral ratings, assessing degree of personality similarity to members of particular groups, accounting for personality changes resulting from treatment or experimental manipulations, and predicting other criterion and construct measures.

## DEVELOPMENT OF THE FIFTH EDITION

Since the first edition of the 16PF was published in 1949, four revisions have followed, with scale refinements distinguishing each (1956, 1962, 1967-69, 1993). The 1993 revision, resulting in the fifth edition, reflects improved psychometric characteristics and gives attention to cultural changes and advances within the profession (e.g., APA's *Standards for Educational and Psychological Testing*, 1985). *The 16PF Fifth Edition Technical Manual* provides complete developmental data relating to the fifth edition (see Cattell, H.E.P., 1994) and to the standardization sample (see Conn & Rieke, 1994a). The sections that follow summarize this developmental data.

### Primary Factor Scales

At the beginning of the fifth edition revision, items were culled from existing 16PF editions on the bases of these criteria: if they correlated highly with their own factor scale and if they did not correlate more highly with another factor scale. The selected items were reviewed for content issues; outdated, ambiguous, or unclear items were rewritten or replaced. Items also were shortened and simplified and were reviewed for race or gender bias (Cattell, H.E.P., 1994).

Next, a series of experimental test forms was administered, and test-taker data were evaluated. At each evaluation stage, items were reduced in number based on reviews of item-scale correlations, scale internal consistencies, and intercorrelations among the scales. The final experimental form included 14 items for each of the factor scales except for Reasoning (Factor B), which had 15 items.

Using six parcels (or groups of items) per factor, a principle components factor analysis of the final experimental form was completed on the basis of a sample of 3,498 examinees from which the national standardization sample was selected. This was followed by a Harris-Kaiser rotation of 19 factors and two hand rotations by Raymond Cattell. The results, shown in Table 13 in Chapter 5, evince strong support for the basic factor structure of the fifth edition because nearly all parcels load on their own factors but not on other factors.

The final experimental form was standardized (see "Standardization" section in this chapter), and items were reduced in number once again, resulting in the 16PF Fifth Edition. Table 7 summarizes sources of the items.

## Reasoning (Factor B) and Response Style Indices

As each experimental form of the fifth edition was evaluated, new items for the Reasoning (Factor B) and Impression Management (IM) scales also were evaluated. Each scale's development is summarized here, and complete developmental information regarding these scales

TABLE 7

SOURCES FOR FIFTH EDITION ITEMS

| Factor Scale | | *Previous Forms* Unchanged | Small Changes | Significant Changes | *New Items* |
|---|---|---|---|---|---|
| A | Warmth | 2 | 4 | 2 | 3 |
| C | Emotional Stability | 2 | 2 | 2 | 4 |
| E | Dominance | 0 | 5 | 3 | 2 |
| F | Liveliness | 5 | 4 | 0 | 1 |
| G | Rule-Consciousness | 3 | 4 | 2 | 2 |
| H | Social Boldness | 8 | 2 | 0 | 0 |
| I | Sensitivity | 3 | 7 | 0 | 1 |
| L | Vigilance | 2 | 1 | 5 | 2 |
| M | Abstractedness | 2 | 0 | 5 | 4 |
| N | Privateness | 1 | 2 | 3 | 4 |
| O | Apprehension | 0 | 2 | 7 | 1 |
| Q1 | Openness to Change | 2 | 5 | 2 | 5 |
| Q2 | Self-Reliance | 4 | 1 | 4 | 1 |
| Q3 | Perfectionism | 1 | 1 | 3 | 5 |
| Q4 | Tension | 0 | 3 | 4 | 3 |
| Total Number | | 35 | 43 | 42 | 38 |
| Percentage | | 22% | 27% | 27% | 24% |

Note. Unchanged = zero to two words changed; small changes = 3-5 words or a phrase changed; significant changes = same idea but rewritten more than several words. From "Development of the 16PF Fifth Edition" by H. E. P. Cattell, 1994. In S. R. Conn & M. L. Rieke (Eds.), *The 16PF Fifth Edition Technical Manual.* Champaign, IL: Institute for Personality and Ability Testing.

is provided in *The 16PF Fifth Edition Technical Manual* (see Rieke & Conn, 1994; Conn & Rieke, 1994e).

Initial revision of the Reasoning (Factor B) scale involved culling items from all existing forms of the 16PF as well as writing and testing new items, resulting in a pool of 43 items. During the process of evaluating the series of experimental forms for the fifth edition, the 43-item pool was reduced to 15, with 5 items relating to each of three types of reasoning skills: verbal, numerical, and logical (Rieke & Conn, 1994). These items were analyzed for their ability to differentiate among levels of ability as well as for bias related to gender and race. The Reasoning (Factor B) scale also was correlated with other brief measures of intelligence. See Chapter 5 for further reliability and validity information relevant to Factor B.

The content of the Impression Management (IM) scale taps socially desirable and undesirable behaviors, feelings, and attitudes (Conn & Rieke, 1994e). Revision of this scale began by culling all applicable items from existing forms of the 16PF and by writing and testing new items. Final items were selected by evaluating item-scale correlations and correlations of the overall scale with other measures of social desirability. For the fifth edition, there are 12 items on the IM scale, which are scored only on this scale and not on any of the primary personality factor scales.

The content of both the Infrequency (INF) and Acquiescence (ACQ) response style indices is based on empirical analyses of item response choice frequencies in the normative sample.

In developing the INF scale, items showing a very low endorsement rate for a particular response alternative (i.e., *a*, *b*, or *c*) were identified and combined into a scale.

A distribution of scores was developed, with percentile values assigned for the range of endorsement frequencies. Finally, a Monte Carlo study was conducted to check the estimated accuracy of INF for detecting randomly generated responses. An elevated INF score indicates that the examinee selected response alternatives that were infrequently chosen in the norm sample. As a result, the possibility exists that the examinee was inattentive to item content or marked responses in a random manner.

The ACQ scale was developed from an empirical approach based on the endorsement frequency of "True" responses on the 16PF. Its purpose is to indicate an examinee's tendency to agree with statements presented in the 16PF, regardless of item content (Conn & Rieke, 1994e).

## Standardization

The final experimental form of the fifth edition was administered to a large group ($\underline{N} = 4,449$), and then a stratified random sampling was used to create the final normative sample of 2,500. Sample stratification was done on the bases of gender, race, age, and educational variables, with the target number for each variable being derived from 1990 U.S. Census figures (Conn & Rieke, 1994a). Demographic details about the norm group are presented in Table 8, including the extent to which the sample matches the census figures. Score means and standard deviations for the norm group are presented in Tables 35 and 36 in Appendix A. The following summarizes the norm sample demographics:

**1.** Size of the norm sample is 2,500: 1,245 males and 1,255 females (49.8% male, 50.2% female).

**2.** Ages range from 15 to 92, with a mean age of 33.3 years.

**3.** Years of education completed range from 7 to 25, with a mean of 13.6 years (standard deviation of 3.30).

**4.** The sample is 80.4% Caucasian, 12.8% African American, 3.0% Asian American, 2.3% Native American, and 9.0% Hispanic. The Hispanic sample crosses racial groups, and for this reason, the total sample exceeds 100%.

**5.** Approximately 16% of those in the sample reside in Northeastern states, 15% in Southeastern states, 28% in North Central states, 14% in South Central states, and 24% in Western states.

## Global Factors

Termed "second-order factors" in previous 16PF editions, the five global factors of personality are Extraversion, Anxiety,

TABLE 8

NORM SAMPLE DEMOGRAPHICS (N=2500, 1245 MALES, 1255 FEMALES)

| GENDER | | Number in Sample | Percent in Sample | Percent in 1990 Census |
|---|---|---|---|---|
| | Male | 1245 | 49.8% | 48.7% |
| | Female | 1255 | 50.2% | 51.3% |

| RACE | | Number in Sample | Percent in Sample | Percent in 1990 Census |
|---|---|---|---|---|
| | African American | 321 | 12.8% | 12.1% |
| | Asian | 76 | 3.0% | 2.9% |
| | Caucasian | 2010 | 80.4% | 80.2% |
| | Native American | 58 | 2.3% | 1.0% |
| | Other | 35 | 1.5% | 3.8% |
| | Hispanic origin | 224 | 9.0% | 9.0% |

Note. Totals add up to over 100% since Hispanics also endorsed one of the five race categories.

| AGE GROUP | Respondents' Age (years) | Number in Sample | Percent in Sample | Percent in 1990 Census |
|---|---|---|---|---|
| | 15 to 17 | 329 | 13.2% | 4.6% |
| | 18 to 24 | 415 | 16.6% | 13.8% |
| | 25 to 44 | 1216 | 48.6% | 41.7% |
| | 45 to 54 | 371 | 14.8% | 12.9% |
| | 55 to 64 | 116 | 4.6% | 10.8% |
| | 65 and over | 53 | 2.2% | 16.2% |

| EDUCATION LEVEL | Respondents' Education | Number in Sample | Percent in Sample | Percent in 1990 Census |
|---|---|---|---|---|
| | H. S. Grad, or less | 1107 | 44.3% | 61.5% |
| | Some College | 617 | 24.7% | 22.7% |
| | College Graduate | 776 | 31.0% | 15.8% |

**Norm Sample Demographics**
**(State Residences of Norm Sample Respondents, by Geographic Region)**
**(N=2500, 1245 males, 1255 females)**

| REGION | Percent in Sample |
|---|---|
| Northeastern | 15.8% |
| Southeastern | 14.8% |
| North Central | 28.0% |
| South Central | 14.3% |
| Western | 24.0% |
| Did not say | 3.1% |

**Regions were defined as follows:**
Northeastern: Connecticut, Delaware, District of Columbia, Maine, Maryland, Massachusetts, New Hampshire, New Jersey, New York, Pennsylvania, Rhode Island, Vermont, Virginia, and West Virginia.
Southeastern: Alabama, Florida, Georgia, Kentucky, Mississippi, North Carolina, South Carolina, and Tennessee.
North Central: Illinois, Indiana, Iowa, Michigan, Minnesota, Nebraska, North Dakota, Ohio, South Dakota, Wisconsin.
South Central: Arkansas, Colorado, Kansas, Louisiana, Missouri, New Mexico, Oklahoma, Texas.
Western: Alaska, Arizona, California, Hawaii, Idaho, Montana, Nevada, Oregon, Utah, Washington, and Wyoming.

**Data Sources:**
U.S. Department of Commerce, Bureau of the Census, Current Population Reports, Series P-70, No. 21. "Educational Background and Economic Status: Spring 1987." (Table was prepared March 1991.)
U.S. Bureau of the Census, Current Population Reports, Series P-20, No. 460, "School Enrollment—Social and Economic Characteristics of Students: October 1990."

Note. Tables from "Characteristics of the Norm Sample" by S. R. Conn and M. L. Rieke, 1994a. In S. R. Conn & M. L. Rieke (Eds.), *The 16PF Fifth Edition Technical Manual*. Champaign, IL: IPAT. Demographic frequencies and percentages for gender, race, age, and education level found in the 16PF Fifth Edition normative sample.

Tough-Mindedness, Independence, and Self-Control. These factors, which are comprised of clusters of related primary factors, describe personality in broader, more general terms than do the primary factors. For the fifth edition, development of the global factors involved submitting the final primary scales to principle component factor analysis on the basis of the same national sample of 3,498 used in the primary scale development, followed by a Harris-Kaiser oblique rotation and three hand rotations (Cattell, H. E. P., 1994). The resultant factor structure is presented in Table 13 in Chapter 5.

The major primary factors loading on each of the five global factors are quite similar to those found in previous second-order factor analyses of the 16PF (Cattell et al., 1970; Krug & Johns, 1986). Chapter 3 gives evidence of the correlations of these scales with the five broad personality dimensions found in other personality measures.

Equations for calculating sten scores on the global factors are presented in Table 13 in Chapter 5, and instructions for handscoring the global factors on the Individual Record Form are given in Chapter 2.

## SUMMARY OF THE 16PF FIFTH EDITION

The 16PF Fifth Edition contains 185 items that comprise 16 primary personality factor scales and the Impression Management (IM) scale. Each scale contains 10 to 15 items. Table 40 in Appendix B presents the items scored for each scale and the keyed direction for each item.

Average test-completion time ranges from 35 to 50 minutes for paper-and-pencil administration and from 25 to 35 minutes for computer administration (Wade & Guastello, 1993). Readability for the fifth edition is estimated at the fifth-grade level (Cattell, H.E.P., 1994). Internal consistency coefficient alpha reliabilities average .74, with a range from .64 to .85. Test-retest reliabilities average .80 for a 2-week interval and .70 for a 2-month interval. (Complete data on scale reliabilities are reported in Chapter 5.) ▼

# CHAPTER

# 5

## RELIABILITY

## AND

## VALIDITY

# 5

## RELIABILITY

## AND

## VALIDITY

## RELIABILITY

**R**eliability gauges the consistency of test results. Two aspects of reliability are addressed in this chapter: (1) the consistency of 16PF results over time as evidenced by test-retest correlations, and (2) the internal consistency, or homogeneity, of the test items as measured by Cronbach's coefficient alpha. Additional information about reliability is provided in *The 16PF Fifth Edition Technical Manual* (see Conn, 1994).

### Test-Retest Reliability

Test-retest coefficients offer evidence of the stability over time of the different traits measured by the 16PF. Pearson Product-Moment Correlations were calculated for two-week and two-month test-retest intervals (see Table 9). Examinees for the two-week interval were 204 (77 male, 127 female) university undergraduate and graduate students. Their mean age was 20.5 years, and their mean education level was 13.8 years. Reliability coefficients for the primary factors ranged from .69 (Reasoning, Factor B) to .86 (Self-Reliance, Factor Q2), with a mean of .80. Test-retest coefficients for the global factors were higher, ranging from .84 to .91, with a mean of .87.

For the two-month interval, the sample consisted of 159 university undergraduates (34 male, 125 female). The mean age of the group was 18.8 years, and the mean education level was 12.6 years. For the primary factors, reliability coefficients ranged from .56 (Vigilance, Factor L) to .79 (Social Boldness, Factor H), with a mean of .70 (see Table 9). Test-retest coefficients for the global factors ranged from .70 to .82, with a mean of .78.

### Internal Consistency

In contrast to test-retest information, internal consistency can be viewed as reliability estimated from a single test administration.

Measurement of the internal reliability of a test provides a source of evidence that all items on a given scale assess the same construct. As the intercorrelations among items within a scale increase, reliability of the scale itself increases. Internal consistency is lowered to the degree that items on the same scale measure different traits or to the extent that scale items are not intercorrelated.

As a measure of scale internal consistency, Cronbach's coefficient alpha essentially calculates the average value of all possible split-half reliabilities (Cronbach, 1951). Cronbach alpha coefficients for the 16PF Fifth Edition were calculated on the general population norm sample of 2,500 adults. Values ranged from .64 (Openness to Change, Factor Q1) to .85 (Social Boldness, Factor H), with an average of .74 (see Table 10).

## VALIDITY

Generally, validity refers to a test's ability to measure the concept it was designed to measure. Construct validity of the 16PF Fifth Edition demonstrates that the test measures 16 distinct personality traits. Criterion validity of the 16PF is demonstrated by its ability to predict various criterion scores, such as Self-Esteem and Creative Potential.

In addition to evidence supporting construct and criterion validities, other types of validity issues may concern 16PF users. For example, an issue might be whether using the 16PF for a specific purpose, such as a job selection device, is "valid." Resolution of this issue relates to determining if personality characteristics measured by the 16PF are relevant to job performance. Another issue might concern whether a client's test results are "valid" and accurate, which bears on response bias. Information about response bias is addressed in Chapter 3.

TABLE 9

TEST-RETEST RELIABILITY DATA

| | | Test-Retest Interval | |
|---|---|---|---|
| Primary Factor | | Two-week ($\underline{N}$ = 204) | Two-month ($\underline{N}$ = 159) |
| A | Warmth | .83 | .77 |
| B | Reasoning | .69 | .65 |
| C | Emotional Stability | .75 | .67 |
| E | Dominance | .77 | .69 |
| F | Liveliness | .82 | .69 |
| G | Rule-Consciousness | .80 | .76 |
| H | Social Boldness | .87 | .79 |
| I | Sensitivity | .82 | .76 |
| L | Vigilance | .76 | .56 |
| M | Abstractedness | .84 | .67 |
| N | Privateness | .77 | .70 |
| O | Apprehension | .79 | .64 |
| Q1 | Openness to Change | .83 | .70 |
| Q2 | Self-Reliance | .86 | .69 |
| Q3 | Perfectionism | .80 | .77 |
| Q4 | Tension | .78 | .68 |
| Mean | | .80 | .70 |
| **Global Factor** | | | |
| Extraversion | | .91 | .80 |
| Anxiety | | .84 | .70 |
| Tough-Mindedness | | .87 | .82 |
| Independence | | .84 | .81 |
| Self-Control | | .87 | .79 |
| Mean | | .87 | .78 |

<u>Note</u>. From "Reliability and Equivalency: Comparison of the 16PF Fifth Edition and Fourth Edition (Form A)" by S. R. Conn, 1994. In S. R. Conn & M. L. Rieke (Eds.), *The 16PF Fifth Edition Technical Manual*. Champaign, IL: Institute for Personality and Ability Testing, Inc.

## Factor-Analytic Results

The 16PF scales are based on factor-analytic methods, and the results of these methods provide evidence about the construct validity of the fifth edition and about its place in the evolution of the 16PF as a test. A summary of the findings related to the fifth edition factor analyses is presented in this section, and complete findings are provided in *The 16PF Fifth Edition Technical Manual* (see Cattell, H.E.P., 1994; Conn, 1994).

### Factor Analysis

That 16PF users grasp all the technical aspects of factor analysis is not relevant to the purposes of understanding and administering the test. What is sufficient is that users know that factor analysis is a statistical technique for discovering, within a large set of variables, a smaller set of variables that explains the larger domain. For the 16PF, factor analysis was used to identify 16 primary factors that explain the larger domain of personality descriptors in the English language. Factor analysis also was used to identify a set of global factors that explain the 16 primary factor scales at a broad level.

A particular aspect of Cattell's factor-analytic method merits explanation because it represents a departure from that used in the development of some other personality inventories. Cattell anticipated that distinct personality traits might nonetheless be related to one another. Therefore, rather than extracting factors forced to be independent of one another and consequently uncorrelated (orthogonal factors), Cattell chose to use oblique factors, which are allowed to intercorrelate. Cattell's assumption is reflected at the global factor level, where related primary factors cluster along the five global scales (e.g., some primary scales relate to Extraversion and others relate to Self-Control).

TABLE 10

INTERNAL RELIABILITY DATA (CRONBACH COEFFICIENT ALPHA) (BASED ON NORM SAMPLE, N=2500)

| Factor | | Alpha |
|---|---|---|
| A | Warmth | .69 |
| B | Reasoning | .77 |
| C | Emotional Stability | .78 |
| E | Dominance | .66 |
| F | Liveliness | .72 |
| G | Rule-Consciousness | .75 |
| H | Social Boldness | .85 |
| I | Sensitivity | .77 |
| L | Vigilance | .74 |
| M | Abstractedness | .74 |
| N | Privateness | .75 |
| O | Apprehension | .78 |
| Q1 | Openness to Change | .64 |
| Q2 | Self-Reliance | .78 |
| Q3 | Perfectionism | .71 |
| Q4 | Tension | .76 |
| Mean | | .74 |

Note. From "Reliability and Equivalency: Comparison of the 16PF Fifth Edition and Fourth Edition (Form A)" by S. R. Conn, 1994. In S. R. Conn & M. L. Rieke (Eds.), *The 16PF Fifth Edition Technical Manual*. Champaign, IL: Institute for Personality and Ability Testing, Inc.

## Primary Factor Pattern

Table 11 presents the results of factor analysis of the broad domain of items in the final experimental form (Form S). The results show that, with few exceptions, parcels of items from a given primary factor scale load on their particular factor scale but not on other factor scales. This pattern provides evidence about the factor structure on which the fifth edition is based.

TABLE 11

**PRIMARY SCALE FACTOR ANALYSIS 16PF, FORM S SECOND SHIFT AFTER HARRIS-KAISER**
**(FACTOR LOADING LESS THAN ABSOLUTE VALUE 0.30 DELETED)**
**(N=3498, 1749 MALES, 1749 FEMALES)**

| Parcel | A | B | C | E | F | G | H | I | L | M | N | O | Q1 | Q2 | Q3 | Q4 | — | — | — | — |
|--------|------|------|------|------|------|------|---|---|---|---|---|---|----|----|----|----|---|------|---|---|
| A1 | 0.66 | | | | | | | | | | | | | | | | | | | |
| A2 | 0.84 | | | | | | | | | | | | | | | | | | | |
| A3 | 0.42 | | | | | | | | | | | | | | | | | | | |
| A4 | 0.39 | | | | | | | | | | | | | | | | | | | |
| A5 | | | | | | | | | | | | | | | | | | 0.53 | | |
| A6 | | | | | | | | | | | | | | | | | | | | |
| B1 | | 0.46 | | | | | | | | | | | | | | | | | | |
| B2 | | 0.54 | | | | | | | | | | | | | | | | | | |
| B3 | | 0.68 | | | | | | | | | | | | | | | | | | |
| B4 | | 0.76 | | | | | | | | | | | | | | | | | | |
| B5 | | 0.70 | | | | | | | | | | | | | | | | | | |
| C1 | | | 0.80 | | | | | | | | | | | | | | | | | |
| C2 | | | 0.52 | | | | | | | | | | | | | | | | | |
| C3 | | | 0.65 | | | | | | | | | | | | | | | | | |
| C4 | | | 0.46 | | | | | | | | | | | | | | | | | |
| C5 | | | 0.79 | | | | | | | | | | | | | | | | | |
| C6 | | | 0.51 | | | | | | | | | | | | | | | | | |
| E1 | | | | 0.41 | | | | | | | | | | | | | | | | |
| E2 | | | | 0.63 | | | | | | | | | | | | | | | | |
| E3 | | | | 0.45 | | | | | | | | | | | | | | | | |
| E4 | | | | 0.47 | | | | | | | | | | | | | | | | |
| E5 | | | | 0.50 | | | | | | | | | | | | | | | | |
| E6 | | | | 0.76 | | | | | | | | | | | | | | | | |
| F1 | | | | | 0.45 | | | | | | | | | | | | | | | |
| F2 | | | | | 0.80 | | | | | | | | | | | | | | | |
| F3 | | | | | 0.43 | | | | | | | | | | | | | | | |
| F4 | | | | | 0.35 | | | | | | | | | | | | | | | |
| F5 | | | | | 0.81 | | | | | | | | | | | | | | | |
| F6 | | | | | 0.54 | | | | | | | | | | | | | | | |
| G1 | | | | | | 0.77 | | | | | | | | | | | | | | |
| G2 | | | | | | 0.54 | | | | | | 0.45 | | | | | | | | |
| G3 | | | | | | 0.58 | | | | | | | | | | | | | | |
| G4 | | | | | | 0.70 | | | | | | | | | | | | | | |
| G5 | | | | | | 0.62 | | | | | | | | | | | | | | |
| G6 | | | | | | 0.70 | | | | | | | | | | | | | | |

Note. From "Reliability and Equivalency: Comparison of the 16PF Fifth Edition and Fourth Edition (Form A)" by S. R. Conn, 1994. In S. R. Conn & M. L. Rieke (Eds.), *The 16PF Fifth Edition Technical Manual.* Champaign, IL: Institute for Personality and Ability Testing, Inc.

TABLE 11, CONTINUED

PRIMARY SCALE FACTOR ANALYSIS 16PF, FORM S SECOND SHIFT AFTER HARRIS-KAISER
(FACTOR LOADING LESS THAN ABSOLUTE VALUE 0.30 DELETED)
(N=3498, 1749 MALES, 1749 FEMALES)

| Parcel | A | B | C | E | F | G | H | I | L | M | N | O | Q1 | Q2 | Q3 | Q4 | — | — | — | — |
|--------|---|---|---|---|---|---|------|------|------|------|------|------|----|----|----|----|------|---|---|---|
| H1 |   |   |   |   |   |   | 0.60 |      |      |      |      |      |    |    |    |    |      |   |   |   |
| H2 |   |   |   |   |   |   | 0.76 |      |      |      |      |      |    |    |    |    |      |   |   |   |
| H3 |   |   |   |   |   |   | 0.74 |      |      |      |      |      |    |    |    |    |      |   |   |   |
| H4 |   |   |   |   |   |   | 0.86 |      |      |      |      |      |    |    |    |    |      |   |   |   |
| H5 |   |   |   |   |   |   | 0.71 |      |      |      |      |      |    |    |    |    |      |   |   |   |
| H6 |   |   |   |   |   |   | 0.73 |      |      |      |      |      |    |    |    |    |      |   |   |   |
| I1 |   |   |   |   |   |   |      |      |      |      |      |      |    |    |    |    | 0.77 |   |   |   |
| I2 |   |   |   |   |   |   | 0.68 |      |      |      |      |      |    |    |    |    |      |   |   |   |
| I3 |   |   |   |   |   |   | 0.42 |      |      |      |      |      |    |    |    |    |      |   |   |   |
| I4 |   |   |   |   |   |   | 0.53 |      |      |      |      |      |    |    |    |    |      |   |   |   |
| I5 |   |   |   |   |   |   |      |      |      |      |      |      |    |    |    |    | 0.66 |   |   |   |
| I6 |   |   |   |   |   |   | 0.32 |      |      |      |      |      |    |    |    |    | 0.52 |   |   |   |
| L1 |   |   |   |   |   |   |      | 0.36 |      |      |      |      |    |    |    |    |      |   |   |   |
| L2 |   |   |   |   |   |   |      | 0.49 |      |      |      |      |    |    |    |    |      |   |   |   |
| L3 |   |   |   |   |   |   |      | 0.60 |      |      |      |      |    |    |    |    |      |   |   |   |
| L4 |   |   |   |   |   |   |      | 0.69 |      |      |      |      |    |    |    |    |      |   |   |   |
| L5 |   |   |   |   |   |   |      | 0.74 |      |      |      |      |    |    |    |    |      |   |   |   |
| L6 |   |   |   |   |   |   |      | 0.58 |      |      |      |      |    |    |    |    |      |   |   |   |
| M1 |   |   |   |   |   |   |      |      | 0.64 |      |      |      |    |    |    |    |      |   |   |   |
| M2 |   |   |   |   |   |   |      |      | 0.42 |      |      |      |    |    |    |    |      |   |   |   |
| M3 |   |   |   |   |   |   |      |      | 0.61 |      |      |      |    |    |    |    |      |   |   |   |
| M4 |   |   |   |   |   |   |      |      | 0.77 |      |      |      |    |    |    |    |      |   |   |   |
| M5 |   |   |   |   |   |   |      |      | 0.69 |      |      |      |    |    |    |    |      |   |   |   |
| M6 |   |   |   |   |   |   |      |      | 0.59 |      |      |      |    |    |    |    |      |   |   |   |
| N1 |   |   |   |   |   |   |      |      |      | 0.69 |      |      |    |    |    |    |      |   |   |   |
| N2 |   |   |   |   |   |   |      |      |      | 0.71 |      |      |    |    |    |    |      |   |   |   |
| N3 |   |   |   |   |   |   |      |      |      | 0.56 |      |      |    |    |    |    |      |   |   |   |
| N4 |   |   |   |   |   |   |      |      |      | 0.63 |      |      |    |    |    |    |      |   |   |   |
| N5 |   |   |   |   |   |   |      |      |      | 0.70 |      |      |    |    |    |    |      |   |   |   |
| N6 |   |   |   |   |   |   |      |      |      | 0.72 |      |      |    |    |    |    |      |   |   |   |
| O1 |   |   |   |   |   |   |      |      |      |      | 0.69 |      |    |    |    |    |      |   |   |   |
| O2 |   |   |   |   |   |   |      |      |      |      | 0.68 |      |    |    |    |    |      |   |   |   |
| O3 |   |   |   |   |   |   |      |      |      |      | 0.48 |      |    |    |    | −0.32 |      |   |   |   |
| O4 |   |   |   |   |   |   |      |      |      |      | 0.41 |      |    |    |    |    |      |   |   |   |
| O5 |   |   |   |   |   |   |      |      |      |      | 0.56 |      |    |    |    |    |      |   |   |   |
| O6 |   |   |   |   |   |   |      |      |      |      | 0.55 |      |    |    |    |    |      |   |   |   |

PRIMARY SCALE FACTOR ANALYSIS 16PF, FORM S SECOND SHIFT AFTER HARRIS-KAISER
(FACTOR LOADING LESS THAN ABSOLUTE VALUE 0.30 DELETED)
(N=3498, 1749 MALES, 1749 FEMALES)

| Parcel | | | | | | | | | | | | | Factor | | | | | | | |
|--------|---|---|---|---|---|---|---|---|---|---|---|---|---|----|----|----|----|---|---|---|
| | A | B | C | E | F | G | H | I | L | M | N | O | Q1 | Q2 | Q3 | Q4 | — | — | — | — |
| Q11 | | | | | | | | | | | | | 0.40 | | | | | | | |
| Q12 | | | | | | | | | | | | | 0.40 | | | | | | | |
| Q13 | | | | | | | | | | | | | 0.52 | | | | | | | |
| Q14 | | | | | | | | | | | | | 0.49 | | | | | | | |
| Q15 | | | | | | | | | | | | | 0.50 | | | | | | | |
| Q16 | | | | | | | | | | | | | 0.48 | | | | | | | |
| Q21 | | | | | | | | | | | | | | 0.59 | | | | | | |
| Q22 | | | | | | | | | | | | | | 0.56 | | | | | | |
| Q23 | | | | | | | | | | | | | | 0.62 | | | | | | |
| Q24 | | | | | | | | | | | | | | 0.62 | | | | | | |
| Q25 | | | | | | | | | | | | | | 0.53 | | | | | | |
| Q26 | | | | | | | | | | | | | | 0.57 | | | | | | |
| Q31 | | | | | | | | | | | | | | | 0.48 | | | | | |
| Q32 | | | | | | | | | | | | | | | 0.56 | | | | | |
| Q33 | | | | | | | | | | | | | | | 0.57 | | | | | |
| Q34 | | | | | | | | | | | | | | | 0.70 | | | | | |
| Q35 | | | | | | | | | | | | | | | 0.61 | | | | | |
| Q36 | | | | | | | | | | | | | | | 0.66 | | | | | |
| Q41 | | | | | | | | | | | | | | | | 0.64 | | | | |
| Q42 | | | | | | | | | | | | | | | | 0.44 | | | | |
| Q43 | | | | | | | | | | | | | | | | 0.73 | | | | |
| Q44 | | | | | | | | | | | | | | | | 0.57 | | | | |
| Q45 | | | | | | | | | | | | | | | | 0.57 | | | | |
| Q46 | | | | | | | | | | | | | | | | 0.69 | | | | |

## Factor Intercorrelations

Although the factor pattern shows that fifth edition items tend to associate with their own scale and not with others, the primary factor scales do evince a predictable pattern of intercorrelations because the factors are oblique. Table 12 presents intercorrelations of the factor scales for the normative group.

## Global Factor Structure

Table 13 presents results of the factor analysis of the primary factor domain, as measured in the fifth edition. Five global (second-order) factors were identified. These five also have appeared with great consistency in factor analyses of previous forms of the 16PF (Cattell et al., 1970; Krug & Johns, 1986).

TABLE 12

PRIMARY AND GLOBAL SCALE INTERCORRELATIONS (STANDARDIZED STEN SCORES)
(BASED ON NORM SAMPLE, N=2500, 1245 MALES, 1255 FEMALES)

|  | A | B | C | E | F | G | H | I | L | M | N | O | Q1 | Q2 | Q3 | Q4 |
|---|---|---|---|---|---|---|---|---|---|---|---|---|---|---|---|---|
| A | 100 | | | | | | | | | | | | | | | |
| B | -02 | 100 | | | | | | | | | | | | | | |
| C | 19 | 12 | 100 | | | | | | | | | | | | | |
| E | 16 | -01 | 25 | 100 | | | | | | | | | | | | |
| F | 31 | -10 | 13 | 24 | 100 | | | | | | | | | | | |
| G | 05 | -01 | 21 | -06 | -24 | 100 | | | | | | | | | | |
| H | 38 | 00 | 38 | 40 | 38 | 02 | 100 | | | | | | | | | |
| I | 19 | 07 | -16 | -12 | -01 | -13 | -03 | 100 | | | | | | | | |
| L | -17 | -27 | -39 | 06 | 06 | -13 | -17 | -05 | 100 | | | | | | | |
| M | -08 | -04 | -38 | -02 | 12 | -41 | -10 | 20 | 31 | 100 | | | | | | |
| N | -40 | -09 | -12 | -12 | -24 | 00 | -36 | -11 | 26 | 03 | 100 | | | | | |
| O | -03 | 04 | -58 | -28 | -07 | -03 | -39 | 16 | 23 | 22 | 02 | 100 | | | | |
| Q1 | 17 | 20 | 09 | 26 | 16 | -25 | 22 | 23 | -08 | 31 | -16 | -08 | 100 | | | |
| Q2 | -43 | 03 | -30 | -14 | -43 | -09 | -35 | 08 | 23 | 21 | 34 | 14 | -05 | 100 | | |
| Q3 | -07 | -10 | 06 | 10 | -15 | 36 | 01 | -10 | 06 | -30 | 09 | 02 | -11 | 06 | 100 | |
| Q4 | -16 | 02 | -43 | 08 | -03 | -22 | -21 | 04 | 30 | 21 | 12 | 34 | -08 | 25 | 00 | 100 |

|  | EX | AX | TM | IN | SC |
|---|---|---|---|---|---|
| EX | 100 | | | | |
| AX | -30 | 100 | | | |
| TM | -27 | -08 | 100 | | |
| IN | 42 | -13 | -34 | 100 | |
| SC | -17 | -20 | 45 | -16 | 100 |

Note. From "Reliability and Equivalency: Comparison of the 16PF Fifth Edition and Fourth Edition (Form A)" by S. R. Conn, 1994. In S. R. Conn & M. L. Rieke (Eds.), *The 16PF Fifth Edition Technical Manual*. Champaign, IL: Institute for Personality and Ability Testing, Inc.

TABLE 13

GLOBAL FACTOR PATTERN AND EQUATIONS (N=3498, 1749 MALES, 1749 FEMALES)

| Factors | Extraversion | Anxiety | Self-Control | Independence | Tough-Mindedness | Factor B |
|---|---|---|---|---|---|---|
| A | 74 | 07 | 14 | -06 | -35 | -04 |
| B | 01 | 01 | -06 | -01 | 02 | 90 |
| C | 05 | -70 | 09 | 15 | 15 | 17 |
| E | 05 | 05 | 09 | 87 | 00 | 00 |
| F | 70 | 19 | -39 | 23 | 12 | -16 |
| G | 02 | -10 | 78 | -21 | 09 | 01 |
| H | 44 | -20 | 00 | 43 | -05 | -03 |
| I | 13 | 09 | 03 | -19 | -75 | -02 |
| L | -15 | 57 | -06 | 31 | 05 | -48 |
| M | -22 | 20 | -58 | 21 | -39 | -22 |
| N | -67 | -04 | -04 | 03 | 17 | -18 |
| O | 21 | 76 | 12 | -29 | -20 | 08 |
| Q1 | -18 | -24 | -26 | 49 | -68 | 17 |
| Q2 | -81 | 07 | 04 | 10 | -22 | 01 |
| Q3 | -11 | 17 | 82 | 23 | -07 | -12 |
| Q4 | 03 | 86 | -05 | 28 | 19 | 23 |

| | | | | | | |
|---|---|---|---|---|---|---|
| Extraversion | = | .3A | +.3F | +.2H | -.3N | -.3Q2 | +4.4 |
| Anxiety | = | -.4C | +.3L | +.4O | +.4Q4 | +1.65 |
| Self-Control | = | -.2F | +.4G | -.3M | +.4Q3 | +3.85 |
| Independence | = | .6E | +.3H | +.2L | +.3Q1 | -2.2 |
| Tough-Mindedness | = | -.2A | -.5I | -.3M | -.5Q1 | +13.75 |

Note. From [H.E.P. Cattell] "Development of the 16PF Fifth Edition" 1994. In S. R. Conn & M. L. Rieke (Eds.), *The 16PF Fifth Edition Technical Manual*. Champaign, IL: Institute for Personality and Ability Testing, Inc.

## Similarity of Structure Across Forms

Intercorrelations of fifth edition scales with 16PF Fourth Edition (Form A) scales are listed in Table 14. Varying degrees of intercorrelation exist between the scales for the two forms because of changes in scale properties for the fifth edition. However, a factor analysis (Conn, 1994) of the two forms together ($N = 462$) reveals support for the factor structure underlying each. Table 15 presents the results of this factor analysis. (Note: Factor loadings lower than .4 were omitted from Table 15.)

According to the data in Table 15, Factor 1 appears to be the Extraversion global factor. Moreover, as in previous factor analyses of the primary scales, Warmth (A+), Liveliness (F+), Social Boldness (H+) and Group-Orientation (Q2-) are major contributors to Extraversion. Unique to the fifth edition, however, is that Forthrightness (N-) loads on the Extraversion global factor.

Factor 2 appears to be the Anxiety global factor, which commonly emerges quite strongly in factor analyses of the 16PF scales. The primary factors from the fifth edition that contribute to Anxiety are the same as those from Form A: Reactivity (C-), Vigilance (L+), Apprehension (O+), and Tension (Q4+).

As the data in Table 15 indicate, similarities between the fifth edition and Form A also emerge on Factors 3 and 4. Dominance (E+), Social Boldness (H+), and Openness to Change (Q1+) load on Factor 3, the Independence global factor, in both test forms. The Independence global factor equation for the fifth edition also includes Vigilance (L+), which is not evident in Table 15 because loadings below .4 were omitted. Both Rule-Consciousness (G+) and Perfectionism (Q3+) load on Factor 4, the Self-Control global factor, in Form A and in the fifth edition. In the fifth edition, however, Abstractedness (M+) loads

**TABLE 14**

**CORRELATIONS BETWEEN 16PF FIFTH EDITION AND 16PF FORM A ($\underline{N}$=462, 209 MALES, 253 FEMALES)**

**Primary Factor Intercorrelations (Sten Scores)**

| | |
|---|---|
| A | .52 |
| B | .55 |
| C | .54 |
| E | .55 |
| F | .71 |
| G | .41 |
| H | .80 |
| I | .55 |
| L | .38 |
| M | .17 |
| N | .26 |
| O | .67 |
| Q1 | .31 |
| Q2 | .66 |
| Q3 | .42 |
| Q4 | .48 |

**Global Factor Intercorrelations (Sten Scores)**

| | |
|---|---|
| Extraversion | .81 |
| Anxiety | .79 |
| Tough-Mindedness | .38 |
| Independence | .70 |
| Self-Control | .65 |

Note. From "Reliability and Equivalency: Comparison of the 16PF Fifth Edition and Fourth Edition (Form A)" by S. R. Conn, 1994. In S. R. Conn & M. L. Rieke (Eds.), *The 16PF Fifth Edition Technical Manual*. Champaign, IL: Institute for Personality and Ability Testing, Inc.

negatively on the Self-Control global factor. This finding is unique to the 16PF Fifth Edition.

Factor 5 is the Tough-Mindedness global factor. Previous analyses have shown Reserve (A–), Utilitarianism (I–), Groundedness (M–), and Traditionalism (Q1–) to load on Tough-Mindedness, and Conn's factor analysis shows that these factors continue to contribute to Tough-Mindedness. In Table 15, Utilitarianism (I–) and Groundedness (M–) load from Form A, and Utilitarianism (I–) and Traditionalism (Q1–) load from the fifth edition. Factor A's loading does not exceed .4 in either form of the test in this study. (Note: The direction of the loadings for Factor 5 are in the *low* Tough-Mindedness, or Receptive, direction.)

Further support for the similarity of structure in both forms is provided by the equations for calculating global factor scores. These equations, in large part, include the same factors for both Form A and the fifth edition. In only two cases did fifth edition factors load onto a global factor in an unprecedented way: (1) Forthrightness (N–) now comes into the Extraversion global factor equation, and (2) Seriousness (F–) and Groundedness (M–) now contribute to the Self-Control global factor equation.

## Correlations with Other Tests

To demonstrate that the 16PF Fifth Edition actually assesses personality traits such as Warmth (A+), Dominance (E+), and Apprehension (O+), scores on the 16 primary factors can be correlated with similar personality constructs measured via other instruments. For example, support for the construct validity of Dominance (Factor E) is shown by its relationship to other measures of dominance (such as the Dominance and Aggression scales from the Personality Research Form [PRF]) and its lack of relationship to measures of different

TABLE 15

FACTOR ANALYSIS OF FIFTH EDITION AND FOURTH EDITION (FORM A)[1] (N=462, 209 MALES, 253 FEMALES)

| | Factor | | | | | |
|---|---|---|---|---|---|---|
| | I | II | III | IV | V | VI |
| **5th Edition Primary Factor** | | | | | | |
| Warmth (A) | 65 | · | · | · | · | · |
| Reasoning (B) | · | · | · | · | · | 64 |
| Emotional Stability (C) | · | –71 | · | · | · | · |
| Dominance (E) | · | · | 63 | · | · | · |
| Liveliness (F) | 65 | · | · | · | · | · |
| Rule-Consciousness (G) | · | · | · | 56 | · | · |
| Social Boldness (H) | 60 | · | 40 | · | · | · |
| Sensitivity (I) | · | · | · | · | 61 | · |
| Vigilance (L) | · | 46 | · | · | · | · |
| Abstractedness (M) | · | · | · | –44 | · | · |
| Privateness (N) | –47 | · | · | · | · | · |
| Apprehension (O) | · | 74 | · | · | · | · |
| Openness to Change (Q1) | · | · | 41 | · | 40 | · |
| Self-Reliance (Q2) | –70 | · | · | · | · | · |
| Perfectionism (Q3) | · | · | · | 68 | · | · |
| Tension (Q4) | · | 57 | · | · | · | · |
| **Form A Primary Factor** | | | | | | |
| Warmth (A) | 57 | · | · | · | · | · |
| Abstract Thinking (B) | · | · | · | · | · | 65 |
| Ego Strength (C) | · | –67 | · | · | · | · |
| Dominance (E) | · | · | 70 | · | · | · |
| Surgency (F) | 73 | · | · | · | · | · |
| Superego Strength (G) | · | · | · | 69 | · | · |
| Boldness (H) | 63 | · | 44 | · | · | · |
| Tender-Mindedness (I) | · | · | · | · | 69 | · |
| Suspiciousness (L) | · | 46 | · | · | · | · |
| Imagination (M) | · | · | · | · | 43 | · |
| Shrewdness (N) | · | · | · | · | · | · |
| Apprehension (O) | · | 77 | · | · | · | · |
| Radicalism (Q1) | · | · | 51 | · | · | · |
| Self-Sufficiency (Q2) | –71 | · | · | · | · | · |
| Control (Q3) | · | · | · | 55 | · | · |
| Tension (Q4) | · | 72 | · | · | · | · |

Note. Decimals omitted; factor loadings less than 0.40 (absolute value) not shown. From "Reliability and Equivalency: Comparison of the 16PF Fifth Edition and Fourth Edition (Form A)" by S. R. Conn, 1994. In S. R. Conn & M. L. Rieke (Eds.), *The 16PF Fifth Edition Technical Manual.* Champaign, IL: Institute for Personality and Ability Testing, Inc.

[1]Rotated (Varimax) Factor loadings from combined analysis of Fifth Edition and Form A Primary Factors

TABLE 16

CORRELATIONS WITH PERSONALITY RESEARCH FORM (PRF) (N=225, 46 MALES, 179 FEMALES)

| PRF Scale | A | B | C | E | F | G | H | I | L | M | N | O | Q1 | Q2 | Q3 | Q4 |
|---|---|---|---|---|---|---|---|---|---|---|---|---|---|---|---|---|
| | | | | | | | *16PF Primary Factor Scale* | | | | | | | | | |
| Abasement | 09 | 06 | -01 | -33* | -01 | 11 | -10 | 07 | -10 | 00 | -02 | 10 | 01 | -08 | -07 | -31* |
| Achievement | -11 | 00 | 16 | 14 | -08 | 30* | -01 | -07 | 01 | -03 | -03 | 01 | 08 | 01 | 35* | -09 |
| Affiliation | 35* | 01 | 27* | 07 | 50* | -07 | 39* | -03 | -18* | -13 | -34* | 02 | -01 | -45* | -11 | -10 |
| Aggression | -04 | -02 | -18* | 34* | 06 | -18* | 08 | -11 | 31* | 06 | 00 | 12 | -11 | 11 | 11 | 46* |
| Autonomy | -26* | 10 | -05 | 04 | -09 | -37* | 11 | -04 | 19* | 25* | 21* | -18* | 20* | 33* | -24* | 01 |
| Change | 05 | -02 | -02 | 11 | 17 | -29* | 23* | 11 | 00 | 26* | -10 | -10 | 42* | -12 | -21* | -10 |
| Cognitive Structure | -10 | -09 | -09 | 09 | -16 | 37* | -21* | -12 | 17 | -28* | 12 | 21* | -25* | 14 | 56* | 16 |
| Defendence | 01 | -05 | -27* | 29* | -04 | 03 | -03 | 01 | 30* | -03 | 15 | 20* | -12 | 18* | 13 | 46 |
| Dominance | 07 | -10 | 26* | 48* | 17 | -03 | 46* | -15 | 09 | 04 | -10 | -28* | 09 | -02 | 15 | 01 |
| Endurance | -09 | -01 | 19* | 17 | -05 | 30* | 08 | -21* | -04 | -10 | -05 | -02 | 02 | -02 | 34* | -14 |
| Exhibition | 30* | -14 | 26* | 31* | 49* | -16 | 71* | -01 | -09 | 11 | -32* | -26* | 11 | -26* | -10 | -01 |
| Harm Avoidance | 18* | 00 | -15 | -13 | -17 | 26* | -25* | 20* | 02 | -26* | 04 | 23* | -17 | -05 | 20* | 08 |
| Impulsivity | 03 | 11 | -03 | 07 | 37* | -47* | 27* | 02 | 00 | 37* | -16 | -05 | 16 | -11 | -45* | 06 |
| Nurturance | 39* | -02 | 09 | -09 | 28* | 13 | 14 | 14 | -16 | -02 | -19* | 23* | 17 | -38* | 08 | -24 |
| Order | -04 | -26* | -01 | 08 | -06 | 33* | -06 | -14 | 06 | -26* | 07 | 10 | -22* | 10 | 66* | 08 |
| Play | 19* | -04 | 13 | 16 | 52* | -30* | 36* | -08 | -08 | 09 | -10 | -12 | 01 | -29* | -29* | -06 |
| Sentience | 04 | 05 | -02 | -01 | 14 | -08 | 15 | 13 | -03 | 21* | -04 | 14 | 30* | -03 | 01 | -16 |
| Social Recognition | 09 | -01 | -11 | -02 | 25* | -01 | -03 | 05 | 01 | -07 | -11 | 26* | -17 | -14 | 03 | 18 |
| Succorance | 27* | -02 | 06 | 03 | 22* | 16 | 06 | 09 | -13 | -11 | -41* | 17 | -10 | -33* | 07 | 04 |
| Understanding | -01 | 09 | 12 | 01 | -10 | 00 | -01 | 25* | -08 | 18* | -09 | -10 | 30* | -06 | -06 | -17 |

Note. Decimals omitted. From "Construct Validation of the 16PF Fifth Edition" by S. R. Conn & M. L. Rieke, 1994b In S. R. Conn & M. L. Rieke (Eds.), *The 16PF Fifth Edition Technical Manual*. Champaign, IL: Institute for Personality and Ability Testing, Inc.

*$p < .01$

concepts (such as the PRF Social Recognition and Understanding scales).

To provide evidence of convergent and discriminant validity, the 16PF Fifth Edition was compared to several tests of normal personality: the Personality Research Form (PRF; Jackson), the California Psychological Inventory (CPI; Gough), the NEO PI-R (Costa & McCrae), and the Myers-Briggs Type Indicator (MBTI; Briggs & Myers). Brief summaries of findings concentrated at the 16PF global factor level and at the highest correlations are provided in the sections that follow and are accompanied by correlation tables. Further information regarding these validity analyses is given in *The 16PF Fifth Edition Technical Manual* (see Conn & Rieke, 1994b).

### Personality Research Form (PRF)

The PRF is a 352-item true-false questionnaire that, like the 16PF, assesses normal personality traits. It contains 20 bipolar scales based on the Murray Need Scales

TABLE 16, CONTINUED

CORRELATIONS BETWEEN 16PF FIFTH EDITION AND PERSONALITY RESEARCH FORM (PRF)
(N=225, 46 MALES, 179 FEMALES).

| PRF Scale | Extraversion | Anxiety | 16PF Global Factor Tough-Mindedness | Independence | Self-Control |
|---|---|---|---|---|---|
| Abasement | 03 | −09 | −04 | −28* | 02 |
| Achievement | −05 | −08 | 03 | 12 | 31* |
| Affiliation | 56* | −18* | −03 | 14 | −13 |
| Aggression | −02 | 36* | 10 | 29* | −06 |
| Autonomy | −25* | 01 | −07 | 17 | −34* |
| Change | 18* | −06 | −34* | 29* | −34* |
| Cognitive Structure | −20* | 21* | 27* | −06 | 54* |
| Defendance | −11 | 42* | 05 | 21* | 09 |
| Dominance | 20* | −17 | 01 | 54* | 01 |
| Endurance | −01 | −14 | 16 | 14 | 33* |
| Exhibition | 54* | −22* | −15 | 47* | −25* |
| Harm Avoidance | −03 | 17 | 00 | −23* | 32* |
| Impulsivity | 23* | 02 | −19* | 19* | −60* |
| Nurturance | 40* | −08 | −23* | 01 | 05 |
| Order | −09 | 08 | 26* | −03 | 54* |
| Play | 38* | −14 | −03 | 22* | −39* |
| Sentience | 10 | 00 | −26* | 14 | −12 |
| Social Recognition | 16 | 20* | 05 | −08 | −01 |
| Succorance | 39* | 01 | −04 | −02 | 11 |
| Understanding | 02 | −16 | −32* | 09 | −07 |

(Murray, 1938) and two validity scales (Desirability and Infrequency).

Both the 16PF Fifth Edition and the PRF-Form E were administered to a sample of 225 university undergraduates (46 males, 179 females; mean age 18.9 years; mean education level 12.6 years). Correlations between the 20 PRF scales and the 16PF primary and global factors are given in Table 16. In the text that follows, all correlations discussed are significant at the $p < .01$ level.

As the data in Table 16 indicate, the Extraversion global factor correlates very highly with PRF scales that suggest the enjoyment of or need for warm interactions with others: Affiliation ($r = .56$), Exhibition ($r = .54$), Nurturance ($r = .40$), Play ($r = .38$), and Succorance ($r = .39$). As can be seen in Table 16, these scales generally correlate with the primary factors that comprise Extraversion. Thus, the highest correlation with 16PF Warmth (Factor A) was Nurturance ($r = .39$), with Liveliness (Factor F) was Play ($r = .52$), with Social Boldness (Factor H) was Exhibition ($r = .71$), with Privateness (Factor N) was Succorance ($r = -.41$), and with Self-Reliance (Factor Q2) was Affiliation ($r = -.45$).

The Anxiety global factor correlates highly with Defendance ($r = .42$) and Aggression ($r = .36$), suggesting emotional hostility. At the primary level, both of the aforementioned PRF scales correlate most strongly with Tension (Factor Q4), an important component of the Anxiety global factor.

The Tough-Mindedness global factor is negatively correlated with Change ($r = -.34$) and Understanding ($r = -.32$). Thus Tough-Mindedness implies a preference for stability as well as a disinterest in intellectualism. At the primary level, Openness to Change (Factor Q1) shows the highest correlations with PRF-Change ($r = .42$) and Understanding ($r = .30$).

The Independence global factor shares its highest correlations with Dominance ($r = .54$) and Exhibition ($r = .47$), scales that concern the desire to influence and control other people and to be the center of attention, respectively. At the primary level, Dominance (Factor E) and Social Boldness (Factor H), which are components of the Independence global factor, correlate with PRF Dominance ($r = .48$ and $r = .46$, respectively). Social Boldness also correlates with PRF Exhibition ($r = .71$). Independence also is related to Aggression ($r = .29$) and Change ($r = .29$), suggesting that Independence contains elements of confrontation and adventuresomeness. Openness to Change (Factor Q1), another component of Independence, shows a strong relationship to PRF Change ($r = .42$).

The Self-Control global factor correlates with Cognitive Structure ($r = .54$), Order ($r = .54$), Endurance ($r = .33$), Harm Avoidance ($r = .32$), and Achievement ($r = .31$)—scales that suggest qualities of self-imposed high standards, the need for order and structure, and the avoidance of uncertainty. In addition, Self-Control correlates negatively with Impulsivity ($r = -.60$), Play ($r = -.39$), Autonomy ($r = -.34$), and Change ($r = -.34$), all scales that suggest aspects of self-restraint, rigidity, and seriousness. At the primary level, most of the aforementioned PRF scales share their highest correlations with Perfectionism (Factor Q3).

## California Psychological Inventory (CPI)

The CPI assesses psychological traits that people refer to when describing or understanding common behaviors. Because of the CPI's use of the "psychological vernacular," its scales are called "folk" scales (Gough, 1987). The test consists of 462 true-false items that result in 20 trait scores. Additionally, there are three structural scales, or vectors, for each of three larger themes underlying the 20 scales: v.1 (Internality), v.2 (Norm-Favoring), and v.3 (Self-realization).

The 16PF Fifth Edition and the CPI were administered to 212 university undergraduates (81 males, 131 females) with a mean age of 20.5 years and a mean education level of 13.7 years. Table 17 contains the correlations between the 16PF factors and the CPI's 20 folk scales and 3 structural scales.

The CPI has been factor analyzed (Gough, 1987), resulting in four factors: "Extraversion," "Control," "Flexibility," and "Consensuality." To simplify the comparison between the 16PF and CPI scales, the CPI scales are described in terms of these broad factors whenever possible. All correlations discussed are significant at $p < .01$.

The 16PF Extraversion global factor correlates (all $r > = .25$) with seven CPI scales that assess interpersonal and extraverted traits: Dominance, Capacity for Status, Sociability, Social Presence, Self-acceptance, Independence, and Empathy. These CPI scales comprise the Extraversion factor of the CPI. In particular, Social Boldness (H+) is highly related to the CPI Extraversion scales, with correlations ranging from .43 to .63. The 16PF primary components of the global factor Extraversion (Warmth [A+], Liveliness [F+], Social Boldness [H+], Forthrightness [N−], and Group-Orientation [Q2−]) correlate with low scores on CPI v.1 (Internality vector). Low v.1 scores imply an outgoing, warm attitude.

TABLE 17

CORRELATIONS WITH CALIFORNIA PSYCHOLOGICAL INVENTORY (CPI) FOLK SCALES
(N=212, 81 MALES, 131 FEMALES)

| CPI Scale | 16PF Primary Factor Scale | | | | | | | | | | | | | | | |
|---|---|---|---|---|---|---|---|---|---|---|---|---|---|---|---|---|
| | A | B | C | E | F | G | H | I | L | M | N | O | Q1 | Q2 | Q3 | Q4 |
| Dominance | 18* | 09 | 36* | 50* | 23* | -04 | 48* | 04 | -18* | -07 | -16 | -32* | 22* | -17 | 05 | -07 |
| Capacity for Status | 24* | 15 | 42* | 22* | 27* | -01 | 50* | 17 | -37* | -01 | -28* | -27* | 28* | -27* | 02 | -33* |
| Sociability | 37* | 08 | 39* | 35* | 50* | -06 | 63* | 07 | -34* | -07 | -30* | -21* | 21* | -45* | -02 | -21* |
| Social Presence | 32* | 01 | 47* | 33* | 51* | -19* | 54* | 11 | -26* | -04 | -30* | -33* | 18* | -39* | -18* | -20* |
| Self-acceptance | 32* | 12 | 34* | 45* | 43* | -08 | 60* | 14 | -21* | 05 | -27* | -25* | 22* | -26* | -06 | -10 |
| Independence | 12 | 11 | 51* | 45* | 15 | -11 | 51* | 16 | -22* | -04 | -15 | -50* | 25* | -11 | 00 | -24* |
| Empathy | 42* | 04 | 40* | 08 | 36* | -03 | 43* | 14 | -40* | -06 | -24* | -20* | 25* | -34* | -13 | -35* |
| Responsibility | 08 | 13 | 20* | -04 | -12 | 36* | 05 | 01 | -34* | -21* | -08 | 04 | 15 | -12 | 17 | -21* |
| Socialization | 06 | 03 | 35* | 06 | -07 | 31* | 00 | -03 | -24* | -44* | -06 | -01 | -10 | -13 | 18* | -01 |
| Self-control | -06 | 03 | 25* | -17 | -38* | 39* | -08 | -04 | -33* | -46* | -01 | 00 | -04 | 05 | 29* | -25* |
| Good Impression | 09 | 00 | 39* | -06 | -16 | 37* | 13 | -04 | -41* | -38* | -08 | -13 | 03 | -13 | 27* | -41* |
| Communality | 14 | 16 | 19* | 10 | 12 | 08 | 00 | -05 | -12 | -18* | -05 | 06 | 08 | -19* | 00 | 04 |
| Well-being | 15 | 08 | 52* | 11 | 00 | 08 | 17 | -01 | -42* | -39* | -11 | -25* | 13 | -25* | 04 | -20* |
| Tolerance | 19* | 10 | 33* | -08 | -03 | 14 | 12 | 13 | -47* | -19* | -19* | -04 | 22* | -19* | -08 | -26* |
| Achievement via Conformance | 10 | 09 | 42* | 22* | -13 | 34* | 15 | 03 | -36* | -41* | -13 | -14 | 02 | -14 | 26* | -13 |
| Achievement via Independence | 14 | 19* | 40* | 11 | -03 | 01 | 11 | 13 | -41* | -13 | -03 | -20* | 32* | -14 | -08 | -26* |
| Intellectual Efficiency | 06 | 22* | 42* | 20* | -01 | 04 | 21* | 04 | -38* | -16 | -12 | -27* | 27* | -12 | -01 | -20* |
| Psychological-mindedness | 03 | 09 | 47* | 26* | -09 | 06 | 19* | 08 | -35* | -17 | -04 | -31* | 35* | -04 | -04 | -27* |
| Flexibility | 20* | 06 | 08 | -12 | 22* | -32* | 11 | 16 | -25* | 29* | -09 | -12 | 26* | -16 | -57* | -19* |
| Femininity/Masculinity | 14 | -11 | -23* | -26* | -09 | 18* | -17 | 19* | -04 | -07 | -07 | 45* | -09 | 00 | 06 | 10 |
| v.1 Externality | -26* | 01 | -22* | -50* | -44* | 14 | -57* | -06 | 09 | -09 | 23* | 32* | -18* | 22* | 00 | 08 |
| v.2 Norm-favoring | 08 | -03 | 19* | 14 | -06 | 34* | 04 | -09 | -01 | -29* | -03 | 09 | -16 | 01 | 26* | 02 |
| v.3 Self-realization | 20* | 15 | 42* | 02 | 01 | 13 | 21* | 12 | -51* | -20* | -21* | -19* | 24* | -23* | -01 | -36* |

Note. Decimals omitted. From "Construct Validation of the 16PF Fifth Edition" by S. R. Conn & M. L. Rieke, 1994b. In S. R. Conn & M. L. Rieke (Eds.), *The 16PF Fifth Edition Technical Manual*. Champaign, IL: Institute for Personality and Ability Testing, Inc.

*$p < .01$

**CORRELATIONS BETWEEN CPI FOLK SCALES AND 16PF FACTOR SCALES**
(N=212, 81 MALES, 131 FEMALES)

| CPI Scale | 16PF Global Factor | | | | |
|---|---|---|---|---|---|
| | Extraversion | Anxiety | Tough-Mindedness | Independence | Self-Control |
| Dominance | 31* | –34* | –14 | 53* | –01 |
| Capacity for Status | 40* | –50* | –27* | 33* | –05 |
| Sociability | 59* | –41* | –18* | 45* | –11 |
| Social Presence | 54* | –46* | –19* | 40* | –25* |
| Self-acceptance | 49* | –33* | –26* | 53* | –17 |
| Independence | 25* | –54* | –21* | 51* | –07 |
| Empathy | 48* | –48* | –26* | 19* | –13 |
| Responsibility | 07 | –24* | –04 | –03 | 32* |
| Socialization | 06 | –22* | 17 | –04 | 40* |
| Self-control | –14 | –28* | 18* | –22* | 54* |
| Good Impression | 08 | –47* | 09 | –07 | 46* |
| Communality | 15 | –07 | 01 | 07 | 08 |
| Well-being | 19* | –49* | 03 | 09 | 20* |
| Tolerance | 18* | –38* | –16 | –04 | 10 |
| Achievement via Conformance | 11 | –37* | 07 | 14 | 44* |
| Achievement via Independence | 11 | –45* | –21* | 13 | 02 |
| Intellectual Efficiency | 13 | –45* | –12 | 22* | 07 |
| Psychological-mindedness | 04 | –50* | –16 | 29* | 10 |
| Flexibility | 21* | –22* | –32* | –02 | –54* |
| Femininity/Masculinity | 01 | 30* | –06 | –27* | 15 |

The Anxiety global factor correlates negatively with all CPI scales except for Femininity/Masculinity, for which the correlation is positive ($r = .30$), and Communality, for which no significant correlation exists. This pattern of correlations probably reflects the social desirability inherent in the CPI scales, which are scored in the "culturally favored expression of the variable" (Gough, 1987, p. 13), whereas admitting to anxiety is socially undesirable. In particular, Anxiety shows strong negative correlations with Intellectual Efficiency (–.45), Tolerance (–.38), and Well-being (–.49), three CPI scales that, when elevated, lend an aspect

of social desirability to a CPI profile (Gough, 1987, p. 13). Two primary components of Anxiety, Emotional Stability (C) and Vigilance (L), also correlate with the majority of CPI scales: Emotional Stability in the positive direction and Vigilance in the negative direction. The primary components of Anxiety also correlate with v.3, the Self-realization vector, such that low anxiety is related to self-realization (or a sense of personal fulfillment). As can be seen in Table 17, high scores on Self-realization relate to high scores on Emotional Stability (C) and low scores on Vigilance (L), Apprehension (O), and Tension (Q4).

The Tough-Mindedness global factor correlates negatively with Flexibility ($r = -.32$), and to some extent with most of the CPI extraversion scales: Capacity for Status ($r = -.27$), Sociability ($r = -.18$), Social Presence ($r = -.19$), Self–acceptance ($r = -.26$), Independence ($r = -.21$), and Empathy ($r = -.26$), alluding to the twofold nature of the Tough-Mindedness factor. That is, the negative correlation with Flexibility suggests resoluteness and the tendency to adhere to the familiar, and the negative correlations with the extraversion scales suggest interpersonal reserve and detachment. This pattern is also reflected in the correlations with the primary components of Tough-Mindedness. Warmth (A) and Openness to Change (Q1), which contribute to the low end of Tough-Mindedness (i.e., Receptivity), correlate positively with the CPI extraversion scales. Openness to Change (Q1 +) and Abstractedness (M), which also contributes to low Tough-Mindedness, correlate with CPI Flexibility ($r = .26$ and $r = .29$, respectively).

The Independence global factor correlates highly with the CPI Extraversion folk scales, suggesting the importance of social interaction. Independence also relates to CPI scales other than those measuring sociability. The correlation between 16PF Independence and the CPI Independence folk scale is higher ($r = .51$) than that between 16PF Extraversion and CPI Independence ($r = .25$). On the other hand, the correlation between 16PF Independence and CPI Empathy is lower ($r = .19$) than that between 16PF Extraversion and CPI Empathy ($r = .48$). The Independence global factor also correlates with Psychological-mindedness ($r = .29$), Intellectual Efficiency ($r = .22$), and Femininity/Masculinity ($r = -.27$), whereas the Extraversion global factor correlates with none of the preceding. This suggests that 16PF Independence (but not 16PF Extraversion) contains aspects of mental toughness and curiosity.

The Self-Control global factor correlates positively with Responsibility, Socialization, Self-control, Good Impression, and Achievement via Conformance (all $r$'s > .30), scales comprising the CPI "Control" factor. This pattern of correlations suggests that 16PF Self-Control measures restraint, conscientiousness, and rule-bound values. Self-Control also correlates negatively with Flexibility ($r = -.54$). This relationship is reflected in the strong negative correlation ($r = -.57$) between Perfectionism (Q3), a component of Self-Control, and CPI Flexibility.

### NEO Personality Inventory, Revised (NEO PI-R)

The NEO PI-R is a 240-item test designed to measure five major dimensions of normal personality: Neuroticism, Extraversion, Openness, Conscientiousness, and Agreeableness. Each of these dimensions is composed of six "facet" scales that tap more specific personality attributes. In fact, the structures of the NEO and 16PF are quite similar, with the 16PF containing 16 primary factors that cluster into five global factors and the NEO containing five global domains that can be divided into 30 facets.

The 16PF Fifth Edition and the NEO PI-R were administered to 257 university undergraduates (69 males, 188 females; mean age 18.9 years; mean education level 12.6 years). Table 18 contains the correlations between the 16PF primary factors and the NEO PI-R facet scales.

Predictably, the 16PF Extraversion global factor and its primary components (Warmth [A], Liveliness [F], Social Boldness [H], Privateness [N], and Self-Reliance [Q2]) correlate most strongly with the NEO Extraversion facets (Warmth [E1], Gregariousness [E2], Assertiveness [E3], Activities [E4], Excitement Seeking [E5], and Positive Emotions [E6]). All primaries comprising 16PF Extraversion correlate

TABLE 18

CORRELATIONS WITH NEO PI, REVISED (NEO PI-R) (N=257, 69 MALES, 188 FEMALES)

| NEO PI-R Facet | 16PF Primary Factor Scale | | | | | | | | | | | | | | | |
|---|---|---|---|---|---|---|---|---|---|---|---|---|---|---|---|---|
| | A | B | C | E | F | G | H | I | L | M | N | O | Q1 | Q2 | Q3 | Q4 |
| Anxiety (N1) | -04 | 02 | -57* | -21* | -11 | 10 | -33* | 15 | 31* | 10 | 20* | 61* | -13 | 11 | 18* | 28* |
| Angry Hostility (N2) | -05 | -05 | -49* | 15 | -07 | -01 | -09 | -01 | 35* | 12 | 11 | 33* | -10 | 24* | 11 | 54* |
| Depression (N3) | -07 | 07 | -69* | -24* | -21* | -01 | -33* | 17 | 39* | 20* | 25* | 54* | -07 | 18* | 06 | 25* |
| Self-Consciousness (N4) | -09 | 11 | -53* | -39* | -20* | 09 | -49* | 18* | 22* | 03 | 21* | 56* | -20* | 20* | 06 | 22* |
| Impulsiveness (N5) | 04 | 12 | -28* | 07 | 14 | -20* | -04 | 08 | 13 | 24* | 02 | 18* | 03 | 04 | -27* | 26* |
| Vulnerability (N6) | -10 | 06 | -59* | -26* | -16 | 00 | -32* | 14 | 18* | 17 | 16 | 41* | -11 | 11 | -04 | 24* |
| Warmth (E1) | 44* | -01 | 27* | 12 | 45* | 04 | 43* | 08 | -25* | -04 | -37* | 02 | 09 | -48* | -14 | -23* |
| Gregariousness (E2) | 46* | -07 | 29* | 23* | 55* | -08 | 51* | 04 | -18* | -03 | -36* | -11 | 09 | -62* | -23* | -10 |
| Assertiveness (E3) | 20* | -06 | 34* | 55* | 35* | 02 | 62* | -19* | -08 | -10 | -29* | -28* | 11 | -26* | 04 | -02 |
| Activity (E4) | 04 | 03 | 26* | 38* | 30* | 13 | 31* | -24* | 00 | -01 | -08 | -09 | 12 | -14 | 10 | 11 |
| Excitement Seeking (E5) | 16 | -02 | 14 | 21* | 57* | -19* | 34* | -12 | -01 | 02 | -14 | -02 | -01 | -28* | -12 | 06 |
| Positive Emotion (E6) | 31* | -01 | 33* | 18* | 41* | -04 | 33* | -01 | -26* | 07 | -29* | -11 | 14 | -36* | -21* | -18* |
| Fantasy (O1) | 16 | -01 | -04 | 04 | 24* | -13 | 14 | 27* | -03 | 44* | -19* | 12 | 27* | -19* | -20* | -09 |
| Aesthetics (O2) | 21* | 00 | -05 | -03 | 16 | -01 | 14 | 43* | -02 | 26* | -12 | 16 | 40* | -21* | -03 | -25* |
| Feelings (O3) | 29* | 05 | -06 | 10 | 16 | -02 | 03 | 26* | 00 | 26* | -18* | 19* | 22* | -12 | -06 | 01 |
| Actions (O4) | -03 | -06 | 09 | 05 | 14 | -21* | 27* | 10 | -08 | 26* | -09 | -19* | 43* | -17 | -24* | -27* |
| Ideas (O5) | -07 | 12 | 11 | 14 | -01 | 09 | 04 | 01 | -03 | 16 | -07 | -07 | 30* | -14 | 08 | -15 |
| Values (O6) | 19* | 09 | 06 | -13 | 11 | -23* | 00 | 24* | -14 | 09 | -02 | 03 | 28* | -16 | -17 | -10 |
| Trust (A1) | 21* | 03 | 40* | -02 | 17 | 05 | 13 | 06 | -62* | -11 | -41* | -11 | 19* | -36* | -09 | -28* |
| Straightforwardness (A2) | 10 | 12 | 11 | -31* | -09 | 23* | -20* | 11 | -33* | -22* | -05 | 03 | 10 | -17 | 01 | -22* |
| Altruism (A3) | 33* | 03 | 11 | -08 | 24* | 13 | 04 | 14 | -14 | -01 | -16 | 14 | 14 | -30* | -07 | -21* |
| Compliance (A4) | 04 | 03 | 10 | -48* | -12 | 07 | -19* | 20* | -20* | -04 | 05 | 00 | -02 | -09 | -09 | -41* |
| Modesty (A5) | 07 | 11 | -13 | -40* | -08 | 06 | -26* | 14 | 00 | 05 | 26* | 23* | 05 | -06 | -04 | -13 |
| Tender-Mindedness (A6) | 27* | 07 | 08 | -10 | 16 | 08 | -02 | 22* | -12 | 03 | -13 | 13 | 17 | -26* | -13 | -17 |
| Competence (C1) | 06 | 00 | 26* | 31* | 04 | 26* | 06 | -13 | -04 | -32* | 03 | -09 | -01 | -08 | 38* | 12 |
| Order (C2) | -07 | -16 | -01 | 08 | -12 | 28* | -06 | -14 | 11 | -33* | 14 | 11 | -23* | 13 | 68* | 14 |
| Dutifulnesss (C3) | 09 | 01 | 14 | 04 | -08 | 36* | -14 | -08 | -03 | -25* | 13 | 01 | -07 | -01 | 35* | -05 |
| Achievement Striving (C4) | -04 | 00 | 18* | 20* | -08 | 32* | -03 | -18* | 03 | -24* | 09 | 02 | -14 | 07 | 44* | 08 |
| Self-Disclosure (C5) | -02 | -04 | 29* | 16 | -02 | 29* | 03 | -17 | -13 | -35* | 06 | -10 | -04 | -04 | 40* | -04 |
| Deliberation (C6) | -05 | -07 | 03 | -05 | -28* | 39* | -25* | -11 | -01 | -33* | 13 | 14 | -17 | 14 | 49* | -03 |

Note. Decimals omitted. From "Construct Validation of the 16PF Fifth Edition" by S. R. Conn & M. L. Rieke, in 1994b. In S. R. Conn & M. L. Rieke (Eds.), *The 16PF Fifth Edition Technical Manual*. Champaign, IL: Institute for Personality and Ability Testing, Inc.

*p < .01

84

Table 18, continued

Correlations with NEO PI, Revised (NEO PI-R) (N = 257, 69 males, 188 females)

| NEO PI-R Scale | Extraversion | Anxiety | 16PF Global Factor Tough-Mindedness | Independence | Self-Control |
|---|---|---|---|---|---|
| Anxiety (N1) | –21* | 63* | –04 | –23* | 11 |
| Angry Hostility (N2) | –16 | 59* | 02 | 12 | 02 |
| Depression (N3) | –28* | 66* | –10 | –22* | –01 |
| Self-Consciousness (N4) | –31* | 55* | 00 | –44* | 09 |
| Impulsiveness (N5) | 02 | 30* | –13 | 07 | –32* |
| Vulnerability (N6) | –22* | 51* | –05 | –28* | –04 |
| Warmth (E1) | 61* | –24* | –17 | 20* | –12 |
| Gregariousness (E2) | 70* | –23* | –15 | 32* | –23* |
| Assertiveness (E3) | 45* | –26* | 03 | 60* | 00 |
| Activity (E4) | 21* | –10 | 06 | 40* | 05 |
| Excitement Seeking (E5) | 39* | –05 | 03 | 25* | –25* |
| Positive Emotion (E6) | 47* | –29* | –14 | 22* | –22* |
| Fantasy (O1) | 26* | 02 | –41* | 15 | –35* |
| Aesthetics (O2) | 24* | –01 | –53* | 15 | –14 |
| Feelings (O3) | 24* | 10 | –37* | 15 | –16 |
| Actions (O4) | 16 | –21* | –31* | 24* | –32* |
| Ideas (O5) | 04 | –12 | –17 | 20* | 02 |
| Values (O6) | 15 | –08 | –33* | –02 | –24* |
| Trust (A1) | 38* | –47* | –14 | –04 | –01 |
| Straightforwardness (A2) | 04 | –19* | –08 | –31* | 20* |
| Altruism (A3) | 32* | –11 | –22* | –02 | –02 |
| Compliance (A4) | –04 | –23* | –10 | –44* | 02 |
| Modesty (A5) | –12 | 09 | –13 | –34* | 01 |
| Tender-Mindedness (A6) | 24* | –07 | –26* | –04 | –06 |
| Competence (C1) | 06 | –11 | 13 | 22* | 39* |
| Order (C2) | –15 | 12 | 28* | –02 | 57* |
| Dutifulness (C3) | –06 | –08 | 12 | –05 | 42* |
| Achievement Striving (C4) | –09 | –03 | 23* | 09 | 44* |
| Self-Discipline (C5) | –01 | –19* | 21* | 08 | 44* |
| Deliberation (C6) | –22* | 03 | 23* | –17 | 57* |

highly with NEO Warmth (E1) (average absolute value |r| = .43) and Gregariousness (E2) (average absolute value |r| = .50). In particular, Liveliness (F+) correlates with Excitement Seeking (r = .57), Social Boldness (H+) correlates with Assertiveness (r = .62), and Self-Reliance (Q2) correlates negatively with Gregariousness (r = –.62).

The Anxiety global factor correlates with the facets of the Neuroticism domain. In particular, the highest correlations with the NEO facet specifically measuring "Anxiety" (Facet N1) are Emotional Stability (Factor C; r = –.57) and Apprehension (Factor O; r = .61). The 16PF primary Tension (Q4) shows a strong relationship to the NEO facet Angry

Hostility (N2; $r = .54$). The Anxiety global factor also correlates negatively with the NEO facet Trust (A1), suggesting that high Anxiety is associated with skepticism and distrust. Vigilance (Factor L), a component of Anxiety, influences this relationship with Facet A1 in particular; the correlation between Vigilance and Trust is $-.62$.

The Tough-Mindedness global factor correlates negatively with the Openness facets (Fantasy, Aesthetics, Feelings, Actions, and Values), except for Ideas (Facet O5), for which the negative correlation is not significant. This pattern of correlations suggests that high scores on Tough-Mindedness entail characteristics of conventionality, conservativeness, and being somewhat closed to new experiences. Each of the NEO Openness facets shares its highest correlation with a different 16PF primary factor, all of which contribute to the low end of Tough-Mindedness (i.e., Receptivity). Fantasy (Facet O1) is highly correlated with Abstractedness (Factor M; $r = .44$); Aesthetics (Facet O2) correlates with Sensitivity (Factor I; $r = .43$); Feelings (Facet O3) correlates with Warmth (Factor A; $r = .29$); Actions (Facet O4) correlates with Openness to Change (Factor Q1; $r = .43$), and Values (Facet O6) correlates with Openness to Change ($r = .28$).

The Independence global factor correlates with the NEO Extraversion facets, especially Assertiveness (Facet E3; $r = .60$). Independence also correlates with Self-consciousness (Facet N4; $r = -.44$), suggesting the lack of feelings of shame or embarrassment. Unlike the Extraversion global factor, Independence correlates negatively with the NEO Agreeableness facets Compliance (A4; $r = -.44$) and Modesty (A5; $r = -.34$), suggesting intractibility and self-assertion.

The Self-Control global factor correlates highest with the NEO Conscientiousness facets, as do three primary factors comprising Self-Control: Rule-Consciousness (G), Abstractedness (M), and Perfectionism (Q3). A strong correlation exists between Perfectionism (Q3+), an important component of Self-Control, and Order (Facet C2; $r = .68$). Self-Control correlates negatively with some Openness facets, in particular Fantasy (O1; $r = -.35$) and Actions (O4; $r = -.32$), which suggests aspects of conventionality and fastidiousness. At the primary level, Abstractedness (Factor M), which contributes to the low end of Self-Control, correlates highly with the Fantasy and Actions facets, whereas Perfectionism (Q3), which contributes to the high end of Self-Control, correlates negatively with both facets.

### Myers-Briggs Type Indicator (MBTI)

The MBTI, Form G, is a 126-item questionnaire based on Carl Jung's theory of Psychological Types (Jung, 1971). This theory posits that individual differences result from the degree to which persons prefer particular styles of perception and judgment. The MBTI identifies four bipolar psychological indices: Extraversion-Introversion, Sensing-Intuitive, Thinking-Feeling, and Judging-Perceptive. Combinations of the four preferences form 16 personality "types."

The 16PF Fifth Edition and the MBTI were administered to a sample of 119 university students (42 males, 77 females; mean age 25.3 years; mean education level 14.4 years). Table 19 contains correlations between the 16PF factors and the MBTI types.

As expected, the 16PF Extraversion global factor correlates positively with the MBTI Extraversion type ($r = .68$), and negatively with the Introversion type ($r = -.61$). All primary factor scales comprising 16PF Extraversion reflect this pattern. To a lesser extent, the Extraversion global factor correlates positively with Feeling, in which judgments tend to be subjective

TABLE 19

CORRELATIONS WITH MYERS–BRIGGS TYPE INDICATOR (MBTI) TYPES
(N=119, 42 MALES, 77 FEMALES)

| MBTI Type | 16PF Primary Factor Scale | | | | | | | | | | | | | | | |
|---|---|---|---|---|---|---|---|---|---|---|---|---|---|---|---|---|
| | A | B | C | E | F | G | H | I | L | M | N | O | Q1 | Q2 | Q3 | Q4 |
| Extraversion | 41* | -09 | 36* | 31* | 48* | -17 | 65* | -10 | -22 | -15 | -40* | -32* | 06 | -49* | -01 | -12 |
| Introversion | -36* | 08 | -23* | -23* | -51* | 17 | -52* | 13 | 13 | 06 | 37* | 19 | -19 | 42* | 02 | 08 |
| Sensing | -06 | -18 | -12 | -22 | -06 | 20 | -16 | -17 | 05 | -41* | 18 | 04 | -59* | 06 | 25* | -12 |
| Intuitive | -03 | 27* | 09 | 19 | -06 | -20 | 19 | 28* | -16 | 41* | -14 | 00 | 54* | -03 | -23* | 03 |
| Thinking | -32* | 10 | 09 | 21 | -03 | -01 | 17 | -19 | 20 | -04 | 27* | -33* | -07 | 08 | 13 | 15 |
| Feeling | 24* | -12 | -09 | -20 | 09 | 01 | -08 | 28* | -12 | 08 | -23* | 27* | 00 | -08 | -11 | -03 |
| Judging | -15 | -03 | -10 | 01 | -22 | 25* | -09 | 18 | 12 | -25* | 19 | 18 | -29* | 20 | 57* | 01 |
| Perceptive | -03 | 02 | 01 | 04 | 11 | -37* | 06 | -13 | -03 | 31* | -18 | -09 | 21 | 06 | -53* | 10 |

| MBTI Type | 16PF Global Factor Scale | | | | |
|---|---|---|---|---|---|
| | Extraversion | Anxiety | Tough-Mindedness | Independence | Self-Control |
| Extraversion | 68* | -38* | -03 | 39* | -13 |
| Introversion | -61* | 23* | 08 | -35* | 17 |
| Sensing | -16 | 04 | 56* | -36* | 38* |
| Intuitive | 08 | -08 | -56* | 32* | -35* |
| Thinking | -18 | -05 | 24* | 22 | 08 |
| Feeling | 19 | 09 | -26* | -19 | -10 |
| Judging | -26* | 15 | 17 | -09 | 54* |
| Perceptive | 09 | -01 | -12 | 11 | -57* |

Note. Decimals omitted. From "Construct Validation of the 16PF Fifth Edition" by S. R. Conn & M. L. Rieke, 1994b. In S. R. Conn & M. L. Rieke (Eds.), *The 16PF Fifth Edition Technical Manual.* Champaign, IL: Institute for Personality and Ability Testing, Inc.

*$p < .01$

and personal ($r = .19$), and negatively with Thinking, in which judgments are objective and impersonal ($r = -.18$). At the primary level, Liveliness (F), Social Boldness (H), and Self-Reliance (Q2) only correlate with MBTI's Extraversion and Introversion. Warmth (Factor A) correlates negatively with Thinking ($r = -.32$) and positively with Feeling ($r = .24$), whereas Privateness (Factor N) shows the opposite pattern, correlating positively with Thinking ($r = .27$) and negatively with Feeling ($r = -.23$). Note that both Warmth (A) and Privateness (N) are more strongly related to the MBTI Extraversion-Introversion scales, however.

The Anxiety global factor correlates negatively with Extraversion ($r = -.38$) and positively with Introversion ($r = .23$), possibly reflecting aspects of social desirability common to low anxiety and high extraversion. At the primary level, only Emotional Stability (C +) and Apprehension (O +) correlate significantly with any of the MBTI types. Emotional Stability correlates positively with MBTI Extraversion ($r = .36$) and negatively with MBTI Introversion ($r = -.23$). Apprehension (O +) correlates negatively with MBTI Extraversion ($r = -.32$), but is not significantly related to MBTI Introversion. Anxiety does not correlate with any other MBTI scales.

The Tough-Mindedness global factor is positively correlated to Sensing ($r = .56$), and negatively correlated to Intuitive ($r = -.56$). This suggests a focus on observation and immediate experience rather than on abstract relationships. In addition, Tough-Mindedness is positively related to Thinking ($r = .24$) and negatively related to Feeling ($r = -.26$), again suggesting a focus on observable, objective processing. The 16PF primary factor Sensitivity (I), an element of low Tough-Mindedness (Receptivity), is positively correlated to Intuitive ($r = .28$) and to Feeling ($r = .28$).

The Independence global factor correlates positively with Extraversion ($r = .39$) and negatively with Introversion ($r = -.35$), indicating a social- or people-orientation. Two primary components of Independence, Dominance (E) and Social Boldness (H), positively correlate with MBTI Extraversion and negatively correlate with MBTI Introversion. Independence also correlates negatively with Sensing ($r = -.36$) and positively with Intuitive ($r = .32$), suggesting an interest in abstract relationships and possibilities. To a lesser extent, Independence correlates positively with Thinking ($r = .22$) and negatively with Feeling ($r = -.19$), a pattern opposite to that shown for the 16PF Extraversion global factor.

The Self-Control global factor correlates positively with Judging ($r = .54$), which involves being oriented to the planning and finalizing of decisions, and negatively with Perceptive ($r = -.57$), in which processing of incoming information is important. Self-Control correlates positively with Sensing ($r = .38$), a focus on immediate experience, and negatively with Intuitive ($r = -.35$), a focus on abstract relationships. Self-Control does not correlate with the other two MBTI pairs. As can be seen in Table 19, Perfectionism (Q3 +) correlates most highly with the Judging/Perceptive pair.

### Reasoning (Factor B)

Because Factor B measures reasoning ability and not personality per se, it was validated separately from the other 16PF factors. Scores on Factor B were correlated with two other measures of general ability: the Information Inventory (Altus, 1948) and Scale 2 of the Culture Fair Intelligence Test (CFIT; IPAT, 1973a, 1973b).

The Information Inventory is a 13-item test of general intelligence, with open-ended questions similar in format to the verbal subtests of the WISC and WAIS (Rieke & Conn, 1994). Previous research has shown the Information Inventory to correlate .66 with the WAIS-R (Moon & Gorsuch, 1988) and .85 with the WAIS for a group of adult mental patients (Pierson & Gorsuch, 1963). The Factor B scale of the 16PF Fifth Edition and the Information Inventory were administered to a group of 296 adults (133 males, 163 females). Mean age of the sample was 28, with a range of 15 to 71 years. Factor B and Information Inventory scores correlated .61.

The CFIT measures inductive reasoning ability, and does not rely on any verbal processing. Scores on each of four subtests that comprise the CFIT (Series, Classification, Matrices, and Conditions) are combined to give an estimate of IQ. The CFIT has been shown to correlate .72 with WISC full scale IQ (Downing, Edgar, Harris, Kornberg, & Storen, 1965). Scale 2 of the test, which is appropriate for the average adult population, was used in this study. The Factor B scale of the 16PF Fifth Edition and the CFIT were administered to a group of 72 college students (3 males, 69 females). The two measures correlated .51.

In an analysis of variance (ANOVA) on the fifth edition norm sample of 2,500 adults, Conn & Rieke (1994a) found a significant main effect of race on the Factor B scale ($F[5,2494] = 81.36$, $p < .003$), and race accounted for 14% of the variance in Factor

B scores. A separate ANOVA showed that education level also had a significant main effect on Factor B ($F[5,2494] = 258.75$, $p < .003$), and accounted for 17% of the variance in Factor B scores. To determine if real race differences existed in Factor B scores, Conn and Rieke compared mean scores on the Factor B scale for three race groups with large enough representations in the sample: Caucasian, African American, and Hispanic. None of the *t*-tests was significant at the .05 level, leading to the conclusion that no significant differences in Factor B scores existed among the three races at the scale level. The authors suggest that the main effect of race could result from the distribution of education in the sample, which was overeducated compared to U.S. Census data. Alternatively, race and education could have a confounding effect on Factor B scores.

To test for the possibility of bias at the item level, two different measures were used to analyze individual Factor B items for race and gender bias: (1) the Standardization Item-Discrepancy Index (SIDI; Dorans & Kulick, 1983, 1988), which assesses differences between expected and observed scores for two groups, and (2) the Mantel-Haenszel Item Discrepancy Index (MHIDI; Holland & Thayer, 1986), which divides up each group by ability level and then compares groups across ability levels. In their analysis, Rieke & Conn (1994) considered a Factor B item to be biased if both indices were significant.

For the gender bias analysis, the sample consisted of 1,375 adults (769 males, median age 27, median education level 12 years; 606 females, median age 31, median education level 13 years). Because no Factor B item was shown to be biased for both methods, the authors concluded that no bias for gender existed.

For the race bias analysis, groups within the sample were equated for age, education, and male-to-female ratio (see Table 20). Asian and Native American samples could not be analyzed because they were too small to

**TABLE 20**

**SAMPLE DEMOGRAPHICS FOR INVESTIGATION OF ITEM BIAS DUE TO RACE**

|  | *Sample Size* | | *Age (years)* | | *Education (yrs complete)* | |
| --- | --- | --- | --- | --- | --- | --- |
|  | **Males** | **Females** | **Range** | **Median** | **Range** | **Median** |
| African Americans | 154 | 129 | 15-78 | 26 | 7-20 | 12 |
| Caucasians | 527 | 443 | 15-75 | 31 | 7-29 | 14 |
| Hispanics | 122 | 110 | 15-60 | 22 | 7-29 | 13 |

<u>Note</u>. From "The Revised Reasoning (Factor B) Scale" by M. L. Rieke and S. R. Conn, 1994. In S. R. Conn & M. L. Rieke (Eds.), *The 16PF Fifth Edition Technical Manual*. Champaign, IL: Institute for Personality and Ability Testing, Inc.

achieve reliable results. Only one item (172) evinced bias, and the bias was shown when Hispanics were compared to Caucasians.

In summary, the Factor B scale is a generally unbiased gauge of reasoning skill that can enrich the interpretation of personality traits. It was not designed, however, as a measure of "intelligence," for which other instruments are available.

## Criterion Validity

Throughout its history, the 16PF has been shown to relate to life behaviors such as interpersonal skills, leadership, and so forth. The sections that follow describe the behavioral criteria predicted from the 16PF Fifth Edition and present correlations of the global and primary factors with the scales of instruments that measure self-esteem, adjustment, social skill, empathy, creative potential, and leadership potential. Full reports on the various behavioral criteria are included in *The 16PF Fifth Edition Technical Manual* (Conn & Rieke, 1994f). Regression equations that predict the criterion of interest also have been developed, and they are available through computerized reports from IPAT.

In this manual, all scales that emerged as significant predictors in the regression analyses are reported. Occasionally in regression analyses, however, factor scales that do not correlate with the criterion nonetheless emerge as predictors of the criterion. Such scales are called suppressor variables (Wiggins, 1973). When a suppressor variable enters the prediction model, it can improve the model by helping to account for more criterion variance. However, it may be doing so because it shares common variance with another predictor variable that *does* correlate with the criterion, while the suppressor variable itself does not. This phenomenon is more likely to occur when predictor variables are correlated, as is the case with the 16PF

primary factor scales. In this manual, to alert the user to the possible presence of a suppressor variable, the designator "s" appears in the regression results tables, next to the name of such a scale.

Although the studies summarized in the following sections document that the 16PF is useful in predicting behavioral criteria such as self-esteem and social skill, **the test must be used cautiously in situations involving occupational selection or the appraisal of specific qualities.** As a test of normal personality, the 16PF has a limited range of prediction value. That is, although personality is an important determinant of some behaviors, other aspects of a person (e.g., motivation, interests, ability) also are important in the prediction of future behavior. In a related vein, the 16PF should never be the sole basis for decision making or selection, although it can be useful as a component of a selection battery.

The APA's *Standards for Educational and Psychological Testing* (1985) and federal employment laws emphasize that the test user is ultimately responsible for demonstrating that a test is an appropriate, nondiscriminatory, and valid predictor for a particular situation. Thus, studies may document that the 16PF predicts "leadership potential," but the testing professional must demonstrate that leadership potential is actually an important criterion for the organization, position of employment, or promotional consideration. (For further information, see Guastello, 1993.)

### Self-esteem

*Self-esteem* often is used as a collective term for qualities ranging from self-confidence to self-concept. Overall, it seems to gauge a person's evaluation of self-worth and thereby influences all aspects of a person's life, from everyday functioning in school or work to interpersonal interactions and overall adjustment level (Conn & Rieke,

1994d). Self-esteem can be an important variable in counseling, particularly since persons with a sense of worthlessness (low self-esteem) often seek counseling. Moreover, such counselees may have a variety of problems associated with low self-esteem and may need different or more sensitive approaches than those with high self-esteem.

To determine how personality traits relate to self-esteem, the 16PF Fifth Edition and the Coopersmith Self-Esteem Inventory (SEI-Adult Form) were administered to a sample of 318 adults (176 males, 142 females) from a variety of personal counseling, vocational counseling, and school settings. The SEI consists of 25 statements that examinees respond to either as "Like Me" or "Unlike Me." The test author defines *self-esteem* as an expression of approval or disapproval, indicating "the extent to which a person believes him- or herself competent, successful, significant, and worthy" (Coopersmith, 1981, p. 5). Table 21 presents correlations between the 16PF factors, both primary and global, and Self-Esteem as measured by the SEI.

Most of the 16 primary factors bear some relationship with Self-Esteem, as measured by the SEI. High Self-Esteem scores correlate with Emotional Stability (Factor C, $r = .64$), low Vigilance (Factor L, $r = -.35$), low Apprehension (Factor O, $r = -.58$), and low Tension (Factor Q4, $r = -.33$), all primary components of the Anxiety global factor. Self-Esteem also relates to Dominance (Factor E, $r = .46$), Social Boldness (Factor H, $r = .54$), and Openness to Change (Factor Q1, $r = .28$) from the Independence global factor. A negative correlation exists between Self-Esteem and Abstractedness (Factor M, $r = -.44$), suggesting that persons high in self-esteem focus on practical solutions rather than imaginative notions.

**TABLE 21**

**CORRELATIONS WITH COOPERSMITH SELF-ESTEEM ($\underline{N}$=318, 176 MALES, 142 FEMALES)**

| 16PF Primary Factor | | Self-Esteem |
|---|---|---|
| A | Warmth | .34* |
| B | Reasoning | .10 |
| C | Emotional Stability | .64* |
| E | Dominance | .46* |
| F | Liveliness | .17 |
| G | Rule-Consciousness | .19 |
| H | Social Boldness | .54* |
| I | Sensitivity | −.10 |
| L | Vigilance | −.35* |
| M | Abstractedness | −.44* |
| N | Privateness | −.20 |
| O | Apprehension | −.58* |
| Q1 | Openness to Change | .28* |
| Q2 | Self-Reliance | −.38* |
| Q3 | Perfectionism | .17 |
| Q4 | Tension | −.33* |

| 16PF Global Factor | Self-Esteem |
|---|---|
| Extraversion | .45* |
| Anxiety | −.64* |
| Tough-Mindedness | −.03 |
| Independence | .49* |
| Self-Control | .26* |

Note. From "Psychological Adjustment and Self–Esteem" by S. R. Conn and M. L. Rieke, 1994d. In S. R. Conn & M. L. Rieke (Eds.), *The 16PF Fifth Edition Technical Manual*. Champaign, IL: Institute for Personality and Ability Testing, Inc.

*$p < .0001$

**TABLE 22**

**SELF-ESTEEM REGRESSION RESULTS ($\underline{N}$=318)**

| $F$-Ratio | Multiple Correlation | Browne's Cross-Validation | Significant Predictors |
|---|---|---|---|
| 39.44 | .76* | .74* | C+, H+, O−, M− A+, Q1+, N+ |

Note. From "Psychological Adjustment and Self–Esteem" by S. R. Conn and M. L. Rieke, 1994d. In S. R. Conn & M. L. Rieke (Eds.), *The 16PF Fifth Edition Technical Manual*. Champaign, IL: Institute for Personality and Ability Testing, Inc.

*$p < .001$

When Self-Esteem was regressed on the 16 primary factors, the most significant predictors were Emotional Stability (C+), Social Boldness (H+), low Apprehension (O−), and low Abstractedness (M−). (See Table 22 for results.)

A summary of the personality traits of individuals with low self-esteem is presented in the next section. The summary is based on correlations between the SEI and 16PF, the regression equation for predicting self-esteem from 16PF primary factors, and mean 16PF profiles of the top (25%) and bottom (25%) of self-esteem scorers. The full report for these analyses is in *The 16PF Fifth Edition Technical Manual* (see Conn & Rieke, 1994d). Because the nature of the relationship between personality traits and self-esteem is unclear, the professional is encouraged to explore whether the client's personality traits lead to low self-esteem or whether low self-esteem manifests itself in those personality traits.

*Personality Traits Related to Low Self-Esteem*
Low self-esteem is related to introversion. Such persons may be impersonal or Reserved (A−), Shy (H−), and Self-Reliant (Q2+).

Persons with low self-esteem tend to show more anxiety traits in contrast to persons with high self-esteem. In particular, persons with low self-esteem tend to be Reactive (C−). This relationship between Reactivity (C−) and self-esteem is especially evident in Factor C item-content, which concerns a sense of satisfaction, of reaching goals, and of coping with setbacks. Therefore, people low on Factor C tend to be dissatisfied with life, may have trouble reaching self-imposed goals, and experience difficulty coping with life's ups-and-downs. Those low in self-esteem also tend to be Vigilant about others' motives (L+) and Apprehensive (O+). Apprehension (O+) seems particularly important; its item content centers around

feelings of inadequacy and guilt (i.e., worrying about others or about decisions, being excessively self-critical or easily upset). Comparisons of the mean 16PF profiles of persons highest and lowest in self-esteem reveals that those high in self-esteem exhibit less frustration and Tension (Factor Q4) than those with low self-esteem (Conn & Rieke, 1994d). Interestingly, the SEI author notes that self-esteem and anxiety should be interrelated, since anxiety often is caused by imminent exposure of "personal inadequacies" (Coopersmith, 1990), and low self-esteem entails more perceived personal inadequacies.

Persons with low self-esteem are less independent than their high self-esteem counterparts. Those with low self-esteem tend to be Shy (H−), Deferential (E−), and Traditional (Q1−) in their outlook.

*Adjustment*
Although a broad term, *adjustment* often alludes to a general sense of psychological balance. In previous editions of the 16PF, Adjustment was considered to be the "healthier" end of a continuum ranging from neurosis to adjustment. The Adjustment criterion equation had been developed on a diverse group of clinically diagnosed neurotics gathered from various counseling and clinical settings in different English-speaking countries (Cattell et al., 1970). In the past, Adjustment was found to be related to Anxiety, with Emotional Stability (C+), low Apprehension (O−) and low Tension (Q4−) predicting high Adjustment. Adjustment also was predicted by Dominance (E+), Liveliness (F+), and low Sensitivity (I−).

To examine the relationship between the 16PF Fifth Edition and adjustment, an objective measure of psychological adjustment, the Adjustment Inventory (Bell, 1961), was chosen in lieu of clinical diagnoses. This inventory measures adjustment on five specific scales: home, health, social, emotional, and occupational. Each of the five scales contains 32 items selected on the basis of whether they could differentiate poorly-adjusted from well-adjusted persons. The scales were validated against clinical diagnoses of adjustment levels. For this study, only three Adjustment Inventory scales (social, emotional, and occupational) were administered, for a total of 96 items.

Social adjustment entails being aggressive in social interactions. For example, high scorers indicate they like to participate in social gatherings, find it easy to talk to strangers, enjoy public speaking, are not self-conscious in social situations, exhibit leadership tendencies, ask to meet important people, and so forth. Emotional adjustment implies emotional stability; high scorers are not upset easily, experience relatively stable moods, do not experience irrational fears, and are not bothered by upsetting thoughts. Occupational adjustment indicates satisfaction with one's current job. High scorers generally have an open line of communication with their employer, are satisfied with their present job responsibilities and benefits, have advancement opportunities, and so forth.

The 16PF Fifth Edition and the social, emotional, and occupational scales of the Adjustment Inventory were administered to a group of 226 adults (108 males, 118 females) from a variety of settings that included personal counseling, vocational counseling, job selection, and schools. Most of the sample was Caucasian (82.9%) and African American (10.6%). Ages ranged from 15 to 67 years (mean = 31.6) and the mean education level was 14 years. Direction of scoring of the Adjustment Inventory was reversed for a more intuitive interpretation of the scales (Conn & Rieke, 1994d). Thus, in this study, high scores indicate good adjustment and low scores indicate poor adjustment. In addition to correlations (see Table 23), a regression equation predicting each adjustment scale from the primary

**TABLE 23**

**CORRELATIONS WITH BELL'S ADJUSTMENT INVENTORY (N=226, 108 MALES, 118 FEMALES).**

| 16PF Primary | | *Adjustment Type* | | | |
| | | Social | Emotional | Occupational | Total |
|---|---|---|---|---|---|
| A | Warmth | 43* | 09 | 15 | 28* |
| B | Reasoning | 09 | 11 | 11 | 11 |
| C | Emotional Stability | 41* | 75* | 45* | 68* |
| E | Dominance | 45* | 18* | –10 | 22* |
| F | Liveliness | 35* | –06 | –09 | 08 |
| G | Rule-Consciousness | 10 | 12 | 18* | 14 |
| H | Social Boldness | 79* | 30* | 14 | 53* |
| I | Sensitivity | 07 | –18* | –10 | –08 |
| L | Vigilance | –32* | –38* | –29* | –41* |
| M | Abstractedness | –10 | –34* | –24* | –28* |
| N | Privateness | –40* | –05 | –07 | –23* |
| O | Apprehension | –48* | –74* | –42* | –71* |
| Q1 | Openness to Change | 30* | 16 | 05 | 22* |
| Q2 | Self-Reliance | –44* | –24* | –21* | –36* |
| Q3 | Perfectionism | 04 | 03 | –06 | –01 |
| Q4 | Tension | –29* | –49* | –27* | –44* |

<u>Note</u>. Decimals omitted. From "Psychological Adjustment and Self–Esteem" by S. R. Conn and M. L. Rieke, 1994d. In S. R. Conn & M. L. Rieke (Eds.), *The 16PF Fifth Edition Technical Manual*. Champaign, IL: Institute for Personality and Ability Testing, Inc.

*$p < .01$

TABLE 24

ADJUSTMENT REGRESSION RESULTS (<u>N</u>=226)

| Adjustment Type | F-Ratio | Multiple Correlation | Browne's Cross-Validation | Significant Factors |
|---|---|---|---|---|
| Emotional | 101.41* | .84 | .82 | O-, C+, Q4-, L-, M- |
| Social | 87.95* | .86 | .84 | H+, E+, L-, O-, Q2-, C+, I+ |
| Occupational | 18.78* | .55 | .53 | C+, O-, E-, L-, A+ |

<u>Note</u>. From "Psychological Adjustment and Self-Esteem" by S. R. Conn and M. L. Rieke, 1994d. In S. R. Conn & M. L. Rieke (Eds.), *The 16PF Fifth Edition Technical Manual.* Champaign, IL: Institute for Personality and Ability Testing, Inc.

*p < .01

factors was developed and cross-validation was estimated using Browne's formula (Browne, 1975). Results are shown in Table 24.

As the data in Table 23 illustrate, all three adjustment scales—along with total adjustment—correlate with the primary factors comprising the Anxiety global factor. High Adjustment is associated with Emotional Stability (C+), Trust (L-), Self-Assurance (O-), and Relaxedness (Q4-). The finding that well-adjusted individuals are typically low in anxiety supports previous research (Cattell & Scheier, 1961; Rickels & Cattell, 1965).

Although low anxiety is associated with all three aspects of adjustment, each of the three scales is, in turn, characterized by different personality traits. In addition to anxiety factors, high Social Adjustment is characterized by Dominance (E+), Social Boldness (H+), Sensitivity (I+), and Group-Orientation (Q2-). Thus, socially adjusted persons prefer interacting with others and may be dominant and venturesome in those exchanges. Emotional Adjustment is clearly predicted by primary factor scales contributing to low Anxiety, with high scorers being Emotionally Stable (C+), Trusting of others (L-), Self-Assured (O-), and Relaxed (Q4-). High scores also are

predicted by low Abstractedness (M-), suggesting that rather than being caught up in the world of ideas, emotionally adjusted persons focus on pragmatic issues. Occupational adjustment is predicted by Warmth (A+) and low Dominance (E-), in addition to factors contributing to low Anxiety. Thus, persons in the sample who indicate satisfaction with their current jobs are relatively unperturbed, enjoy warm interactions with other people, but are deferential rather than forceful.

### Social Skill

The ability to communicate with other people has far-reaching consequences for personal adjustment, vocational prospects, and, in general, for most areas of life. For example, lack of assertiveness, poor interpersonal relationships, and loneliness can all stem from inadequate social skills (Riggio, 1989). The Social Skills Inventory (SSI; Riggio, 1989) is a 90-item self-report measure of basic social communication skills. Although primarily used in research on social processes, the SSI also can be used to help individuals develop social skills or in applied settings for training and development.

The SSI evaluates skill in three areas of social communication: sending information or "expressivity," receiving information or "sensitivity," and controlling information.

TABLE 25

CORRELATIONS WITH THE SOCIAL SKILLS INVENTORY (N=256, 146 FEMALES, 110 MALES)

| Primary Factor | | SSITOT | EE | ES | EC | SE | SS | SC |
|---|---|---|---|---|---|---|---|---|
| A | Warmth | .48* | .35* | .39* | −.21* | .45* | .17* | .27* |
| B | Reasoning | .14 | .09 | .13 | .12 | .32* | −.01 | .12 |
| C | Emotional Stability | .03 | −.03 | −.08 | .06 | .15 | −.39* | .39* |
| E | Dominance | .27* | .30* | .16 | .04 | .20* | −.20* | .37* |
| F | Liveliness | .51* | .42* | .24* | −.12 | .62* | .14 | .20* |
| G | Rule-Consciousness | −.01 | −.18* | .04 | −.03 | −.06 | .13 | .04 |
| H | Social Boldness | .57* | .42* | .15 | .01 | .68* | −.22* | .70* |
| I | Sensitivity | .12 | .13 | .16 | −.10 | .78* | .05 | .08 |
| L | Vigilance | −.19* | −.14 | −.01 | .05 | −.21* | .11 | −.39* |
| M | Abstractedness | .06 | .13 | .16 | .04 | .00 | .05 | −.15 |
| N | Privateness | −.41* | −.45* | −.20* | .28* | −.44* | −.14 | −.23* |
| O | Apprehension | .03 | .03 | .18* | −.28* | −.08 | .54* | −.36* |
| Q1 | Openness to Change | .21* | .15 | .26* | .02 | .21* | −.19* | .26* |
| Q2 | Self-Reliance | −.46* | −.37* | −.16 | .15 | −.54* | −.13 | −.27* |
| Q3 | Perfectionism | −.02 | −.13 | −.05 | .04 | −.08 | .00 | .09 |
| Q4 | Tension | −.11 | .05 | −.07 | −.14 | −.18* | .30* | −.28* |

| Global Factor | SSITOT | EE | ES | EC | SE | SS | SC |
|---|---|---|---|---|---|---|---|
| Extraversion | .65* | .55* | .33* | −.22* | .73* | .13 | .42* |
| Anxiety | −.10 | .00 | .07 | −.17* | −.22* | .49* | −.50* |
| Tough-Mindedness | −.28* | −.25* | −.34* | .07 | −.24* | .02 | −.17* |
| Independence | .41* | .37* | .25* | .05 | .39* | −.26* | .49* |
| Self-Control | −.16 | −.07 | −.02 | .15 | −.25* | −.23* | .07 |

Note. For SSI, SSITOT = Total SSI Score; EE = Emotional Expressivity; ES = Emotional Sensitivity; EC = Emotional Control; SE = Social Expressivity; SS = Social Sensitivity; SC = Social Control. From "Interpersonal Skills and Empathy" by M. L. Rieke, S. J. Guastello, and S. R. Conn, 1994a. In S. R. Conn & M. L. Rieke (Eds.), *The 16PF Fifth Edition Technical Manual*. Champaign, IL: Institute for Personality and Ability Testing, Inc.

*$p < .01$

Each skill is assessed at two levels: nonverbal (termed "Emotional") and verbal (termed "Social"). The resulting six scales (Emotional Expressivity, Emotional Sensitivity, Emotional Control, Social Expressivity, Social Sensitivity, Social Control) are summed to get a total measure of social skills. Theoretically, a socially skilled communicator would show a balance among the scales, with no scale being too much higher or lower than the others (Riggio, 1989).

To determine how personality traits relate to social skills, the 16PF Fifth Edition and SSI were administered to 254 individuals, 222 of whom were university students and 32 of whom were retired persons. There were 110 males and 146 females, with ages ranging from 18 to 92 (mean = 26.8). Scores for 16PF primary and global factors were correlated with SSI scales (see Table 25). Separate regression equations were developed to predict each SSI scale from the 16PF

TABLE 26

SOCIAL SKILLS REGRESSION RESULTS (N=256)

| SSI Scale | F-Ratio | Multiple Correlation | Browne's Cross-Validation | Significant Predictors |
|---|---|---|---|---|
| EE | 29.7 | .61* | .59* | N-, H+, E+, G-, Q4+$_s$ |
| ES | 30.0 | .44* | .42* | A+, Q1+ |
| EC | 16.9 | .41* | .39* | O-, N+, B+ |
| SE | 110.8 | .80* | .79* | H+, F+, N-, Q1+ |
| SS | 30.5 | .65* | .63* | O+, A+, C-, Q1-, H-, Q4+ |
| SC | 62.8 | .78* | .76* | H+, L-, Q1+, E+, Q3+, B+ |
| Total | 60.2 | .71* | .69* | H+, F+, A+, B+ |

Note. EE = Emotional Expressivity; ES = Emotional Sensitivity; EC = Emotional Control; SE = Social Expressivitiy; SS = Social Sensitivitiy; SC = Social Control; Total = Total SSI Score; s = may be operating as a suppressor variable. From "Interpersonal Skills and Empathy" by M. L. Rieke, S. J. Guastello, and S. R. Conn, 1994a. In S. R. Conn & M. L. Rieke (Eds.), *The 16PF Fifth Edition Technical Manual.* Champaign, IL: Institute for Personality and Ability Testing, Inc.

*$p < .01$

primaries. Results are presented in Table 26. The total SSI score (SSITOT) is strongly related to Extraversion at the global factor level. Correlations with the primary factors comprising Extraversion are all high. Correspondingly, overall social skill is predicted by Extraversion components of Warmth (A+), Liveliness (F+), and Social Boldness (H+), plus good Reasoning ability (B+). In general, being socially skilled seems to entail an orientation toward other people, a willingness to initiate such interaction, and good problem-solving abilities.

*SSI Expressivity Scales*

*Expressivity,* whether verbal or nonverbal, entails interacting with others and initiating communication. Accordingly, primary personality traits related to Extraversion also relate to Emotional and Social Expressivity.

Emotional Expressivity (EE) concerns the ability to communicate nonverbally. Persons who score high on EE are highly expressive emotionally and are able to arouse or inspire others with their ability to transmit feelings. Emotionally expressive people are Dominant (E+), Socially Bold (H+), and Forthright about personal matters (N-). They also have a tendency to operate by their own set of rules and to be Expedient (G-).

Social Expressivity (SE) involves skill in verbal expression and the ability to engage others in social discourse. High scores on SE suggest individuals who are comfortable in initiating and guiding conversations. Just as for Emotional Expressivity, Extraversion factors are important to Social Expressivity. However, Sensitivity (Factor I) is very highly correlated with Social Expressivity, suggesting an element of sensitivity differentiating it from Emotional Expressivity. Socially expressive persons also show Openness to Change and to new ideas or activities (Q1+).

*SSI Sensitivity Scales*

*Sensitivity* refers to the ability to receive and interpret information, yet the two SSI Sensitivity scales differ markedly in their personality correlates. In fact, the scales do not intercorrelate on the SSI (Riggio, 1989).

Emotional Sensitivity (ES) entails skill in understanding and interpreting nonverbal, often subtle, messages. Persons high on ES may be so affected by other people's emotional states that they experience the emotions themselves. Warmth (A+) and Openness to Change (Q1+), both components of the Tough-Mindedness global factor, relate highly to Emotional Sensitivity. Thus, persons low on Tough-Mindedness are high on Emotional Sensitivity.

Social Sensitivity (SS) pertains to the ability to understand the verbal communications of others. High scorers are sensitive to social behaviors, manners, and presentation. They tend to be very conscious of their own behaviors and how they present themselves. Social Sensitivity is the only SSI scale not related to Extraversion. In fact, high Social Sensitivity is predicted by anxiety-related traits: emotional Reactivity (C−), Apprehension (O+), and Tension (Q4+). Socially sensitive persons also are Shy (H−), indicating that skill in interpreting verbal messages is not necessarily equated to being "people-oriented." Instead, socially sensitive persons may be somewhat socially insecure, perhaps as a result of focusing too much on others' actions or being overly self-conscious. Unlike persons high on Emotional Sensitivity, persons high on Social Sensitivity are traditional (Q1−) rather than open to new experiences.

*SSI Control Scales*

Neither of the SSI Control scales directly relates to the 16PF global factor of Self-Control, in part because the SSI and 16PF tend to define *control* differently. In contrast

to the SSI's use of the term to describe the external regulating and/or directing of information, the 16PF uses the term to define a more internal, psychoanalytic connotation of impulse control and self-discipline (concerning moral standards and conscience).

Emotional Control (EC) relates to the ability to regulate emotional and nonverbal displays. Persons who are high on EC may conceal their feelings or adapt their display of emotion to a given situation. EC is the only SSI scale negatively correlated with the Extraversion global factor. Specifically, EC correlates with Reserved interactions (A−) and Privateness (N+). In addition to Privateness, high EC scores are predicted by Self-Assuredness (O−) and good Reasoning ability (B+).

Social Control (SC) entails skill in role-playing and social self-presentation. Persons high on SC may interact comfortably in most social situations and may lead conversations. Unlike Emotional Control, Social Control correlates with the Extraversion global factor and its primaries. SC persons are quite independent. High scorers are Dominant (E+), Socially Bold (H+), and Open to Change (Q1+). Good Reasoning (B+) is also important.

*Empathy*

*Empathy* is the capacity to identify with another individual's situation or feelings. The California Psychological Inventory (CPI) contains a 38-item Empathy folk scale based on the Hogan Empathy scale. The empathy scale has an estimated coefficient alpha reliability of .58 based on 400 college students (Gough, 1988). To determine which personality factors were related to empathy, a group of 212 university undergraduates (81 males, 131 females) was given the 16PF Fifth Edition and the CPI. The Empathy scale score was regressed on the 16PF primary factors to identify personality traits predicting empathy. Correlations and regression results are shown in Tables 27 and 28. High scores on Empathy are characterized by high Extraversion and low Anxiety. Empathy correlated with the primary factors comprising Extraversion (in the extraverted direction): Warmth (A+), Liveliness (F+), Social Boldness (H+), Forthrightness (N-), and Group-Orientation (Q2-). In addition, Warmth (A+), Liveliness (F+), and Social Boldness (H+) predicted Empathy. Overall, this suggests that empathic persons are warm, helping, and enjoy the company of others. Empathy also was predicted by Emotional Stability (C+), low Vigilance (L-), and low Tension (Q4-), components of the Anxiety global factor. Thus, empathic persons could be described as emotionally mature and largely satisfied with their lives, and as being generally trusting of and patient with other people. In addition, Empathy was predicted by Openness to Change (Q1+), suggesting that one must be open-minded to see another's point of view.

### Creative Potential

*Creativity*, although measured and defined in numerous ways, usually entails elements of original, imaginative thought and expression. *Creativity* can be considered domain-specific (Barron & Harringron, 1981), as for example with musical talent, or as a general trait that crosses domains (Cattell & Drevdahl, 1955; Guastello, Bzdawka, Guastello, & Rieke, 1991). Obviously, creativity is a broad concept, and personality is but one of its elements; other sources may include mental and physical ability, motivation, and/or environmental context (Rieke, Guastello, & Conn, 1994b).

For the 16PF Fourth Edition (Form A) and other previous editions, predictions of creative potential were based on a personality profile of a group of artists who were listed in *Who's Who in American Art* and writers who had published prodigiously (Drevdahl & Cattell, 1958). Factors of

## TABLE 27

### CORRELATIONS WITH EMPATHY (N=212, 81 MALES, 131 FEMALES)

| Primary Factor | | Empathy |
|---|---|---|
| A | Warmth | .42* |
| B | Reasoning | .04 |
| C | Emotional Stability | .40* |
| E | Dominance | .08 |
| F | Liveliness | .36* |
| G | Rule-Consciousness | -.03 |
| H | Social Boldness | .43* |
| I | Sensitivity | .14 |
| L | Vigilance | -.40* |
| M | Abstractedness | -.06 |
| N | Privateness | -.24* |
| O | Apprehension | -.20* |
| Q1 | Openness to Change | .25* |
| Q2 | Self-Reliance | -.34* |
| Q3 | Perfectionism | -.13 |
| Q4 | Tension | -.35* |

Note. From "Interpersonal Skills and Empathy" by M. L. Rieke, S. J. Guastello, and S. R. Conn, 1994a. In S. R. Conn & M. L. Rieke (Eds.), *The 16PF Fifth Edition Technical Manual*. Champaign, IL: Institute for Personality and Ability Testing, Inc.

*p<.01.

## TABLE 28

### EMPATHY REGRESSION RESULTS (N=211)

| F-Ratio | Multiple Correlation | Browne's Cross-Validation | Significant Predictors |
|---|---|---|---|
| 21.4 | .65* | .62* | H+, L-, A+, C+ Q1+, Q4-, F+ |

Note. From "Interpersonal Skills and Empathy" by M. L. Rieke, S. J. Guastello, and S. R. Conn, 1994a. In S. R. Conn & M. L. Rieke (Eds.), *The 16PF Fifth Edition Technical Manual*. Champaign, IL: Institute for Personality and Ability Testing, Inc.

*p<.01

particular importance included: Extraversion factors (in the introverted direction) of Reserved (A–), Seriousness (F–), and Self-Reliance (Q2+); Independence factors of Dominance (E+), Social Boldness (H+), Forthrightness (N–), and Openness to Change (Q1+); and a high Reasoning (Factor B) score. Note that Factor N is now on the Extraversion global factor rather than Independence; *The 16PF Fifth Edition Technical Manual* gives more detail (see Rieke, Guastello, & Conn, 1994b).

To determine how creativity relates to personality as measured by the 16PF Fifth Edition, a self-report measure of creativity was chosen: Something About Myself (SAM; Khatena & Torrance, 1976). SAM is a 50-item checklist that assesses creativity along three dimensions: personality characteristics, thinking strategies, and creative output. The 16PF Fifth Edition and SAM were administered to 376 adults (174 male, 202 female). Ages ranged from 15 to 75 years with a mean of 30; mean education level was 13.2 years. Approximately 70% of the sample was Caucasian and 18% was African American.

Although SAM consists of six creativity subscales, three scales intuitively related to personality were chosen for the analysis and combined into a total score (Rieke, Guastello, & Conn, 1994b). The three subscales were: (1) Initiative, which concerns participation in the fine arts and drama, producing new formulas and prod-ucts, and effecting change, (2) Self-strength, which assesses self-confidence, resourceful-ness, flexibility, and motivation, and (3) Intellectuality, which assesses curiosity, imagination, and willingness to try new activities.

Correlations of the individual SAM scales with the 16PF primary and global factors are shown in Table 29. In addition, the three creativity scales were combined and

TABLE 29

CORRELATIONS WITH SOMETHING ABOUT MYSELF (SAM) (N= 376, 202 FEMALES, 174 MALES)

| Primary Factor | | Correlation |
|---|---|---|
| A | Warmth | .07 |
| B | Reasoning | .07 |
| C | Emotional Stability | .06 |
| E | Dominance | .28* |
| F | Liveliness | .13 |
| G | Rule-Consciousness | .00 |
| H | Social Boldness | .30* |
| I | Sensitivity | −.03 |
| L | Vigilance | .01 |
| M | Abstractedness | .09 |
| N | Privateness | −.13 |
| O | Apprehension | −.15 |
| Q1 | Openness to Change | .29* |
| Q2 | Self-Reliance | −.05 |
| Q3 | Perfectionism | .03 |
| Q4 | Tension | −.12 |

| Global Factor | Correlation |
|---|---|
| Extraversion | .18* |
| Anxiety | −.12 |
| Tough-Mindedness | −.16* |
| Independence | .38* |
| Self-Control | −.05 |

Note. From "Leadership and Creativity" by M. L. Rieke, S. J. Guastello, & S. R. Conn, 1994b. In S. R. Conn & M. L. Rieke (Eds.), *The 16PF Fifth Edition Technical Manual.* Champaign, IL: Institute for Personality and Ability Testing, Inc.

*$p < .01$

regressed on the 16 primary factors. Results of the regression are shown in Table 30.

As with the 16PF Fourth Edition creativity equation, Independence is the personality trait most related to creative potential. Specifically, high scores for the fifth edition creative potential equation were predicted by three independence-related primary scales: Dominance (E+), Social Boldness (H+), and Openness to Change (Q1+). In addition, creative potential was predicted by Abstractedness (M+) and by Perfectionism (Q3+). Since personality is but one component of creativity, aspects such as motivation and cognitive skills should also be considered (Rieke, Guastello, & Conn, 1994b).

Correlation between the new Creative Potential equation and the fourth edition equation (Drevdahl & Cattell, 1958) was not high (.27). Unlike the previous equation, the new Creative Potential lacks the aspect of Introversion (Factors A, F, and Q2). This result may stem from the difference in the samples tested: the mean profiles of artists and writers show them to be more introverted than the general population (Cattell et al., 1970). The different measurement criteria also may have influenced the correlation between the creativity equations.

Reasoning (Factor B) did not correlate or predict creativity for the fifth edition. Some level of general mental ability may be necessary for high creative functioning, but greater amounts of reasoning skills do not necessarily translate into greater creative potential (Rieke, Guastello, & Conn, 1994b).

### Leadership Potential

The Leadership Potential equation for the 16PF Fifth Edition evolved from the Leadership Potential Index first developed by Cattell and Stice (1954, 1960). In their study, 800 military personnel, all males, were organized into groups of 10 and asked to perform various group tasks. Team

TABLE 30

CREATIVITY REGRESSION RESULTS ($\underline{N}$=376)

| $F$-Ratio | Multiple Correlation ($\underline{n}$=247) | Browne's Cross-Validation ($\underline{n}$=129) | Significant Predictors |
|---|---|---|---|
| 11.65 | .44* | .39* | H+, Q3+$_s$, M+, E+, Q1+ |

Note. $s$ = may be operating as a suppressor variable. From "Leadership and Creativity" by M. L. Rieke, S. J. Guastello, & S. R. Conn, 1994b. In S. R. Conn & M. L. Rieke (Eds.), *The 16PF Fifth Edition Technical Manual.* Champaign, IL: Institute for Personality and Ability Testing, Inc.

leaders were elected during an early phase of the experiment and, at later stages, were either replaced or reelected. Additionally, observers rated leadership and group performance. The Leadership Potential Index was derived from the personality characteristics of the effective elected leaders.

To determine whether the Leadership Potential equation generalized to other situations, Guastello and Rieke (1993b) conducted a literature review and found an average correlation of .75 with membership in a successful leadership group, .55 with performance, and .46 with other self-report indicators of leadership.

To obtain a Leadership Equation for the 16PF, 462 subjects (208 males, 254 females) completed both the 16PF Fourth Edition (Form A) and the 16PF Fifth Edition. Using the fourth edition Leadership Potential (LP) equation, a LP score was obtained from the fourth edition primary scale scores. Next, this fourth edition LP score was predicted from fifth edition primary scale scores by using multiple regression. That is, the fourth edition LP score was regressed on the fifth edition primary scales. The resulting regression equation was scaled on the norm sample for the fifth edition, and became the Leadership Potential equation for the fifth edition. Regression results are shown in Table 31. The new equation is very similar to the original equation, and the correlation between the two is .81. Mean LP scores for men and women did not differ significantly for either the fourth edition equation or the fifth edition equation; results are shown in Table 32. Thus, even though the original Leadership Potential equation was developed on males, the equation can be applied to females.

As can be seen in Table 31, high leadership potential is characterized by extraversion and, in particular, by Social Boldness (H+), Liveliness (F+), and Group-Orientation (Q2-).

**TABLE 31**

**LEADERSHIP POTENTIAL REGRESSION RESULTS ($\underline{N}$=462)**

| $F$-Ratio | Multiple Correlation | Browne's Cross-Validation | Significant Predictors |
|---|---|---|---|
| 91.94* | .81 | .80 | H+, F+, M-, C+, Q3+ E+, Q4-, I-, B+$_s$, Q2- |

Note. $s$ = may be operating as a suppressor variable. From "Leadership and Creativity" by M. L. Rieke, S. J. Guastello, & S. R. Conn, 1994b. In S. R. Conn & M. L. Rieke (Eds.), *The 16PF Fifth Edition Technical Manual.* Champaign, IL: Institute for Personality and Ability Testing, Inc.

*$p < .0001$

**TABLE 32**

**MEAN GENDER DIFFERENCES ON LEADERSHIP EQUATIONS ($\underline{N}$=462, 208 MALES, 254 FEMALES)**

*Fourth Edition, Form A Equation*

| Gender | Mean | Standard Deviation | Z-score Difference |
|---|---|---|---|
| Females | 6.15 | 1.67 | |
| Males | 5.35 | 1.76 | .64 |

*Fifth Edition Equation*

| Gender | Mean | Standard Deviation | Z-score Difference |
|---|---|---|---|
| Females | 5.77 | 1.77 | |
| Males | 5.51 | 1.96 | .45 |

Note. From "Leadership and Creativity" by M. L. Rieke, S. J. Guastello, and S. R. Conn, 1994b. In S. R. Conn & M. L. Rieke (Eds.), *The 16PF Fifth Edition Technical Manual.* Champaign, IL: Institute for Personality and Ability Testing, Inc.

High scorers also show minimal anxiety. They are characterized by high Emotional Stability (C+) and low Tension (Q4–). High scorers tend to have a Utilitarian, objective outlook (I–) and are solution-oriented and practical (M–). They also indicate Perfectionistic tendencies that suggest a need for order (Q3+). As has been shown in previous research, leadership potential is predicted by high scores on Reasoning (B+) and by Dominance (E+).

## Invalid Test Results

Detecting invalid test results is a separate validity issue that is addressed in Chapter 3 of this manual.▼

# 6

**16PF® BASIC**

**INTERPRETIVE**

**REPORT**

**(BIR)**

# 6

## 16PF® BASIC

## INTERPRETIVE

## REPORT

## (BIR)

**T**he 16PF Basic Interpretive Report (BIR) is a computer-generated interpretation of an examinee's test scores. Even though the BIR is unique to the fifth edition, longtime 16PF users probably will note similarities between the BIR and the Narrative Score Report (NSR), generated from the 16PF Fourth Edition.

The BIR displays the overall pattern of an examinee's personality traits, provides interpretations of predominant personality factors, and presents information about related interpersonal, vocational, and behavioral criteria. The scope of the BIR is quite broad, covering domains helpful in both personal and vocational counseling. In addition to the BIR, a scores-only report, the Basic Score Report (BSR), is available from the fifth edition. Although this chapter focuses on the BIR, much of the information also is applicable to the BSR.

Like the test from which it is generated, the BIR is intended to be used only by qualified professionals who understand the limits of psychological testing and interpretation and possess a fundamental understanding of psychometrics. They also should be familiar with the APA's *Standards for Educational and Psychological Testing*. BIR contents are not intended to be shared directly with the client.

### FORMAT OF THE BIR

The interpretive strategy discussed in Chapter 3 provides the framework for the format of the BIR. In brief, the recommended strategy involves this sequence of steps: (1) review the response style indices for unusual response tendencies, (2) evaluate the global factors of personality to obtain a broad picture of the examinee, and (3) evaluate the primary factors to obtain details of the personality picture. As professionals become accustomed to using the report, they may wish to tailor the strategy to fit a specific testing application.

The BIR begins with a Profile Section, which includes the examinee's scores for the three response style indices and profiles of the examinee's sten scores on the five global factors and the 16 primary factors. Thus, at a glance, the professional can obtain an overview of the examinee's personality pattern. The Profile Section also serves as a handy reference tool during review of the interpretive text sections of the BIR.

The remainder of the BIR is divided into four main sections. The Global Factors Section presents personality trait information consisting of a profile and interpretive statements for each global factor and its associated primaries. The Criterion Scores Section provides criterion scores and explanations for various interpersonal, interest, and behavioral measures related to personality. In the Vocational Interests Section, the examinee's personality characteristics are used to predict similarity to six vocational orientations based on the Holland Occupational Types (Holland, 1985a). Scores for the six types, or themes, are profiled, and the examinee's highest themes are discussed in detail. The final page of the report is the Item Summary Section, which includes statistics concerning the number and percentage of a, b, c, and missing responses as well as raw scores for the 16 primary factors.

The content of the BIR, section by section, is discussed in the text that follows.

## CONTENT OF THE BIR

### I. Title Page
This cover page presents the report's title, copyright information, the examinee's name or I.D. number or both, and the date of test processing. Also appearing is a statement that stresses the BIR's appropriate application and its confidential nature. The statement cautions that the BIR is not to be used as the sole basis for personnel or counseling decisions. Instead, the report is intended for use in conjunction with other sources of data, such as interviews, biographical data, and other assessment results.

### II. Profile Section
The Profile Section is on page 2 of the BIR. The heading of the page provides the examinee's name or I.D. number or both, and the date of test processing. The selected norm group (male, female, or combined gender) is printed as well. (For explanations of the normative options, refer to Chapter 2.)

The body of this page contains scores for the three response style indices and profiles of sten scores on the five global factors and 16 primary personality factors. Descriptions of these follow.

#### Response Style Indices
The BIR reports an examinee's scores on three response style indices: Impression Management (IM), Infrequency (INF), and Acquiescence (ACQ). These indices measure particular test-taking attitudes that may influence how an examinee responds to 16PF personality items. Values beyond the average range indicate that test scores may reflect a particular response bias rather than "pure" personality traits. A high score on any of the three indices as well as a low score on IM should prompt the professional to consider response bias. Statements indicating this consideration appear in the report if a score reaches the 95th percentile (also the 5th percentile for low IM), with cutoffs being based on the general adult population norm sample ($\underline{N} = 2,500$). Depending on the individual and the test setting, the professional may wish to use different cutoffs, and instructions for calculating these are in Appendix C of this manual and also in

*The 16PF Fifth Edition Technical Manual* (see Conn & Rieke, 1994e).

A test having 12 or fewer incomplete items can be computer-processed. When an examinee omits over half the items on any single factor scale, a cautionary statement appears. The professional can identify the affected factor or factors and the omitted items by referring to the Item Summary Section of the BIR.

The response style indices are intended to serve only as warning flags that suggest the possibility of response bias. Whether to accept the test results or to retest is a decision best made by the professional on the bases of the examinee's testing history and interview information. Therefore, during test processing, personality scores are neither adjusted nor "corrected" when one or more response style indices are elevated, a scoring policy different from that used for previous 16PF editions.

Descriptions of the three response indices follow; additional information concerning these indices is in Chapter 3 of this manual and in *The 16PF Fifth Edition Technical Manual* (see Conn & Rieke, 1994e).

*Impression Management (IM)*
The only bipolar scale of the three response style indices, IM taps social desirability. A high score indicates that the examinee has endorsed traits or behaviors deemed desirable in society, or has denied undesirable characteristics. The tendency to portray oneself in an unrealistically positive light sometimes is seen in job placement settings. However, the possibility always exists that an examinee's high score may reflect sincere responses. For example, socially desirable answers may be accurate for certain persons, such as members of the clergy. A high IM score also may reflect an idealized self-image rather than deliberate "faking." In this case, the profile appears more socially

desirable than the person's actual behavior, but the "distortion" probably was introduced unconsciously, given the examinee's idealized self-image.

A low IM score suggests that the examinee has presented himself or herself in an unfavorable light by endorsing items that reflect or even exaggerate undesirable qualities. The examinee may be extremely self-critical or may be reinforcing a need for counseling or for attention.

*Infrequency (INF)*
In part because it was empirically derived, the INF scale is comprised of all *b* responses, the question mark *(?)* option; that is, the scale consists of items for which the overwhelming majority of the norm sample selected the *a* or *c* response choice. Each of the scale's 32 items was endorsed less than 6.5% of the time by the general population norm sample of 2,500 adults.

A high score on the INF scale indicates that the examinee endorsed responses seldom chosen by others and therefore suggests random responding. Alternatively, a high INF score may indicate an inability or unwillingness to make a commitment to specific response choices. In rare cases, a high INF score may reflect the accurate responses of an extremely unique individual.

The BIR's Item Summary Section reports the examinee's response choice to each 16PF item as well as the number and percentage of *b* responses. If necessary, the professional can use this information in conjunction with Table 44 to address specific items in considering possible response bias.

*Acquiescence (ACQ)*
The purpose of the ACQ scale is to detect the tendency of an examinee to endorse an item as self-descriptive, regardless of the item's content. Therefore, when an acquiescent response pattern occurs, it

affects the entire test. A high score on the scale reflects an extremely high number of *TRUE* responses, which are the *a* choices to fifth edition personality items.

An acquiescent response style may indicate a high need for acceptance. Another possible explanation for a high ACQ score is test sabotage; that is, the examinee may have deliberately chosen mostly or all *a* responses.

The BIR's Item Summary Section reports the examinee's response choice to each 16PF item as well as the number and percentage of *a* responses, thus enabling the professional to address specific items in considering a possible acquiescent pattern. Table 47 in Appendix C lists items belonging to the ACQ scale.

### Profiles of Global and Primary Factor Scores

In the BIR's Profile Section, scores on the five global factors and the 16 primary personality factors are profiled separately and are reported as stens ranging from 1-10, with a mean of 5.5 and a standard deviation of 2.0. Figure 5 in Chapter 3 is a bell-curve diagram that shows the nature of the sten distribution. Because the 16PF scales are bipolar in nature, scores at each end of the scale are psychologically meaningful; that is, low scores are not necessarily "bad" and high scores are not necessarily "good." Within the profiles, the left and right poles of each factor are designated by key behavioral descriptors. For example, the left pole descriptor for the Extraversion global factor is "Introverted," and the right pole descriptor is "Extraverted." (See Chapter 3 for comprehensive descriptions of the factors.)

Between the descriptors for the opposite poles of each factor is a bar. The bar begins in the middle of the profile and extends to the right or to the left, depending on the examinee's sten score on the factor. The sten score is printed at the end of the bar. A short bar in the shaded middle region indicates that the score is within the average range for the factor; a long bar extending outside the shaded area shows that the score is extreme and therefore reflects a trait that is quite representative of the examinee.

When interpreting a score, the professional is advised to refer to a sten score of 5 or 6 as "average," or as balanced between the two behavioral descriptors at the extremes of a factor's pole. A score of 1, 2, or 3 (bar extended to the left) is explained as corresponding to the factor's left-pole descriptor. A score of 8, 9, or 10 (bar extended to the right) is explained as corresponding to the factor's right-pole descriptor. Borderline scores of 4 and 7 are described as "low-average" and "high-average," respectively. This terminology reflects the measurement imprecision (i.e., standard error of measurement [$SE_M$]) that is inherent in any test. For example, since the $SE_M$ for most factors is approximately plus or minus one sten, a person scoring 4 (low-average) could just as likely score a 3 (low) and be characterized by low-end traits on a retest. (For more information on $SE_M$, see Chapter 3.)

### III. Global Factors Section

Starting with page 3, the BIR presents information in profile and text form on the personality traits measured by the 16PF Fifth Edition. This information is organized around the examinee's scores on the global factors, which are presented in order from most extreme to average. Thus, the first profile for an examinee's scores would consist of his or her most extreme global factor along with its affiliated primary traits presented in the standard alphabetical order. Interpretive statements are provided for each global factor score as well as for each primary factor score outside the average range. **No statements are generated for average scores**. (See Chapter 3 for detailed explanations of the global and primary factors.)

## IV. Criterion Scores Section

This section of the BIR contains interpersonal and behavioral information based on relationships between the examinee's scores on the 16 primary factors and various criterion measures. Interpretive comments are generated from prediction equations of criterion scores. Predictor regression analyses were cross-validated whenever sample size (300 or more subjects) permitted. When the sample was smaller than 300, Browne's formula (Browne, 1975) was used to estimate the cross-validated regression coefficient.

A brief explanation of each criterion follows. Most of the criterion studies are described in Chapter 5 of this manual, and professionals should review this chapter when interpreting scores. *The 16PF Fifth Edition Technical Manual* (see Conn & Rieke, 1994f) provides in-depth coverage of all criterion studies.

### Self-Esteem

The score on Self-Esteem is based on a general population sample of 318 adults who completed the 25-item Coopersmith Self-Esteem Inventory (SEI-Adult Form) and the 16PF Fifth Edition.

High self-esteem is nearly always interpreted as a sign of a well-adjusted individual. High scorers possess a strong sense of self-worth. They feel comfortable expressing their opinions, do not succumb to conformity pressures, and generally reach their personal goals (Coopersmith, 1981). Their personality characteristics indicate emotional maturity, good coping skills, and a general satisfaction with life. They are friendly and can be quite forward and venturesome in their interactions with others. Moreover, they are not overly concerned with how others might perceive them. Persons with high self-esteem tend to concentrate on practical matters and can stay focused on issues at hand.

In extreme cases, persons with very high self-esteem may not admit to personal shortcomings and therefore may assume more responsibilities than they can reasonably expect to handle (Conn & Rieke, 1994d). Because the presentation of high self-esteem is socially desirable, the professional may wish to explore the possibility that an extremely high score is artificially inflated, especially if the Impression Management (IM) score is also elevated.

Persons low in self-esteem, according to Coopersmith (1981), view themselves as inferior to most people. Additionally, they may have problems with intimacy. Fifth edition results show that low scorers tend to have trouble coping with day-to-day problems. They can be emotionally reactive, worrying about their actions and other people's perceptions. Typically they are aloof and somewhat timid. Moreover, they may be distractible or absentminded. Low scorers may be likely to seek counseling and, in fact, may have a variety of problems associated with low self-esteem. Rather than reflecting a poor self-image, a moderately low self-esteem score could be a sign of humility, which is considered a desirable trait in some cultures (Conn & Rieke, 1994d). Ultimately, the professional should decide whether intervention is necessary.

Self-Esteem is predicted by the 16PF factors of Warmth (A+), Emotional Stability (C+), Social Boldness (H+), low Abstractedness (M−), Privateness (N+), low Apprehension (O−), and Openness to Change (Q1+).

### Adjustment

Although a broad term, *adjustment* often alludes to a general sense of psychological balance. As measured by the Adjustment Inventory (Bell, 1961), adjustment is predicted for two specific areas: emotional and social. The Occupational Adjustment scale is not presented in the BIR because, based on item content, the scale seemed to measure state-dependent aspects of job satisfaction rather than a stable trait. (Refer to Chapter 5 for information regarding Occupational Adjustment.)

Equations predicting Emotional and Social Adjustment from the 16PF primary factors were developed on a sample of 226 adults who completed the Adjustment Inventory and the 16PF Fifth Edition (Conn & Rieke, 1994d). Cross-validation was estimated using Browne's formula. Results are shown in Table 24 in Chapter 5.

Regardless of the specific area, high adjustment correlated with low anxiety in the criterion study. In general, well-adjusted individuals were Emotionally Stable (C+), Trusting (L−), Self-Assured (O−), and Relaxed (Q4−), all components of the Anxiety global factor.

*Emotional Adjustment*
This scale indicates emotional stability. Overall, the scale seems to reflect low anxiety and a sense of well-being. In the criterion study, high scorers endorsed Adjustment Inventory items suggesting a self-assured, imperturbable demeanor. Their 16PF results suggest that high scorers are emotionally mature and capable of coping with life's ups-and-downs. They are patient with other people and situations. Low scorers tend to be worried, nervous, or easily upset.

Emotional Adjustment is predicted by the 16PF factors of Emotional Stability (C+), low Vigilance (L−), low Abstractedness (M−), low Apprehension (O−), and low Tension (Q4−).

*Social Adjustment*
This scale indicates aggressive social behavior. In the criterion study, high scorers typically endorsed Adjustment Inventory items reflecting an outgoing and audacious social orientation. High scorers tend to be bold and forceful during social interactions, whereas low scorers tend to be meek and accommodating (Bell, 1961). As reflected by 16PF results, persons high on this scale are self-confident and generally satisfied with their lives. They seek out group interaction, and are typically assertive and uninhibited in social arenas. They are trusting of peoples' motives and actions.

Social Adjustment is predicted by the 16PF factors of Emotional Stability (C+), Dominance (E+), Social Boldness (H+), Sensitivity (I+), low Vigilance (L−), low Apprehension (O−), and low Self-Reliance (Q2−).

*Social Skill*
Scores are reported for components of overall social skill as measured by the Social Skills Inventory (SSI; Riggio, 1989), a self-report measure of social interaction abilities. According to Riggio, social interaction can be based on both verbal (termed *Social*) and nonverbal (termed *Emotional*) communication. Furthermore, each type of communication can be broken down into three components: the sending, receiving, and controlling of information (termed *Expressivity*, *Sensitivity*, and *Control*, respectively). Separate scores are predicted for each of the resulting six scales. The research was based on a sample of 254 college students and retirees who completed the SSI and the 16PF Fifth Edition.

In addition to considering an examinee's scores on the six individual scales, the professional should review the general pattern of scores because overall social competence is believed to be reflected by a relative balance among the six components (Riggio, 1989). As reported in *The 16PF Fifth Edition Technical Manual* (see Rieke, Guastello, & Conn, 1994a), total social skill is predicted by extraversion; high scorers enjoy being around other people, and their interactions with others are animated, lively, and venturesome. In contrast to low scorers, persons high in total social skill report more experience with public contact through activities such as sales, acting, or public speaking (Riggio, 1989, 1986).

When interpreting scores relating to Social Skill, professionals should remember that the characterizations apply *only* to social situations. Definitions for each scale are from the SSI manual; personality descriptions are derived from 16PF test results.

*Emotional Expressivity (EE)*
High scorers are skilled in sending information through nonverbal means, which typically entails communicating via expression of emotions or attitude. EE people can be quite theatrical. They are capable of evoking emotional displays from others; that is, their emotional state may be contagious. In general, females tend to score higher than males (Riggio, 1989).

When interacting with others, high scorers can be forceful and dominant. They tend to be socially bold and forthright about personal matters, openly manifesting their feelings. They tend to value their individualism and sometimes their actions may be based on self-interest.

EE is predicted by the 16PF factors of Dominance (E+), low Rule-Consciousness (G-), Social Boldness (H+), low Privateness (N-), and Tension (Q4+).

*Emotional Sensitivity (ES)*
High scorers are skilled in receiving nonverbal communications. They excel at interpreting emotional cues as they continually analyze other people's gestures, feelings, and interactions. High scorers can empathize with or even get drawn into emotional exchanges. Females tend to score higher than males on this scale (Riggio, 1989).

ES persons are warm and sociable. They also tend to be open to new ideas, opinions, and experiences.

ES is predicted by the 16PF factors of Warmth (A+) and Openness to Change (Q1+).

*Emotional Control (EC)*
High scorers are skilled in regulating nonverbal communication. They may be able to display (or hide) emotions intentionally. Depending on the social situation, they may assume personae. Males tend to score higher than females on this scale (Riggio, 1989).

EC individuals tend to be skilled reasoners. Because they are personally guarded and private, they typically know other people better than others know them. They also tend to be self-assured.

EC is predicted by the 16PF factors of Reasoning (B+), Privateness (N+), and low Apprehension (O-).

*Social Expressivity (SE)*
High scorers are verbally fluent and gregarious. Typically, they are skilled conversationalists or writers or both. SE persons usually make a good first impression (Riggio, 1989). They can easily engage others in conversation; however, a lack of restraint can result in their making impulsive remarks.

SE relates to Social Control (SC), and, in fact, to Total Social Skill; intercorrelations among these three scales all exceed .65 (Riggio, 1989). This suggests that high SE pertains to overall social competence. On the other hand, when a person high in SE lacks traits relating to SC, he or she may speak without thinking and thereby suffer the consequences (Riggio, 1989).

Persons high in SE enjoy being the center of attention and do not consider themselves to be shy. They indicate enjoyment of lively or festive social interactions. They reveal personal matters about themselves and are usually open-minded about new ideas or experiences.

SE is predicted by the 16PF factors of Liveliness (F+), Social Boldness (H+), low Privateness (N−), and Openness to Change (Q1+).

### Social Sensitivity (SS)

High scorers are skilled in receiving and interpreting verbal messages. They attend to social behavior and the appropriateness of their own actions, with social norms being very important to them. If an individual is extremely self-conscious, social interaction may be difficult (Riggio, 1989). To explore this possibility, the professional can look for a high Anxiety global factor score as well as low scores on Social Expressivity (SE) and Social Control (SC).

Many 16PF anxiety traits relate to the SS scale. SS persons admit to difficulty in dealing with day-to-day problems and setbacks. Often they are filled with worry and self-doubt. They also tend to get frustrated easily. They are warm and enjoy being in the company of others, even if they prefer to remain in the background.

SS is predicted by the 16PF factors of Warmth (A+), low Emotional Stability (C−), low Social Boldness (H−), Apprehension (O+), Low Openness to Change (Q1−), and Tension (Q4+).

### Social Control (SC)

High scorers are skilled in regulating verbal communication. More specifically, these people are skilled in role-playing and self-presentation (Riggio, 1989). They are tactful yet confident in social situations, and they can guide conversation.

SC people are trusting of others and have good reasoning ability. They show a need for an ordered, structured environment. They also tend to be independent; their interactions with others are characterized by dominance, boldness, and a willingness to try new ideas or outlooks.

SC is predicted by the 16PF factors of Reasoning (B+), Dominance (E+), Social Boldness (H+), low Vigilance (L−), Openness to Change (Q1+), and Perfectionism (Q3+).

### Empathy

*Empathy* is the capacity to identify with another individual's situation or feelings. Its applications are broad: empathy has been shown to relate to management style, counseling and nursing effectiveness, and parenting, among other areas (Guastello & Rieke, 1993a; Guastello, Choi, Rieke, & Billings, 1993). To determine which personality factors relate to empathy, 212 university undergraduates (81 males, 131 females) were administered the 16PF Fifth Edition and the California Psychological Inventory (CPI), which contains a 38-item Empathy scale based on the Hogan Empathy Scale. The students' scores on the CPI Empathy scale were correlated with fifth edition primary factor scales, and a prediction equation was developed to predict Empathy from primary scores. Results are shown in Tables 27 and 28 in Chapter 5.

Persons scoring high on Empathy understand the feelings of others. Overall, they are characterized by high Extraversion and low Anxiety. As one might expect, empathic persons are outgoing and enjoy social contact. They are warm and friendly and enjoy helping others. Their interactions tend to be lively and dynamic. Empathic persons are emotionally mature and generally satisfied with their lives. They are confident in themselves. In addition, they are generally trusting of and patient with other people, and they remain open-minded about different ideas or opinions.

Empathy is predicted by the 16PF factors of Warmth (A+), Emotional Stability (C+), Liveliness (F+), Social Boldness (H+), low Vigilance (L-), Openness to Change (Q1+), and low Tension (Q4-).

### Leadership Potential

The Leadership Potential equation for the 16PF Fifth Edition evolved from the Leadership Potential index first developed by Cattell and Stice (1954, 1960). The original index was derived from the personality characteristics of effective leaders who emerged from teams performing group tasks. All participants in the study were males.

To obtain a Leadership Equation for the fifth edition, both the fourth edition (Form A) and fifth edition of the 16PF were administered to 462 subjects (208 males, 254 females). First, the fourth edition Leadership Potential score was obtained from fourth edition primary scale scores. Next, the fourth edition Leadership Potential score was predicted from fifth edition factor scale scores by using multiple regression. Regression results are shown in Table 31 in Chapter 5.

The new Leadership Potential equation for the fifth edition correlates with the original equation (.81). Mean Leadership Potential scores for men and women do not differ significantly for either 16PF edition, as shown in Table 32 in Chapter 5. Thus, even though the original Leadership Potential equation was developed on males, it also applies to females.

Leadership Potential is characterized by extraversion and low anxiety. High scorers tend to be socially bold and not easily offended. They prefer interacting with

others rather than being alone, and their interactions are lively and animated. High scorers enjoy good coping skills and are generally relaxed and tolerant. They tend to focus on objective, utilitarian matters and are solution-oriented. Indications of perfectionistic tendencies suggest that high scorers have a need for a structured environment. As shown in previous research (Cattell & Stice, 1954, 1960), leaders are characterized by forcefulness and dominance (E+).

For the 16PF Fifth Edition, Leadership Potential is predicted by the factors of Reasoning (B+), Emotional Stability (C+), Dominance (E+), Liveliness (F+), Social Boldness (H+), low Sensitivity (I-), low Abstractedness (M-), low Self-Reliance (Q2-), Perfectionism (Q3+), and low Tension (Q4-).

### Creative Potential

*Creative Potential*, as defined in the BIR, contains elements of enterprise, confidence, and general curiosity. The creative potential score is a combination of three subscales from Something About Myself (SAM; Khatena & Torrance, 1976). SAM is a self-report measure of creativity that assesses the personality characteristics, cognitive operations, and products of creative pursuits. Although SAM consists of six creativity subscales, only the three subscales intuitively related to personality were chosen for the criterion study and combined into a total score (Rieke, Guastello, & Conn, 1994b). These subscales are (1) Initiative, which concerns participation in the fine arts and drama, producing new formulas and products, and effecting change; (2) Self-strength, which assesses self-confidence, resourcefulness, flexibility, and motivation; and (3) Intellectuality, which measures curiosity, imagination, and willingness to try new activities. Scores on the three SAM subscales were combined, and the total creativity score was regressed on the 16 primary factors of the fifth edition. The results of the regression are shown in Table 30 in Chapter 5.

Creative persons show definite elements of independence: their interactions with others are characterized by a tendency for competitive and dominant behaviors. They are boldly self-expressive and venturesome, being open to new ideas, opinions, and experiences. Creative persons are imaginative and "idea-oriented." As measured by the SAM inventory, creativity contains elements of initiative, resourcefulness, and openness, suggesting that persons scoring high on Creative Potential not only generate new ideas but implement them as well (Rieke, Guastello, & Conn, 1994b).

Creative Potential is predicted by the 16PF factors of Dominance (E+), Social Boldness (H+), Abstractedness (M+), Openness to Change (Q1+), and Perfectionism (Q3+).

### Creative Achievement

In addition to personal qualities, another aspect of creativity concerns its expression, or output, whether in the form of products or ideas. A research instrument called the Artistic and Scientific Activities Study (ASAS; Guastello, 1991) measures rate of creative achievement. The ASAS is basically a checklist wherein subjects indicate the extent to which they have produced creative output in eight areas: visual arts, music, literature, theater, science and engineering, business, apparel design, and video and photography. Since creative output in each of the eight areas was so highly correlated, the eight scales were aggregated into a total creative output score (Guastello & Shissler, 1993).

To determine the link between creative output and personality traits, a mixed group of 440 undergraduates and job incumbents (including artists, musicians, research scientists, engineers, beauticians, and graduate students in the preceding fields) took the 16PF Fifth Edition and the ASAS. A regression analysis was done to predict total creative achievement from the personality factor scores of the 16PF. The multiple regression coefficient was .42; the cross-validation coefficient, using Browne's formula, was .39.

Like the Creative Potential equation, Creative Achievement is characterized by an openness to new ideas, opinions, and experiences. In addition, high Creative Achievement scorers tend to be immersed in ideas and imagination. These elements indicate an underlying aspect of Independence, which also characterizes Creative Potential. Creative Achievement tends to be characterized by lively social interaction and a certain openness about personal matters. However, high scorers may prefer to rely on themselves rather than to seek group support. This broad and unusual mix of personality characteristics may reflect aspects of Creative Achievement not specific to any particular creative endeavor.

Creative Achievement is predicted by the 16PF factors of low Warmth (A−), Liveliness (F+), Abstractedness (M+), low Privateness (N−), Openness to Change (Q1+), Self-Reliance (Q2+), and Perfectionism (Q3+).

## V. Vocational Interests Section

Measures of personality and of vocational interests are used to guide, or even to predict, an individual's occupational choices. Vocational interests predicted in this section of the BIR are defined according to Dr. John Holland's typology (Holland, 1973, 1985a). Holland posits six general occupational "types," or themes, which describe not only people who prefer particular occupations but also actual work environments. The themes are Realistic, Investigative, Artistic, Social, Enterprising, and Conventional. Central to Holland's theory is the assumption of certain personality traits that serve to describe the general characteristics of persons who gravitate toward a theme. The themes also are evidenced in the activities, competencies, interests, and skills of individuals.

To examine the ties between personality and vocational interest, the 16PF Fifth Edition and the Self-Directed Search, Form R (SDS; Holland, 1985b) were administered to 194 individuals, the majority of whom were university students. The sample was composed of 79 males and 115 females whose mean age was 24.8 years and whose mean education level was 13.5 years.

The SDS is a 228-item inventory that measures Holland's six general occupational themes. Each theme is evaluated by responses on four scales: Activities, Competencies, Occupations, and Self-Estimates. For the Activities scale, examinees indicate whether they would LIKE or DISLIKE a listed activity; for Competencies, examinees indicate (YES/NO) whether they can do a stated activity competently; for Occupations, examinees indicate (YES/NO) whether they are interested in a given occupation; for Self-Estimates, examinees rate specific abilities on a seven-point scale (1 = low, 7 = high). Scale points are summed for each theme. The three themes with the highest totals form the Summary Code (e.g., EIS for Enterprising, Investigative, Social), which indicates a person's pattern of interests that could guide his or her occupational search. The first letter of the code represents the strongest theme matching the person's interests; the second letter, the second strongest theme; and the last letter, the third strongest theme.

For the criterion study, total scores on each of the SDS themes were correlated with the 16PF global and primary factors. The results are shown in Table 33. Next, each Holland theme was regressed on the 16PF primary factors to obtain separate prediction equations for the themes. These results are presented in Table 34. Full details of the study are in *The 16PF Fifth Edition Technical Manual* (see Karol, 1994).

The BIR displays a profile of an examinee's predicted sten score for each of Holland's six general occupational themes. Any theme for which the examinee scored a sten of eight or above is discussed in the text of the report. If the examinee did not score highly on any themes, his or her two highest scores are discussed. When interpreting scores, the professional should not focus exclusively on the top score; all high scores are notable. In some instances—especially because the scores are predicted rather than measured directly—the top theme may not be significantly higher than the second highest. Moreover, real-life occupations are rarely "pure" and cannot be classified under a single theme. More commonly, occupations encompass aspects of a few themes. For example, a math teacher might be Investigative (mathematics) and Social (teaching), or an advertising executive might be Artistic (design aspects) and Enterprising (business aspects).

In a related vein, research has replicated specific relationships among the themes (Holland & Gottfredson, 1992; Karol, 1994). Highly related themes are located close to one another on a hexagon-shaped model; unrelated themes are located at opposite points on the model. If an individual's highest scores occur for two themes adjacent to one another on the model, he or she has compatible interests. If a person's highest scores occur for two themes opposite each other on the model, he or she has incompatible interests, or ill-defined interests.

The BIR indicates the compatibility of an examinee's highest themes, based on the hexagonal model. An examinee has a good chance of finding an occupation that encompasses aspects of compatible themes. An examinee's chance of finding an occupation

TABLE 33

## CORRELATIONS WITH HOLLAND THEMES (N=194, 115 FEMALES, 79 MALES)

| 16PF Primary Factor | | R | I | A | S | E | C |
|---|---|---|---|---|---|---|---|
| A | Warmth | −.19* | −.31* | .17 | .55* | .37* | .02 |
| B | Reasoning | .08 | .32* | .05 | −.06 | −.04 | .04 |
| C | Emotional Stability | .16 | −.08 | −.05 | .09 | .24* | .16 |
| E | Dominance | .13 | .00 | .06 | .21* | .43* | .01 |
| F | Liveliness | −.01 | −.16 | .17 | .27* | .32* | −.05 |
| G | Rule-Consciousness | −.01 | −.03 | −.21* | .01 | .02 | .23* |
| H | Social Boldness | .09 | −.06 | .30* | .45* | .45* | −.03 |
| I | Sensitivity | −.45* | −.27* | .29* | .07 | −.27* | −.21* |
| L | Vigilance | .04 | .00 | .03 | −.08 | .03 | −.13 |
| M | Abstractedness | .04 | .15 | .39* | .05 | −.02 | −.38* |
| N | Privateness | .10 | .09 | −.10 | −.30* | −.10 | .09 |
| O | Apprehension | −.28* | −.07 | −.07 | −.05 | −.30* | −.06 |
| Q1 | Openness to Change | .10 | .14 | .41* | .21* | .13 | −.23* |
| Q2 | Self-Reliance | −.01 | .15 | −.01 | −.28* | −.21* | .00 |
| Q3 | Perfectionism | −.03 | −.13 | −.18 | .05 | .15 | .32* |
| Q4 | Tension | −.09 | −.11 | .00 | −.16 | −.02 | −.09 |

| Global Factor | R | I | A | S | E | C |
|---|---|---|---|---|---|---|
| Extraversion | −.08 | −.22* | .19* | .51* | .39* | −.04 |
| Anxiety | −.20* | −.04 | .00 | −.14 | −.21* | −.15 |
| Tough-Mindedness | .22* | .09 | −.52* | −.29* | .00 | .34* |
| Independence | .15 | .03 | .27* | .33* | .46* | −.10 |
| Self-Control | −.03 | −.09 | −.34* | −.05 | .01 | .38* |

Note. R = Realistic; I = Investigative; A = Artistic; S = Social; E = Enterprising; C = Conventional. From "Holland Occupational Typology and the 16PF" by D. L. Karol, 1994. In S. R. Conn & M. L. Rieke (Eds.), *The 16PF Fifth Edition Technical Manual.* Champaign, IL: Institute for Personality and Ability Testing, Inc.

*p < .01

TABLE 34

## HOLLAND THEME REGRESSION RESULTS (N=194, 115 FEMALES, 79 MALES)

| Theme | F– Ratio | Multiple Correlation | Browne's Cross–Validation | Significant Predictors |
|---|---|---|---|---|
| Realistic | 18.22* | .57 | .54 | I−, A−, O−, Q1+, Q4− |
| Investigative | 12.75* | .57 | .52 | A−, I−, B+, Q4−, M+, N−$_s$, Q1+ |
| Artistic | 21.44* | .56 | .53 | I+, M+, H+, Q1+ |
| Social | 21.45* | .60 | .57 | A+, H+, G+$_s$, C−$_s$, Q1+ |
| Enterprising | 20.73* | .60 | .57 | A+, E+, H+, I−, N+$_s$, |
| Conventional | 16.63* | .46 | .43 | M−, Q3+, I− |

Note. s = may be operating as a suppressor variable. From "Holland Occupational Typology and the 16PF" by D. L. Karol, 1994. In S. R. Conn & M. L. Rieke (Eds.), *The 16PF Fifth Edition Technical Manual.* Champaign, IL: Institute for Personality and Ability Testing, Inc.

*p < .01

that involves incompatible themes is smaller. *The Dictionary of Holland Occupational Codes* (Gottfredson & Holland, 1989) is a useful resource for exploring career options by theme.

Each theme is described in the text that follows. These descriptions and those printed within the BIR are based on (1) typical SDS-item endorsement, (2) the 16PF personality characteristics that typify each theme, and (3) occupations for which high scorers indicate definite preferences on the SDS. Professionals should note that vocational interest can be influenced by a wide range of variables unrelated to personality (e.g., an individual's abilities, educational opportunities, monetary resources, expectations for standard of living, etc.). Such variables should be considered in conjunction with 16PF results; the 16PF should never serve as the sole evaluative measure.

*Realistic Theme*
The Realistic theme centers around manipulation of tools and knowledge of mechanical principles. Persons scoring high on this theme show interest in activities such as repairing mechanical apparatuses, working on cars, mechanical drawing, and outdoor activities such as farming, hunting, and fishing. In a related vein, they often show experience and skill in mechanical drawing, operating machinery, and repairing automobiles, furniture, or electrical devices. They rate themselves as high in mechanical ability and manual skills.

Holland claims that Realistic persons may lack social skills, and this is evinced by the personality data. The data indicate many aspects of tough-mindedness, including reticence, reserve, and an objective and unsentimental outlook. However, Realistic persons may be open to new ideas, which is not an aspect of tough-minded persons, who tend to be conservative. Realistic persons

also are characterized by aspects of low anxiety; they are self-assured and laid-back, and they are typically relaxed and tolerant.

Realistic persons indicate interest in mechanical or outdoor professions such as mechanic, electrician, firefighter, carpenter, fish and wildlife specialist, and surveyor.

Similarities between personality characteristics and the Realistic theme are predicted by these 16PF factors: low Warmth (A–), low Sensitivity (I–), low Apprehension (O–), Openness to Change (Q1+), and low Tension (Q4–).

*Investigative Theme*
The Investigative theme is characterized by analytical skill and curiosity. High scorers show interest in the manipulation of ideas or scientific principles. They enjoy reading scientific books or articles, working in a laboratory—especially on a science project or theory—applying math to problems, and taking courses in science or math. They are well-versed in scientific and math principles, and are experienced in the use of associated tools such as calculators, microscopes, and computers. They rate themselves as high in scientific and math ability.

Investigative people's personality characteristics are quite diverse. As would be expected, they show above-average reasoning ability. They tend to be reserved and reticent rather than sociable, and are also objective and unsentimental. Regression analyses indicate that the Investigative type is predicted by a willingness to entertain new perspectives and opinions, along with an inward focus on ideas and abstract possiblities. This latter combination may be related to some aspect of scientific creativity. When in potentially frustrating situations, Investigative persons tend to be patient.

Investigative persons indicate interest in the scientific professions (e.g., biologist, chemist, zoologist, geologist, physicist, etc.) and also in editing and writing scientific books and journals.

Similarities between personality characteristics and the Investigative theme are predicted by these 16PF factors: low Warmth (A−), Reasoning (B+), low Sensitivity (I−), Abstractedness (M+), low Privateness (N−), Openness to Change (Q1+), and low Tension (Q4−).

*Artistic Theme*

The Artistic theme concerns self-expression, particularly in the creation of artistic ideas or products. Interests of high scorers typically cover vast areas of art and entertainment, including drawing and painting, acting, musical performance, composing, writing, photography, and design. Not unexpectedly, artistic persons have experience in musical performance, acting, artwork, writing, designing, and so forth. They rate themselves as highly skilled in artistic and musical ability.

Artistic persons are characterized by tender-mindedness; they usually are sensitive and sentimental, and they show strong aesthetic tastes. They also can be abstracted, fanciful, and idea-oriented. They are open to change and to new experiences. Additionally, Artistic persons tend to be bold and uninhibited. Correlations and mean profiles indicate that Artistic persons may be low in self-control; they may go against the grain and question tradition as part of their creative process.

Artistic persons prefer occupations in the arts and entertainment industry. They indicate interest in the evident options of being an artist, sculptor, or painter, and they also express interest in occupations involving cartooning, creative writing (poet, playwright, novelist, free-lance writer, journalist), music (musician, musical arranger, singer, composer, symphony conductor), and acting.

Similarities between personality characteristics and the Artistic theme are predicted by these 16PF factors: Social Boldness (H+), Sensitivity (I+), Abstractedness (M+), and Openness to Change (Q1+).

*Social Theme*

The Social theme pertains to the desire to help and care for others. High scorers show interest in working for charitable organizations, taking care of children, studying juvenile delinquency, teaching, and studying psychology and human relations. They find it easy to talk with all kinds of people, to lead group discussions, to explain things to people, and, in general, to teach others. They participate in charity drives, are good at helping people who are upset or troubled, and indicate that others seek them out to tell their troubles. They rate themselves highly in the ability to teach and in the skill of understanding others.

Not surprisingly, Social persons are extraverted. Correlations show them to be exuberant, forthright, and group-oriented. They tend to be warm, personable, and sociable, but also bold and venturesome in social contacts. They remain open to new ideas and experiences, perhaps facilitating their interplay with diverse individuals.

High Social scorers prefer working in helping professions such as teaching and school administration; counseling-related positions such as marriage counselor, speech therapist, social worker, and vocational counselor; human-relations jobs such as director of a welfare agency or youth camp director; and positions relating to work in general fields such as psychology and sociology.

Similarities between personality characteristics and the Social theme are predicted by these 16PF factors: Warmth (A+), low Emotional Stability (C−),

Rule-Consciousness (G+), Social Boldness (H+), and Openness to Change (Q1+).

*Enterprising Theme*

The Enterprising theme involves persuasion of others, leadership, and generally a high need for achieving objectives. High scorers indicate interest in influencing others, leading a group, or taking charge of a political campaign. They are drawn to business-related activities such as sales and attending sales conferences, running their own business, and learning business success strategies. Additionally, they show interest in taking courses in business, administration, or leadership. Enterprising persons report that they have won awards for sales or leadership. They have experience in managing a small business or service or a sales campaign; they may have a reputation for being able to deal with difficult people. They have organized others' work, and admit to being ambitious, assertive, and persuasive. They rate themselves as having above-average sales and leadership abilities as well as good managerial and public-speaking skills.

Enterprising persons are sociable and friendly, yet they have a tendency to exert their will over others. They tend to be bold in social settings and may enjoy being the focus of a group's attention. They have an unsentimental and objective outlook. Correlations show them to be exuberant and self-assured.

Enterprising persons prefer business occupations such as speculator, buyer, advertising executive, salesperson, business executive, restaurant manager, realtor, travel guide, radio/TV announcer, and emcee.

Similarities between personality characteristics and the Enterprising theme are predicted by these 16PF factors: Warmth (A+), Dominance (E+), Social Boldness (H+), low Sensitivity (I–), and Privateness (N+).

*Conventional Theme*

The Conventional theme entails a preference for organizing and maintaining information. High scorers indicate interest in filling out income tax forms, typing, bookkeeping and business computations, operating business machines and computers, setting up and keeping detailed records, doing inventory, and taking courses in business, bookkeeping, or commercial math. Such persons are competent typists and data processors; they can operate business machines, have experience doing tasks such as taking short-hand and filing, can do large amounts of paperwork in little time, and can keep detailed and accurate records. They rate themselves as having above-average clerical ability and office skills.

Personality characteristics of Conventional people include having an objective, unsentimental outlook and being practical and solution-oriented. These people show a high need for order, and they are self-disciplined, if not perfectionistic.

Conventional persons prefer clerical and record-keeping professions such as book-keeper, tax expert, certified public accountant, credit investigator, financial analyst, payroll clerk, bank examiner, bank teller, court stenographer, and inventory controller.

Similarities between personality characteristics and the Conventional theme are predicted by these 16PF factors: low Sensitivity (I–), low Abstractedness (M–), and Perfectionism (Q3+).

## VI. Item Summary Section

The Item Summary Section appears on the final page of the BIR. This section contains an item-by-item listing of an examinee's response choices as well as summary statistics regarding the response choices. In addition, the examinee's raw score on each factor is presented.▼

Basic Interpretive Report
Profile

NAME:  John Sample
DATE:  November 5, 1993

Norms:  Male

### Response Style Indices

| Index | RS | |
|---|---|---|
| Impression Management | 14 | within expected range |
| Infrequency | 4 | within expected range |
| Acquiescence | 59 | within expected range |

All response style indices are within the normal range.

### Global Factors

| Sten | Factor | Left Meaning | 1 2 3 4 5 : 6 7 8 9 10 | Right Meaning |
|---|---|---|---|---|
| 5 | Extraversion | Introverted | 5 | Extraverted |
| 1 | Anxiety | Low Anxiety | 1 | High Anxiety |
| 7 | Tough–Mindedness | Receptive | 7 | Tough–Minded |
| 8 | Independence | Accomodating | 8 | Independent |
| 5 | Self–Control | Unrestrained | 5 | Self–Controlled |

low    average    high

### 16PF Profile

| Sten | Factor | Left Meaning | 1 2 3 4 5 : 6 7 8 9 10 | Right Meaning |
|---|---|---|---|---|
| 4 | Warmth (A) | Reserved | 4 | Warm |
| 7 | Reasoning (B) | Concrete | 7 | Abstract |
| 9 | Emotional Stability (C) | Reactive | 9 | Emotionally |
| 9 | Dominance (E) | Deferential | 9 | Dominant |
| 5 | Liveliness (F) | Serious | 5 | Live |
| 4 | Rule–Consciousness (G) | Expedient | 4 | |
| 6 | Social Boldness (H) | Shy | 6 | |
| 3 | Sensitivity (I) | Utilitarian | 3 | |
| 4 | Vigilance (L) | Trusting | 4 | |
| 6 | Abstractedness (M) | Grounded | | |
| 5 | Privateness (N) | Forthright | | |
| 3 | Apprehension (O) | Self–Assured | | |
| 6 | Openness to Change (Q1) | Tradit | | |

BASIC INTERPRETIVE REPORT SAMPLE GLOBAL FACTORS PAGE

Basic Interpretive Report
Global Factors

NAME:    John Sample
DATE:    November 5, 1993

**Anxiety**

| Sten | Factor | Left Meaning | 1 2 3 4 5 6 7 8 9 10 | Right Meaning |
|------|--------|--------------|---------------------|---------------|
| 1 | Anxiety | Low Anxiety | | High Anxiety |
| 9 | Emotional Stability (C) | Reactive | | Emotionally Stable |
| 4 | Vigilance (L) | Trusting | | Vigilant |
| 3 | Apprehension (O) | Self–Assured | | Apprehensive |
| 2 | Tension (Q4) | Relaxed | | Tense |

low        average        high

** At the present time, Mr. Sample presents himself as less anxious than most people. This could reflect his characteristic, imperturbable style, or it could reflect his behavior in the absence of significant stressors. At times, low scores can reflect a tendency to minimize difficulties and negative affect.

* This individual shows confidence in his ability to meet challenges with calm and inner strength. Overall, he tends to have an optimistic disposition.

* He shows a tendency to be trusting and accepting of other people and their motives.

* This person typically feels sure about himself. That is, he does not harbor doubts about his behavior and does not worry about how others perceive him.

* At present, he is relaxed and composed. He is tolerant of others and has few feelings of frustration.

**Independence**

| Sten | Factor | Left Meaning | 1 2 3 4 5 6 7 8 9 10 | Right Meaning |
|------|--------|--------------|---------------------|---------------|
| 8 | Independence | Accommodating | | Independent |
| 9 | Dominance (E) | Deferential | | Dominant |
| 6 | Social Boldness (H) | Shy | | Socially Bo |
| 4 | Vigilance (L) | Trusting | | Vigi |
| 6 | Openness to Change (Q1) | Traditional | | |

low        average        hi

** Mr. Sample's preferred lifestyle is highly independent an
achieve control of others and the environment. He te
persuasiveness. He prefers to form his own o

* In interpersonal relationships, he le
getting his way.

* This person is some

This individual is likely to present well in most social situations. He may consider the appropriateness of speaking up and may be able to present himself according to the demands of a given situation. Social Control is high–average (7).

Mr. Sample is usually able to put aside his own worries and opinions in order to listen to other people's feelings and points of view. At times, others may seek him out for sympathy and support. Empathy is high–average (7).

### Leadership and Creativity

In a group of peers, potential for leadership is predicted to be relatively high (8). He is likely to possess the resilience and patience that characterize effective leaders.

At the client's own level of abilities, potential for creative functioning is high–average (7). He probably has the inherent resourcefulness and imagination instrumental for pursuing creative interests.

Should this individual choose to pursue creative activities, his rate of productivity is predicted to be above average (7).

### Vocational Activities

Different occupational interests have been found to be associated with personality qualities. The following section compares Mr. Sample's personality to these known associations. The information below indicates the degree of similarity between Mr. Sample's personality characteristics and each of the six Holland Occupational Types (Self Directed Search; Holland, 1985). Those occupational areas for which Mr. Sample's personality profile shows the highest degree of similarity are described in greater detail. Descriptions are based on item content of the Self Directed Search as well as the personality predictions of the Holland types as measured by the 16PF.

**BASIC INTERPRETIVE REPORT SAMPLE VOCATIONAL INTERESTS PAGE**

Basic Interpretive Report
Vocational Activities (continued)

NAME:  John Sample
DATE:  November 5, 1993

### Vocational Activities

Remember that this information is intended to expand Mr. Sample's range of career options rather than to narrow them. All comparisons should be considered with respect to other relevant information about Mr. Sample, particularly his interests, abilities, and other personal resources.

**Holland Themes**

| Sten | | 1 2 3 4 5 6 7 8 9 10 |
|------|------|------|
| 10 | Investigative | |
| 9 | Realistic | |
| 7 | Enterprising | |
| 6 | Conventional | |
| 5 | Artistic | |
| 3 | Social | |

**Investigative=10**
Mr. Sample shows personality characteristics similar to Investigative persons. Such persons typically have good reasoning ability and enjoy the challenge of problem–solving. They tend to have critical minds, are curious, and consider new ideas and solutions. Investigative persons tend to be reserved and somewhat impersonal; they may prefer working independently. They tend to be concerned with the function and purpose of materials rather than aesthetic principles. Mr. Sample may enjoy working with ideas and theories, especially in the scientific realm. It may be worthwhile to explore whether Mr. Sample enjoys doing research, reading technical articles, or solving challenging problems.

Occupational Fields: Science
Math
Research
Medicine and Health
Computer Science

**Realistic=9**
Mr. Sample shows personality characteristics similar to Realistic persons
theme indicate a preference for physical activity and for workin
be reserved and somewhat aloof with others and may not lik
which can be pursued independently may be more
function and purpose of objects. They are
Many Realistic persons indicate a procli
motive products, or a willingne
whether Mr. Sampl
principle

APPENDIX

A

TABLE 35

PRIMARY SCALE RAW SCORE MEANS AND STANDARD DEVIATIONS

| Primary Factor | | Combined (N = 2500) | | Males (n = 1245) | | Females (n = 1255) | |
|---|---|---|---|---|---|---|---|
| | | Mean | S.D. | Mean | S.D. | Mean | S.D. |
| A | Warmth | 14.25 | 4.63 | 12.83 | 4.53 | 15.67 | 4.28 |
| B | Reasoning | 9.12 | 3.42 | 8.94 | 3.56 | 9.31 | 3.27 |
| C | Emotional Stability | 13.25 | 5.22 | 13.69 | 5.10 | 12.81 | 5.30 |
| E | Dominance | 13.00 | 4.19 | 13.60 | 3.86 | 12.40 | 4.42 |
| F | Liveliness | 11.84 | 4.88 | 11.54 | 4.67 | 12.13 | 5.06 |
| G | Rule-Consciousness | 13.63 | 5.19 | 13.57 | 5.23 | 13.69 | 5.15 |
| H | Social Boldness | 10.72 | 6.22 | 10.79 | 6.06 | 10.65 | 6.37 |
| I | Sensitivity | 12.29 | 5.55 | 8.91 | 4.69 | 15.64 | 4.13 |
| L | Vigilance | 11.11 | 4.72 | 11.50 | 4.63 | 10.72 | 4.78 |
| M | Abstractedness | 8.17 | 5.27 | 8.57 | 5.24 | 7.78 | 5.26 |
| N | Privateness | 11.44 | 4.95 | 12.22 | 4.66 | 10.67 | 5.11 |
| O | Apprehension | 11.42 | 5.47 | 10.03 | 5.30 | 12.79 | 5.30 |
| Q1 | Openness to Change | 16.73 | 5.33 | 16.32 | 5.12 | 17.13 | 5.50 |
| Q2 | Self-Reliance | 8.38 | 5.28 | 8.74 | 5.33 | 8.02 | 5.20 |
| Q3 | Perfectionism | 11.85 | 4.83 | 11.80 | 4.78 | 11.91 | 4.88 |
| Q4 | Tension | 11.07 | 5.13 | 10.80 | 5.17 | 11.34 | 5.08 |

Note. From "Characteristics of the Norm Sample" by S. R. Conn & M. L. Rieke, 1994a. In S. R. Conn & M. L. Rieke (Eds.), *The 16PF Fifth Edition Technical Manual.* Champaign, IL: Institute for Personality and Ability Testing, Inc.

TABLE 36

STEN SCORE MEANS AND STANDARD DEVIATIONS

| Primary Factor | | Mean | S.D. |
|---|---|---|---|
| A | Warmth | 5.70 | 2.08 |
| | Males | 5.55 | 1.98 |
| | Females | 5.85 | 2.17 |
| B | Reasoning | 5.51 | 2.10 |
| C | Emotional Stability | 5.60 | 2.02 |
| E | Dominance | 5.61 | 2.00 |
| | Males | 5.74 | 2.02 |
| | Females | 5.47 | 1.98 |
| F | Liveliness | 5.65 | 1.80 |
| G | Rule-Consciousness | 5.33 | 1.95 |
| H | Social Boldness | 5.61 | 1.96 |
| I | Sensitivity | 5.58 | 2.10 |
| | Males | 5.33 | 2.02 |
| | Females | 5.83 | 2.14 |
| L | Vigilance | 5.67 | 2.04 |
| M | Abstractedness | 5.58 | 1.98 |
| N | Privateness | 5.49 | 1.81 |
| O | Apprehension | 5.42 | 2.00 |
| Q1 | Openess to Change | 5.55 | 1.95 |
| Q2 | Self-Reliance | 5.42 | 1.92 |
| Q3 | Perfectionism | 5.42 | 1.85 |
| Q4 | Tension | 5.37 | 1.88 |

| Global Factor | Mean | S.D. |
|---|---|---|
| Extraversion | 5.65 | 1.87 |
| Anxiety | 5.44 | 2.14 |
| Self-Control | 5.38 | 1.94 |
| Independence | 5.66 | 1.81 |
| Tough-Mindedness | 5.63 | 1.76 |

Note. From "Characteristics of the Norm Sample" by S. R. Conn & M. L. Rieke, 1994a. In S. R. Conn & M. L. Rieke (Eds.), *The 16PF Fifth Edition Technical Manual*. Champaign, IL: Institute for Personality and Ability Testing, Inc.

## TABLE 37

### PRIMARY SCALE RAW SCORE STANDARD ERRORS OF MEASUREMENT ($SE_M$)

| Factor | | Combined | $SE_M$ Males | Females |
|---|---|---|---|---|
| A | Warmth | 2.58 | 2.52 | 2.38 |
| B | Reasoning | 1.64 | 1.71 | 1.57 |
| C | Emotional Stability | 2.45 | 2.39 | 2.49 |
| E | Dominance | 2.44 | 2.25 | 2.58 |
| F | Liveliness | 2.58 | 2.47 | 2.68 |
| G | Rule-Consciousness | 2.60 | 2.62 | 2.58 |
| H | Social Boldness | 2.41 | 2.35 | 2.47 |
| I | Sensitivity | 2.66 | 2.25 | 1.98 |
| L | Vigilance | 2.41 | 2.36 | 2.44 |
| M | Abstractedness | 2.69 | 2.67 | 2.68 |
| N | Privateness | 2.48 | 2.33 | 2.56 |
| O | Apprehension | 2.57 | 2.49 | 2.49 |
| Q1 | Openness to Change | 3.20 | 3.07 | 3.30 |
| Q2 | Self-Reliance | 2.48 | 2.50 | 2.44 |
| Q3 | Perfectionism | 2.60 | 2.57 | 2.63 |
| Q4 | Tension | 2.51 | 2.53 | 2.49 |

Note. From "Characteristics of the Norm Sample" by S. R. Conn & M. L. Rieke, 1994a. In S. R. Conn & M. L. Rieke (Eds.), *The 16PF Fifth Edition Technical Manual.* Champaign, IL: Institute for Personality and Ability Testing, Inc.

TABLE 38

STEN SCORE STANDARD ERRORS OF
MEASUREMENT $(SE_M)$

| Primary Factor | | $SE_M$ |
|---|---|---|
| A | Warmth | 1.16 |
| | Males | 1.10 |
| | Females | 1.21 |
| B | Reasoning | 1.01 |
| C | Emotional Stability | .98 |
| E | Dominance | 1.17 |
| | Males | 1.18 |
| | Females | 1.15 |
| F | Liveliness | .95 |
| G | Rule-Consciousness | .98 |
| H | Social Boldness | .76 |
| I | Sensitivity | 1.01 |
| | Males | .97 |
| | Females | 1.03 |
| L | Vigilance | 1.04 |
| M | Abstractedness | 1.01 |
| N | Privateness | .91 |
| O | Apprehension | .94 |
| Q1 | Openness to Change | 1.17 |
| Q2 | Self-Reliance | .90 |
| Q3 | Perfectionism | 1.00 |
| Q4 | Tension | .92 |

| Global Factor | |
|---|---|
| Extraversion | 0.84 |
| Anxiety | 1.17 |
| Self-Control | 0.89 |
| Independence | 0.79 |
| Tough-Mindedness | 0.75 |

Note. From "Characteristics of the Norm Sample" by S. R. Conn &
M. L. Rieke, 1994a. In S. R. Conn & M. L. Rieke (Eds.), *The 16PF*
*Fifth Edition Technical Manual.* Champaign, IL: Institute for
Personality and Ability Testing, Inc.

APPENDIX

B

TABLE 39

GENERAL POPULATION NORMS (COMBINED MALES AND FEMALES) ($\underline{N}$=2500, 1245 MALES, 1255 FEMALES)

| Factor | Sten1 | Sten2 | Sten3 | Sten4 | Sten5 | Sten6 | Sten7 | Sten8 | Sten9 | Sten10 |
|---|---|---|---|---|---|---|---|---|---|---|
| A | 0-4 | 5-6 | 7-9 | 10-12 | 13-15 | 16-17 | 18-19 | 20 | 21-22 | - |
| Male | 0-3 | 4-5 | 6-7 | 8-10 | 11-13 | 14-15 | 16-17 | 18-19 | 20 | 21-22 |
| Female | 0-5 | 6-8 | 9-11 | 12-13 | 14-15 | 16-17 | 18-19 | 20 | 21 | 22 |
| B | 0-2 | 3 | 4-5 | 6-7 | 8-9 | 10-11 | 12 | 13 | 14 | 15 |
| C | 0-1 | 2-4 | 5-7 | 8-10 | 11-13 | 14-16 | 17-18 | 19 | 20 | - |
| E | 0-3 | 4-6 | 7-9 | 10-11 | 12-13 | 14-15 | 16-17 | 18 | 19· | 20 |
| Male | 0-4 | 5-7 | 8-9 | 10-11 | 12-13 | 14-15 | 16-17 | 18 | 19 | 20 |
| Female | 0-2 | 3-5 | 6-7 | 8-10 | 11-12 | 13-15 | 16-17 | 18 | 19 | 20 |
| F | 0-1 | 2-3 | 4-5 | 6-8 | 9-11 | 12-14 | 15-17 | 18 | 19-20 | - |
| G | 0-2 | 3-5 | 6-8 | 9-11 | 12-14 | 15-17 | 18-19 | 20-21 | 22 | - |
| H | - | 0 | 1-3 | 4-6 | 7-10 | 11-14 | 15-17 | 18-19 | 20 | - |
| I | 0-1 | 2-3 | 4-6 | 7-9 | 10-12 | 13-15 | 16-18 | 19-20 | 21 | 22 |
| Male | 0 | 1-2 | 3-4 | 5-6 | 7-8 | 9-11 | 12-14 | 15-16 | 17-18 | 19-22 |
| Female | 0-6 | 7-8 | 9-10 | 11-13 | 14-15 | 16-17 | 18-19 | 20 | 21 | 22 |
| L | 0-1 | 2-3 | 4-5 | 6-8 | 9-11 | 12-13 | 14-15 | 16-17 | 18-19 | 20 |
| M | - | 0 | 1-2 | 3-4 | 5-7 | 8-10 | 11-13 | 14-16 | 17-19 | 20-22 |
| N | 0-1 | 2-3 | 4-5 | 6-8 | 9-11 | 12-14 | 15-17 | 18-19 | 20 | - |
| O | 0 | 1-2 | 3-5 | 6-8 | 9-12 | 13-15 | 16-17 | 18 | 19-20 | - |
| Q1 | 0-5 | 6-8 | 9-11 | 12-13 | 14-16 | 17-19 | 20-22 | 23-24 | 25-26 | 27-28 |
| Q2 | - | 0 | 1-2 | 3-5 | 6-8 | 9-11 | 12-14 | 15-17 | 18-19 | 20 |
| Q3 | 0-1 | 2-3 | 4-6 | 7-9 | 10-12 | 13-15 | 16-17 | 18 | 19-20 | - |
| Q4 | 0 | 1-3 | 4-5 | 6-8 | 9-11 | 12-14 | 15-17 | 18-19 | 20 | - |

**Converting IM Raw Scores to Percentile Ranks**

| If Raw Score = | 0-1 | 2 | 3 | 4 | 5 | 6 | 7 | 8 | 9 | 10 | 11 | |
|---|---|---|---|---|---|---|---|---|---|---|---|---|
| Percentile = | 1 | 2 | 5 | 6 | 12 | 15 | 24 | 28 | 38 | 42 | 52 | |
| If Raw Score = | 12 | 13 | 14 | 15 | 16 | 17 | 18 | 19 | 20 | 21 | 22 | 23-24 |
| Percentile = | 57 | 68 | 72 | 79 | 82 | 88 | 90 | 94 | 95 | 97 | 98 | 99 |

Note. Male and Female norms presented separately for Factors A, E, and I

TABLE 40

## ARRANGEMENT OF ITEMS WITH RESPECT TO FACTORS

| | | Number of Items | Position of High Scoring Response | | |
|---|---|---|---|---|---|
| | | | (a) | (b) | (c) |
| A | Warmth | 11 | 1, 31, 33, 96, 127, 159 | | 63, 65, 98, 129, 161 |
| B | Reasoning | 15 | 171, 173, 174, 176 | 177, 181, 182, 183, 184, 185 | 172, 175, 178, 179, 180 |
| C | Emotional Stability | 10 | 2, 64, 97, 128, 160, 162 | | 32, 35, 67, 131 |
| E | Dominance | 10 | 36, 66, 99, 130, 132 ,163, 165 | | 3, 38, 102 |
| F | Liveliness | 10 | 6, 39, 68, 100, 103, 134, 164 | | 4, 37, 70 |
| G | Rule-Consciousness | 11 | 5, 7, 40, 69, 104 ,168 | | 72, 106, 133, 136, 166 |
| H | Social Boldness | 10 | 9, 73, 135, 137 | | 41, 71, 105, 107, 167, 169 |
| I | Sensitivity | 11 | 10, 42, 44, 74, 77, 108 | | 8, 110, 138, 140, 170 |
| L | Vigilance | 10 | 11, 13, 43, 76, 112, 141 | | 45, 78, 109, 139 |
| M | Abstractedness | 11 | 12, 14 ,79, 111, 142, 145 | | 17, 46, 49, 81, 114 |
| N | Privateness | 10 | 47, 50, 80, 113, 143, 148 | | 15, 18, 84, 117 |
| O | Apprehension | 10 | 51, 54, 87, 116, 150 | | 19, 21, 82, 119, 146 |
| Q1 | Openness to Change | 14 | 22, 53, 83, 88, 118, 120, 149 | | 20, 24, 52, 55, 86, 147, 151 |
| Q2 | Self-Reliance | 10 | 27, 59, 89, 121, 152 | | 25, 56, 92, 123, 156 |
| Q3 | Perfectionism | 10 | 61, 93, 125, 157 | | 26, 29, 57, 90, 122, 154 |
| Q4 | Tension | 10 | 28, 30, 62, 126, 155 | | 60, 91, 94, 124, 158 |
| IM | | 12 | 16 | | 23, 34, 48, 58, 75, 85, 95, 101, 115, 144, 153 |

Note. Test items belonging to each factor are listed above, along with the scoring direction. The alternative (a) or (c) always indicates the response which contributes +2 to the factor score concerned. A "b" or "?" answer always contributes +1 in such cases, the only exception to this being Factor B (reasoning ability), where the numbers indicated score +1 in each case.

APPENDIX C

TABLE 41

IMPRESSION MANAGEMENT (IM):
RAW TO PERCENTILE CONVERSIONS
(BASED ON NORM SAMPLE, N=2500)

| IM | Percentile |
|---|---|
| 0-1 | 1 |
| 2 | 2 |
| 3 | 5 |
| 4 | 6 |
| 5 | 12 |
| 6 | 15 |
| 7 | 24 |
| 8 | 28 |
| 9 | 38 |
| 10 | 42 |
| 11 | 52 |
| 12 | 57 |
| 13 | 68 |
| 14 | 72 |
| 15 | 79 |
| 16 | 82 |
| 17 | 88 |
| 18 | 90 |
| 19 | 94 |
| 20 | 95 |
| 21 | 97 |
| 22 | 98 |
| 23-24 | 99 |

Note. From "Response Style Indices" by S. R. Conn and M. L. Rieke, 1994e. In S. R. Conn & M. L. Rieke (Eds.), *The 16PF Fifth Edition Technical Manual.* Champaign, IL: Institute for Personality and Ability Testing, Inc.

TABLE 42

IMPRESSION MANAGEMENT (IM)
ITEMS/SCORING KEY

| Item Number | Direction of Keyed Response |
|---|---|
| 16 | *a* |
| 23 | *c* |
| 34 | *c* |
| 48 | *c* |
| 58 | *c* |
| 75 | *c* |
| 85 | *c* |
| 95 | *c* |
| 101 | *c* |
| 115 | *c* |
| 144 | *c* |
| 153 | *c* |

Note. From "Response Style Indices" by S. R. Conn & M. L. Rieke, 1994e. In S. R. Conn & M. L. Rieke (Eds.), *The 16PF Fifth Edition Technical Manual.* Champaign, IL: Institute for Personality and Ability Testing, Inc.

TABLE 43

**INFREQUENCY (INF): RAW TO PERCENTILE CONVERSIONS (BASED ON NORM SAMPLE, <u>N</u>=2500)**

| Raw Score | Percentile |
|-----------|------------|
| 0-1 | 51 |
| 2 | 68 |
| 3 | 78 |
| 4 | 84 |
| 5 | 88 |
| 6 | 91 |
| 7 | 93 |
| 8 | 95 |
| 9 | 96 |
| 10-11 | 98 |
| 12-32 | 99 |

<u>Note</u>. From "Response Style Indices" by S. R. Conn & M. L. Rieke, 1994e. In S. R. Conn & M. L. Rieke (Eds.), *The 16PF Fifth Edition Technical Manual.* Champaign, IL: Institute for Personality and Ability Testing, Inc.

**TABLE 44**

**INFREQUENCY ITEMS/SCORING KEY (ALL ITEMS ARE SCORED TO "B" RESPONSE: "B"=1, 0 OTHERWISE)**

**Item Numbers:**

6, 16, 18, 23, 24, 26, 34, 35, 36, 41, 51, 62, 75, 76, 80, 90, 92, 94, 99, 100, 101, 105, 111, 116, 125, 140, 148, 152, 155, 156, 161, 165

**INSTRUCTIONS:** Infrequency is scored by tallying the number of "*b*" responses in the set of 32 items listed here. Simply score 1 point for each *b*–response, and 0 points otherwise.

<u>Note</u>. From "Response Style Indices" by S. R. Conn & M. L. Rieke, 1994e. In S. R. Conn & M. L. Rieke (Eds.), *The 16PF Fifth Edition Technical Manual.* Champaign, IL: Institute for Personality and Ability Testing, Inc.

TABLE 45

OVERALL HIT RATES FOR VARIOUS INFREQUENCY CUTOFF SCORES
(WITH A BASE RATE OF 5% RANDOM PROTOCOLS)

| Cutoff Scores | Valid Group | Random Group | Overall Hit Rate |
|---|---|---|---|
| 3 | 77.7 | 99.9 | 78.8 |
| 4 | 83.7 | 99.9 | 84.5 |
| 5 | 87.6 | 99.2 | 88.2 |
| 6 | 90.4 | 98.0 | 90.8 |
| 7 | 92.8 | 96.6 | 93.0 |
| 8 | 94.6 | 88.7 | 95.3 |
| 9 | 96.1 | 79.1 | 95.3 |
| 10 | 97.7 | 65.9 | 96.1 |

**INSTRUCTIONS:** IPAT interpretive reports issue warning statements for INF scores above the 95th percentile of the Fifth Edition norm sample. If you determine the expected base rate of random responding and select the hit rate for correctly classifying random and nonrandom tests, you can set a different cutoff value for INF.

To choose the cutoff, first estimate the base rate of random responding expected in your sample. A base rate of 5% is reasonable (Conn & Rieke, 1994e). However, a lower rate may be applicable for settings in which test-takers are motivated to attend to item content (as for example in employment settings), or a higher rate may be useful in forced testing (i.e., court ordered) testing situations. Next, consider the accuracy needed in correctly classifying valid and invalid tests. In other words, would it be more costly to accept test results as valid when they are actually invalid, or to reject tests classified as invalid when they are valid? Once these issues have been addressed, the hit rate for different cutoff scores and different base rates can be calculated. The instructions that follow are reprinted from the 16PF Fifth Edition Technical Manual (Conn & Rieke, 1994e).

**Instructions on how to construct overall hit rate tables for various base rates:**

The first step in constructing an overall hit rate table is to estimate the base rate. The base rate indicates the percentage of random protocols expected in a particular population (Berry et al., 1991).

With the base rate, the entries in the "Valid Group" (VG) and "Random Group" (RG) columns in Table 45, below, can be used in the following formula to calculate the overall hit rate at the different cutoff scores.

Before using the formula, multiply the base rate (BR) by 100 [e.g., for a base rate of 3% enter 3 for BR and 97 for (100-BR)]. Then,

$$HIT\ RATE = (VG\ entry \times (100\text{-}BR)) + (RG\ entry \times BR)$$

For example, choose a base rate of 3% and a cutoff of 6. Thus, BR = 3 and (100-BR) = 97. From Table 9, at the INF cutoff score of 6, VG entry = .904 and RG entry = .980. From the formula above, the overall hit rate is:

Hit Rate = (.904 x 97) + (.980 x 3)
= 87.69 + 2.94
= 90.63%

Note. From "Response Style Indices" by S. R. Conn & M. L. Rieke, 1994e. In S. R. Conn & M. L. Rieke (Eds.), *The 16PF Fifth Edition Technical Manual.* Champaign, IL: Institute for Personality and Ability Testing, Inc.

# TABLE 46

## ACQUIESCENCE (ACQ): RAW TO PERCENTILE CONVERSION (BASED ON NORM SAMPLE, N=2500)

| Raw Score | Percentile |
|-----------|------------|
| 0-33 | 1 |
| 34-36 | 2 |
| 37-38 | 3 |
| 39-40 | 4 |
| 41 | 5 |
| 42 | 7 |
| 43 | 8 |
| 44 | 9 |
| 45 | 11 |
| 46 | 13 |
| 47 | 15 |
| 48 | 17 |
| 49 | 20 |
| 50 | 22 |
| 51 | 26 |
| 52 | 29 |
| 53 | 33 |
| 54 | 37 |
| 55 | 42 |
| 56 | 47 |
| 57 | 52 |
| 58 | 56 |
| 59 | 60 |
| 60 | 65 |
| 61 | 69 |
| 62 | 73 |
| 63 | 76 |
| 64 | 80 |
| 65 | 83 |
| 66 | 86 |
| 67 | 88 |
| 68 | 91 |
| 69 | 93 |
| 70 | 94 |
| 71 | 96 |
| 72-73 | 97 |
| 74-75 | 98 |
| 76-103 | 99 |

Note. From "Response Style Indices" by S. R. Conn & M. L. Rieke, 1994e. In S. R. Conn & M. L. Rieke (Eds.), *The 16PF Fifth Edition Technical Manual*. Champaign, IL: Institute for Personality and Ability Testing, Inc.

TABLE 47

ACQUIESCENCE ITEMS/SCORING KEY (ALL ITEMS ARE
SCORED TO "A" RESPONSE: "A"=1, 0 OTHERWISE)

**Item Numbers:**

1, 2, 6, 9, 10, 11, 12, 13, 14, 15, 22, 23, 25, 27, 28, 29, 33, 34, 35, 36, 39, 40, 41, 43, 44, 47, 48, 49, 50, 52, 54, 57, 58, 59, 60, 61, 62, 63, 64, 65, 66, 68, 69, 71, 72, 76, 77, 79, 83, 85, 87, 89, 90, 91, 93, 94, 96, 97, 99, 100, 103, 105, 106, 107, 108, 110, 111, 112, 113, 114, 116, 118, 124, 125, 126, 128, 130, 132, 133, 134, 135, 137, 138, 140, 141, 142, 145, 146, 148, 150, 151, 152, 155, 157, 158, 159, 162, 164, 165, 166, 167, 168, 169

**INSTRUCTIONS:** Recall that the Acquiescent Style gauges the tendency of an individual to endorse an item as "TRUE" of him/herself, regardless of the item's actual content. Therefore, Acquiescence is scored by tallying the number of TRUE responses in the subset of 103 True-False questions contained within the 16PF. For each item listed below, an "a" response (TRUE response) receives 1 point; otherwise, no points are assigned. NOTE: Only the test questions in Table 47 are used to tally the Acquiescence score; do not use the total number of "a" responses for the whole test.

Note. From "Response Style Indices" by S. R. Conn & M. L. Rieke, 1994e. In S. R. Conn & M. L. Rieke (Eds.), *The 16PF Fifth Edition Technical Manual.* Champaign, IL: Institute for Personality and Ability Testing, Inc.

REFERENCES

Allport, G. W., & Odbert, H. S. (1936). Trait-names: A psycholexical study. *Psychological Monographs, 47,* 171.

Altus, W. D. (1948). The validity of an abbreviated information test used in the Army. *Journal of Consulting Psychology, 12,* 270-275.

American Psychological Association. (1985). *Standards for educational and psychological testing.* Washington, DC: American Psychological Association, Inc.

Barron, F., & Harringron, D. M. (1981). Creativity, intelligence, and personality. *Annual Review of Psychology, 32,* 439-476.

Bell, H. M. (1961). *Manual for the Adjustment Inventory.* Palo Alto, CA: Consulting Psychologists Press, Inc.

Berry, D. T., Wetter, M. W., Baer, R. A., Widiger, T. A., Sumpter, J. C., Reynolds, S. K., & Hallam, R. A. (1991). Detection of random responding on the MMPI-2: Utility of F, Back F, and VRIN scales. *Psychological Assessment, 3,* 418-423.

Browne, M. W. (1975). Predictive validity of a linear regression equation. *British Journal of Mathematical and Statistical Psychology, 18,* 79-87.

Cattell, H. B. (1989). *The 16PF: Personality in depth.* Champaign, IL: Institute for Personality and Ability Testing, Inc.

Cattell, H. E. P. (1994). Development of the 16PF Fifth Edition. In S. R. Conn & M. L. Rieke (Eds.), *The 16PF Fifth Edition technical manual.* Champaign, IL: Institute for Personality and Ability Testing, Inc.

Cattell, R. B. (1957, April). The conceptual and test distinction of neuroticism and anxiety. *Journal of Clinical Psychology, 13*(3), 221-233.

Cattell, R. B., Cattell, A. K., & Cattell, H. E. (1993). *Sixteen Personality Factor Questionnaire, Fifth Edition.* Champaign, IL: Institute for Personality and Ability Testing, Inc.

Cattell, R. B., & Drevdahl, J. E. (1955). A comparison of the personality profile (16PF) of eminent researchers with that of eminent teachers and administrators, and the general population. *British Journal of Psychology, 46,* 248-261.

Cattell, R. B., Eber, H. W., & Tatsuoka, M. M. (1970). *Handbook for the 16PF.* Champaign, IL: Institute for Personality and Ability Testing, Inc.

Cattell, R. B., & Scheier, I. H. (1961). *The meaning and measurement of neuroticism and anxiety.* NY: Ronald Press.

Cattell, R. B., & Stice, G. F. (1954). Four formulae for selecting leaders on the basis of personality. *Human Relations, 7*(4), 493-507.

Cattell, R. B., & Stice, G. F. (1960). *The dimensions of groups and their relations to the behavior of members.* Champaign, IL: Institute for Personality and Ability Testing, Inc.

Conn, S. R. (1993, August). *Relationship between 16PF Fifth Edition Global Factors and the Personality Research Form, California Psychological Inventory, NEO Personality Inventory, and the Myers-Briggs Type Indicator: A study of construct validity.* In P. Farber (Chair), The Revised 16PF—Psychometric Issues. Symposium presented at the 101st Annual Conference of the American Psychological Association, Toronto, Ontario, Canada, August 23, 1993.

Conn, S. R. (1994). Reliability and equivalency: comparision of the 16PF Fifth Edition and Fourth Edition (Form A). In S. R. Conn & M. L. Rieke (Eds.), *The 16PF Fifth Edition technical manual.* Champaign, IL: Institute for Personality and Ability Testing, Inc.

Conn, S. R., & Rieke, M. L. (1994a). Characteristics of the norm sample. In S. R. Conn & M. L. Rieke (Eds.), *The 16PF Fifth Edition technical manual.* Champaign, IL: Institute for Personality and Ability Testing, Inc.

Conn, S. R., & Rieke, M. L. (1994b). Construct validation of the 16PF Fifth Edition. In S. R. Conn & M. L. Rieke (Eds.), *The 16PF Fifth Edition technical manual.* Champaign, IL: Institute for Personality and Ability Testing, Inc.

Conn, S. R., & Rieke, M. L. (1994c). Leisure activities and the 16PF Fifth Edition. In S. R. Conn & M. L. Rieke (Eds.), *The 16PF Fifth Edition technical manual.* Champaign, IL: Institute for Personality and Ability Testing, Inc.

Conn, S. R., & Rieke, M. L. (1994d). Psychological adjustment and self-esteem. In S. R. Conn & M. L. Rieke (Eds.), *The 16PF Fifth Edition technical manual.* Champaign, IL: Institute for Personality and Ability Testing, Inc.

Conn, S. R., & Rieke, M. L. (1994e). Response style indices. In S. R. Conn & M. L. Rieke (Eds.), *The 16PF Fifth Edition technical manual.* Champaign, IL: Institute for Personality and Ability Testing, Inc.

Conn, S. R., & Rieke, M. L. (Eds.), (1994f). *The 16PF Fifth Edition technical manual.* Champaign, IL: Institute for Personality and Ability Testing, Inc.

Coopersmith, S. (1967). *The antecedents of self-esteem.* San Fransisco: Freeman.

Coopersmith, S. (1975). Building self-esteem in the classroom. *In Developing motivation in young children.* Palo Alto, CA: Consulting Psychologists Press, Inc.

Coopersmith, S. (1981). *Self-esteem inventories.* Palo Alto, CA: Consulting Psychologists Press, Inc.

Costa, P. T., & McCrae, R. R. (1992). *NEO PI-R professional manual.* Odessa, FL: PAR, Inc.

Cronbach, L. J. (1951). Coefficient alpha and the internal structure of tests. *Psychometrika, 16,* 297-334.

Crowne, D., & Marlowe, D. (1960). A new scale of social desirability independent of psychopathology. *Journal of Consulting and Clinical Psychology, 24,* 349-354.

Crowne, D., & Marlowe, D. (1964). *The approval motive: Studies in evaluative dependence.* New York: Wiley.

Dorans, N., & Kulick, E. (1983). *Assessing unexpected differential item performance of female candidates on SAT and TSWE forms administered in December 1977: An application of the standardization approach* (Research Rep. No. 83-9). Princeton, NJ: Educational Testing Service.

Dorans, N. J., & Kulick, E. (1988). *The standardization approach to assessing differential speededness* (Research Rep. No. 88-31). Princeton, NJ: Educational Testing Service.

Downing, G. L., Edgar, R. W., Harris, A. J., Kornberg, L., & Storen, H. F. (1965). *The preparation of teachers for schools in culturally deprived neighborhoods.* Cooperative Research Project No. 935. Flushing: Queens College of the City University of New York.

Drevdahl, J. E., & Cattell, R. B. (1958). Personality and creativity in artists and writers. *Journal of Clinical Psychology, 14,* 107-111.

Eysenck, H. J. (1960). *Handbook of abnormal psychology.* London: Pitman.

Goldberg, L. R. (1992). The development of markers for the big-five factor structure. *Psychological Assessment, 4*(1), 26-42.

Gottfredson, G. D., & Holland, J. L. (1989). *Dictionary of Holland occupational codes* (2nd ed.). Odessa, FL: Psychological Assessment Resources, Inc.

Gough, H. G. (1987). *California Psychological Inventory administrator's guide.* Palo Alto, CA: Consulting Psychologists Press, Inc.

Guastello, S. J. (1991). *Artistic and Scientific Activities Survey.* Milwaukee, WI: Marquette University, Department of Psychology.

Guastello, S. J. (1993). *Implications of recent legislation for pre-employment personality testing.* Unpublished paper, Marquette University Department of Psychology.

Guastello, S. J., Bzdawka, A., Guastello, D. D., & Rieke, M. L. (1991). Cognitive measures of creative behavior: CAB-5 and consequences. *Journal of Creative Behavior, 26,* 260-267.

Guastello, S. J., Choi, J. J., Rieke, M. L., & Billings, S. W. (1993). *Personality and volunteer service orientation.* Manuscript submitted for publication.

Guastello, S. J., & Rieke, M. L. (1993a). *Selecting successful salespersons with the 16PF: Form A validity studies.* Champaign, IL: Institute for Personality and Ability Testing, Inc.

Guastello, S. J., & Rieke, M. L. (1993b). *The 16PF and leadership: Summary of research findings* 1954-1992. Champaign, IL: Institute for Personality and Ability Testing, Inc.

Guastello, S. J., & Shissler, J. E. (1993). *A two-factor taxonomy of creative behavior* (Technical Report). Milwaukee, WI: Marquette University, Department of Psychology.

Holland, J. L. (1973). *Making vocational choices.* Englewood Cliffs, NJ: Prentice-Hall.

Holland, J. L. (1985a). *Making vocational choices: A theory of vocational personalities and work environments.* Englewood Cliffs, NJ: Prentice-Hall.

Holland, J. L. (1985b). *SDS: The Self-Directed Search professional manual.* Odessa, FL: Psychological Assessment Resources, Inc.

Holland, J. L., & Gottfredson, G. D. (1992). Studies of the hexagonal model: an evaluation (or, the perils of stalking the perfect hexagon). [Comment] *Journal of Vocational Behavior, 40*, 158-170.

Holland, P. W., & Thayer, D. T. (1986). *Differential item functioning and the Mantel-Haenszel procedure.* Paper presented at the meeting of the American Educational Research Association, San Francisco.

IPAT (1973a). *Measuring intelligence with the Culture Fair Tests: Manual for Scales 2 and 3.* Champaign, IL: Institute for Personality and Ability Testing, Inc.

IPAT (1973b). *Technical supplement for the Culture Fair Intelligence Tests Scales 2 and 3.* Champaign, IL: Institute for Personality and Ability Testing, Inc.

Jackson, D. N. (1989). *Personality Research Form manual.* Port Huron, MI: Sigma Assessment Systems, Inc.

Jung, C. G. (1971). *Psychological types* (H. G. Baynes, Trans. revised by R. F. C. Hull). Volume 6 of *The collected works of C. G. Jung.* Princeton, NJ: Princeton University Press. (Original work published in 1921)

Karol, D. L. (1994). Holland occupational typology and the 16PF. In S. R. Conn & M. L. Rieke (Eds.), *The 16PF Fifth Edition technical manual.* Champaign, IL: Institute for Personality and Ability Testing, Inc.

Karson, S., & O'Dell, J. W. (1976). *A guide to the clinical use of the 16PF.* Champaign, IL: Institute for Personality and Ability Testing, Inc.

Khatena, J., & Torrance, E. P. (1976). *Khatena Torrance Creative Perception Inventory instruction manual.* Chicago: Stoelting.

Krug, S. E. (1981). *Interpreting 16PF profile patterns.* Champaign, IL: Institute for Personality and Ability Testing, Inc.

Krug, S. E., & Johns, E. F. (1986, October). A large-scale cross-validation of second-order personality structure defined by the 16PF. *Psychological Reports, 59,* 683-693.

McKechnie, G. E. (1974). *Leisure Activities Blank.* Palo Alto, CA: Consulting Psychologists Press, Inc.

McKechnie, G. E. (1976). *Manual for the Leisure Activities Blank.* Palo Alto, CA: Consulting Psychologists Press, Inc.

Moon, G. M., & Gorsuch, R. L. (1988). Information Inventory: The quicker quick test of intelligence. *Journal of Clinical Psychology, 44,* 248-251.

Murray, H. A. (1938). *Explorations in personality.* NY: Oxford University Press.

Myers, I. B., & McCaulley, M. H. (1985). *Manual: A guide to the development and use of the Myers-Briggs Type Indicator.* Palo Alto, CA: Consulting Psychologists Press, Inc.

Paulhus, D. L. (1990). Assessing self-deception and impression management in self-reports: The balanced inventory of desirable responding. Unpublished paper, University of British Columbia Department of Psychology, Vancouver.

Pierson, G., & Gorsuch, R. L. (1963). Clinical validation and usefulness of the Altus in screening for intelligence. *Psychological Reports, 13,* 87-89.

Rickels, K., & Cattell, R. B. (1965). The clinical factor validity and trueness of the IPAT verbal and objective batteries for anxiety and regression. *Journal of Clinical Psychology, 21*, 257-264.

Rieke, M. L., & Conn, S. R. (1994). The revised reasoning (Factor B) scale. In S. R. Conn & M. L. Rieke (Eds.), *The 16PF Fifth Edition technical manual.* Champaign, IL: Institute for Personality and Ability Testing, Inc.

Rieke, M. L., Guastello, S. J., & Conn, S. R. (1994a). Interpersonal skills and empathy. In S. R. Conn & M. L. Rieke (Eds.), *The 16PF Fifth Edition technical manual.* Champaign, IL: Institute for Personality and Ability Testing, Inc.

Rieke, M. L., Guastello, S. J., & Conn, S. R. (1994b). Leadership and creativity. In S. R. Conn & M. L. Rieke (Eds.), *The 16PF Fifth Edition technical manual.* Champaign, IL: Institute for Personality and Ability Testing, Inc.

Riggio, R. E. (1986). Assessment of basic social skills. *Journal of Personality and Social Psychology, 51*, 649-660.

Riggio, R. E. (1989). *Social Skills Inventory manual.* Palo Alto, CA: Consulting Psychologists Press, Inc.

U.S. Bureau of the Census. (1991). Current population reports, series P-70, No. 21, *Educational Background and Economic Status: Spring 1987*. Washington, DC: U. S. Government Printing Office. (Table was prepared March 1991)

U.S. Bureau of the Census. (1992). Current population reports, series P-20, No. 460, *School enrollment—social and economic characteristics of students: October 1990*. Washington, DC: U.S. Government Printing Office.

Wade, A. M., & Guastello, S. J. (1993). *Comparison of scores on the 16PF administered in conventional versus automated format*. Marquette University Department of Psychology. Unpublished paper.

Wiggins, J. S. (1973). *Personality and prediction: Principles of personality assessment*. Reading, MA: Addison-Wesley.

AUTHOR INDEX

Allport, G. W., 59
Altus, W. D., 88
American Psychological Association
    (APA), 60, 90, 105
Barron, F., 98
Bell, H. M., 92, 109, 110
Berry, D. T., 141
Billings, S. W., 112
Briggs, K. C., 78
Browne, M. W., 94, 109, 110, 114
Bzdawka, A., 98
Cattell, H. B., 43, 45, 46, 49, 50
Cattell, H. E. P., 60, 61, 64, 65, 71
Cattell, R. B., 13, 30, 32, 64, 74, 92, 94, 98,
    100, 103
Choi, J. J., 112
Conn, S. R., 17, 21, 22, 23, 24, 25, 43, 44
    48, 51, 60, 62, 69, 71, 76, 78, 88, 89, 90,
    92, 93, 98, 99, 100, 107, 109, 110, 113,
    114
Coopersmith, S., 44, 48, 91, 92, 109
Costa, P. T., 78
Cronbach, L. J., 70
Crowne, D., 23
Dorans, N., 89
Downing, G. L., 88
Drevdahl, J. E., 98, 100
Eber, H. W., 13, 30, 32, 64, 74, 92, 100
Edgar, R. W., 88
Eysenck, H. J., 30
Goldberg, L. R., 30, 31
Gorsuch, R. L., 88
Gottfredson, G. D., 115, 117
Gough, H. G., 78, 80, 82, 97
Guastello, S. J., 8, 51, 65, 90, 98, 99, 100,
    101, 110, 112, 113, 114
Harringron, D. M., 98
Harris, A. J., 88
Harris, C. W., 61, 64
Holland, J. L., 89, 106, 114, 115, 117
IPAT, 3, 4, 8, 12, 13, 88, 90

Jackson, D. N., 32, 78
Johns, E. F., 64, 74
Jung, C. G., 30, 86
Kaiser, H. F., 61, 64
Karol, D. L., 115
Karson, S., 42, 44
Khatena, J., 99, 113
Kornberg, L., 88
Krug, S. E., 50, 64, 74
Kulick, E., 89
Marlowe, D., 22
McCrae, R. R., 78
Moon, G. M., 88
Murray, H. A., 79
Myers, I. B., 78
O'Dell, J. W., 42, 44
Odbert, H. S., 59
Paulhus, D. L., 23
Pierson, G., 88
Rickels, K., 94
Rieke, M. L., 17, 21, 22, 23, 24, 25, 43, 44,
    48, 51, 60, 62, 78, 88, 89, 90, 92, 93, 98,
    99, 100, 101, 107, 109, 110, 112, 113, 114
Riggio, R. E., 94, 95, 97, 110, 111, 112
Scheier, I. H., 94
Shissler, J. E., 114
Stice, G. F., 100, 113
Storen, H. F., 88
Tatsuoka, M. M., 13, 30, 32, 64, 74, 92, 100
Thayer, D. T., 89
Torrance, E. P., 99, 113
Wade, A. M., 8, 65
Wiggins, J. S., 90

SUBJECT INDEX

Keys *see* Scoring Keys
    *also see* Scoring, by hand

L Factor *see* Vigilance (L+)
Leadership, **100-102**, 113, 119
Liveliness (F+), 46
    related to other 16PF scales, 25, 26,
        30, 35, 42, 48, 54, 76
    related to other measures, 79, 80, 83,
        85, 87, 92, 96, 98, 101, 112, 113, 114

M Factor *see* Abstractedness (M+)
Machine scoring *see* Scoring, by
    computer
MBTI *see* Myers-Briggs Type Indicator
    (MBTI)
Measurement limits, *20*
Missing responses
    *see* Scoring, missing responses
Multiple regression, **90**, 92, 93, 95, 97, 115
    results, 91, 94, 96, 98, 100, 101, 116
Myers-Briggs Type Indicator (MBTI), 31,
    33, 35, 42, 43, 46, 49, 51, 52, 53, 54, 55,
    78, **86-88**

N Factor *see* Privateness (N+)
NEO PI-R (Costa & McRae), 78, **83-86**
Norms
    completing norm choice on answer
        sheet, 9, 13
    norm table, 133
    norm sample demographics, 62-64
    sex-specific option, 42, 45, 49
    using norm table, 10-11

O Factor *see* Apprehension (O+)
OnFax 4, 13 *see also* Scoring
Openness to Change (Q1+), **53-54**, 70, 76
    related to other 16PF scales, 33, 43,
        45, 48, 49, 50, 51
    related to other measures, 80, 83, 86,
        91, 96, 97, 98, 99, 100, 109, 111, 112,
        113, 114, 117, 118, 119

Perfectionism (Q3+), 23, **55**
    related to other 16PF scales, 35, 47, 76
    related to other measures, 80, 83, 86,
        88, 100, 102, 112, 113, 114, 119
Personality, 3, 4, 13, 17, 19, 60, 70, 71, 77, 90
Personality Research Form (PRF), 31, 32,
    33, 34, 35, 42, 43, 45, 46, 47, 48, 49, 50,
    51, 52, 53, 54, 55, 56, 77, **78-80**
Prediction *see* Criterion Validity
PRF *see* Personality Research Form
    (PRF)
Primary Factor Scales, 17, 21, 25, 41, 60,
    71, 74
    interpretive material *see* specific
    factor by scale name or letter (e.g.,
    Warmth, or A factor)
Privateness (N+), 41, **52**
    related to other 16PF scales, 26
    related to other measures, 79, 83, 87,
        97, 109, 111, 112, 114, 118, 119
Profile sheet *see* Individual Record Form
Prorating scores for missing data
    *see* Scoring, missing responses

Q1 Factor *see* Openness to Change (Q1+)
Q2 Factor *see* Self-Reliance (Q2+)
Q3 Factor *see* Perfectionism (Q3+)
Q4 Factor *see* Tension (Q4+)
Qualifications *see* User qualifications

Race, 4, 43, 62, 63, 88-89
Random responding *see* Response Style
    Indices; Infrequency
Raw scores, 10, 11, 24, 25, 42, 45, 106
Readability, 3, 7, 65
Reasoning, **43**, **88-90**
    development of scale, 61-62
    related to other 16PF scales, 45
    related to other measures, 96, 97, 99,
        100, 102, 111, 112, 113, 118
    related to scoring, 7, 10